Received On

JAN -- 2017

Magnolia Library

NO LONGER PRO
SEATTLE

D1108450

THE LIFE AND SHIP MODELS OF
❖ NORMAN OUGH ❖

THE LIFE AND SHIP MODELS OF
❖ NORMAN OUGH ❖

ALISTAIR ROACH

FOREWORD BY PHILIP REED

NAVAL INSTITUTE PRESS

ANNAPOLIS, MARYLAND

In Memory of
Norman Arthur Ough
10 November 1898 – 3 August 1965

Copyright © Alistair Roach 2016
First published in Great Britain in 2016 by
Seaforth Publishing,
Pen & Sword Books Ltd,
47 Church Street,
Barnsley S70 2AS

Published and distributed in the
United States of America and Canada by the
Naval Institute Press,
291 Wood Road, Annapolis,
Maryland 21402-5034

www.nip.org

Library of Congress Control Number: 2016947222

ISBN 978 1 59114 617 9

This edition authorized for sale only in the United States of America, its territories
and possessions, and Canada.

All rights reserved. No part of this publication may be reproduced or transmitted in any form or by any means,
electronic or mechanical, including photocopying, recording, or any information storage and retrieval system,
without prior permission in writing of both the copyright owner and the above publisher.

The right of Alistair Roach to be identified as the author of this work has been asserted by him in accordance
with the Copyright, Designs and Patents Act 1988.

Typeset and designed by Neil Sayer
Printed by Printworks Global Ltd., London & Hong Kong

❖

❖ CONTENTS ❖

❖

❖ Acknowledgements ❖

Maggie Aherne, for her editing skills and expertise.
Jenny Durrant, Assistant Curator at the Royal Albert Memorial Museum, Exeter.
Richard Eddy, for sharing his personal correspondence with Norman Ough.
Nancy Frankel, for her assistance with cataloguing the MacGregor Plans Collection.
Paul Freshney, Editor of *Model Boats* magazine, for his guidance.
Earl Howe, for his help with identifying models held by the Howe family.
Richard Jordan-Baker, Director of the Broadlands Estate, for access to the
Mountbatten collection.
Brian Lavery, for assistance with model recognition.
David Lindridge, Collections Research Manager of the National Maritime Museum.
Julian Mannering, Seaforth Publications, for all his help and guidance.
William Mowll, for his advice and inspiration.
Jenny Orwin, Archivist at Bootham School.
Nigel Overton, Curator of Maritime Heritage, Plymouth City Museum.
Julien Parsons, Curator of the Royal Albert Memorial Museum, Exeter.
Neera Puttapipat, at the Imperial War Museum, for help with photographs.
Philip Reed, for writing the Foreword.
John Rooney, Archivist at Hartley Library, Southampton University.
Simon Stephens, Curator of Ship Models, National Maritime Museum.
David Weller, for sharing his reminiscences about Norman Ough.

I am particularly indebted to Rhona Bolger at 'MyTimeMedia' and to Eleni Papavasileiou,
Head Curator of Library and Archives (ss Great Britain Trust). Also, to Martin Ough Dealy
who has supplied me with many copies of letters and photographs from the Ough family.
It is only because of these people's and organisations' generosity, in allowing original articles
and plans to be republished, and for permitting me to use the family archive, that this book
has come to fruition. Hopefully it will serve as a tribute to Norman Ough's life and work.

Finally, I thank my wife, Daphne, for her support and encouragement, as well as her
forbearance, while every available surface in our house has been taken over either by piles
of papers and books or by model boats.

❖ Foreword ❖

Back in the late 1950s and early '60s I was an art student living in south London, hoping in some way to pursue a life involved in fine art. I would occasionally take days off, and with a friend, head for the West End to visit art galleries and hunt through the many bookshops to be found around the Charing Cross Road in those days. This always ended up with a visit to Foyles Bookshop followed by a coffee in a small café on the edge of Soho where we would peruse our spoils. Had I only known, just across the road from Foyles, several storeys up, was working a man who was later to have a quite profound influence on my life and work. That man was Norman Ough.

It was in 1971, when my career in fine art was failing, that I discovered, through a series of coincidences, the world of ship modelling. Right from the start it became the passion that has dominated my life ever since. Initially my work was with sailing vessels of the late nineteenth century but then a visit to the Imperial War Museum and a re-acquaintance with Norman's work started me on a series of Second World War warships. As time went on I assembled articles, plans and photographs relating to and by Norman that were used both as research tools and as artistic inspiration.

A few of Norman's models can still be seen in some of our national museums but, as seems to be the fashion nowadays, usually just the odd model displayed as part of an extended exhibition covering a wider event or battle; others languish in secure storage facilities. I and many others would maintain that his best works are worthy of recognition as outstanding works of art in their own right, and that they should be exhibited as such with due recognition given to the artist, as would be the case were he working with paint and canvas. He brought together a truly remarkable knowledge of his subjects at a time when most official information was restricted, and he had a true artist's ability to put an individual stamp on his work, in a manner never before achieved.

In this volume Alistair Roach has given us a very timely and complete overview of Norman's life and work, something for which I have been waiting and hoping for many years. I would dearly love to see a retrospective exhibition of his work; much is still in public hands, so it's not such a mammoth task. Perhaps this present volume might nudge things in that direction.

Although we never met, Norman has been an ongoing inspiration and presence in my life over the years. Through chance meetings in museums and while undertaking modelling commissions, I have come into contact with many people who knew Norman well. All had a tale to tell. He was without doubt a man of genius, who lived a unique life outside the conventions of the day. He was dedicated to his work, always willing to help the young and aspiring modelmakers, and a true and delightful eccentric into the bargain. If the present volume brings his work to a wider audience it will have more than achieved its purpose.

Philip Reed

❖ INTRODUCTION ❖
SHIP MODELS AND THE WORK OF NORMAN OUGH

'However intrinsically valuable or perfect a model may be she becomes far more intriguing if she has an appeal to the imagination and to the emotions; if one knows what ship she represents, or has at any rate some kind of inkling of the man who made her ...'

(C FOX SMITH, 1951)

When Cicely Fox Smith (1882–1954) made this statement in the introduction of her book *Ship Models* she epitomised why people, regardless of gender or age, are fascinated by ship models from all periods of history – it's about imagination and emotions.

The *Oxford English Dictionary* defines a model, in its present sense, as 'A representation in three dimensions of some projected or existing structure, or some material object, showing the proportions and arrangements of its parts – especially on a smaller scale'. It is also known that people relate to miniatures for a variety of reasons: for example, they have a personal or intimate relationship with the piece, there is perhaps an illusion of control, or they admire the technical challenges overcome by the maker and are fascinated by the human effort involved.

Ship models not only have a special place in maritime history but also are unique among the various forms of evidence for maritime history and archaeology. They provide information that is sometimes lacking in two-dimensional representations such as drawings, pictures or paintings, and also in low relief depictions as seen on medals, coins or seals. Models, even if not true to scale, have proved to be a useful primary source of information as they may have been the subject of contemporary criticism. Sometimes they may be perceived as a class of objects among the 'minor arts'

reflecting one of the most widespread and perennial traits of many people around the world, that is, their close relationship with and dominance over the sea. It has often been recognised that – certainly in any pre-industrial society – a ship was among the largest and most complex movable structures produced, and water, whether it be lake, sea or river, has influenced developments in other spheres such as mythology, religion, language and communication, and power structures within the ideology of particular populations.

The true value of any old ship model is primarily historical, although it appears that collectors often acquire them for their aesthetic qualities – or perhaps now for their monetary value. Reasons for making models in the first place could be many and various, for example religion, presentation or commemoration, aid in building or design, decoration, reconstruction, invention or training, or perhaps for leisure purposes as toys. The often quoted lines from Samuel Pepys's diary probably exemplify the enthusiasm of ship model owners through-out past centuries. On 11 August 1662 he wrote:'Mr Deane, the assistant [shipwright] at Woolwich came to me ... He promises me also a model of a ship, which will please me exceedingly, for I do want one of my owne.' People such as Pepys used models to teach themselves the parts and rigging of a ship but also loved them for their own sake. Model ships often had personal connotations as well as being pleasing to look at and, as ornaments, have been very much in vogue at various times in history.

The main problem with the average wooden ship model is that it is delicate and not made of particularly durable materials. Most are made up from many types of organic material such as wood or bone, and textiles for rigging and sails, and so on. All these materials are sensitive to variations in light levels, and in temperature and relative humidity, which lead to distortion and degradation and the growth of bacteria and fungi. The use of some metals such as lead also poses difficult conservation problems as the metal parts of models may tend to corrode in certain conditions or perhaps set up chemical reactions with other metals or wood they come into contact with.

Put simply, I believe the importance of model ships is that they can be seen as a reflection of the deepest interests of societies which were, and in some cases still are, dependent on the sea and ships. They are a cultural and historical resource that has been much undervalued, if indeed ever recognised, and it is hoped that a publication such as this will help to do something to redress the balance.

Norman Ough

Norman Ough's life and work will be looked at more fully in later chapters, but for now his work can perhaps be summed up by a quote from a local newspaper of the time, which read: 'for beautiful craftsmanship, for accuracy of detail and design, Mr Ough's models are unsurpassed'.

Ough's drawings and models have, over the years, been looked upon as masterpieces. In some circles he was thought of as a genius, in others an eccentric, while many believed he was both. His whole life revolved around model making, and in spite of his genius it appears he never had any money nor ever married. Once, when asked why he had not married, his simple and immediate reply was 'I'm too much of a model maker: I wouldn't inflict it on any woman'. With regard to money, another eminent model maker of the 1950s, Donald McNarry, asked Ough

Model maker - Ough at work on his model of HMS *Daring* for Mountbatten. (Courtesy the Ough family)

Draughtsman – Ough drawing up plans for HMS *Curacoa*. (Courtesy British Pathé)

for advice on what to charge for making models. With professional common sense Ough replied that the work had to look worth £1 an hour and if you got a quarter of that you were lucky!

Those readers 'of a certain age' will certainly remember Ough's warship drawings which were sold firstly directly by him and later through the David MacGregor Plans Service. He is also remembered for his series of articles in *Model Maker and Model Boats* magazine on 'All Steel Construction' and 'Warship Detail' which were published from 1958 until just before his death in 1965. We know from family correspondence that it was Ough's intention to continue writing these articles and eventually have them published in book form. Unfortunately his untimely death prevented him from doing this but, hopefully, this book will go some way towards fulfilling his wishes by reproducing many of his articles,

illustrated by his own drawings and pictures of his models.

A superb draughtsman, Ough paid great attention to detail and his drawings are very attractive in their own right in addition to being authentic. Most of his warship plans are drawn to a scale of 1/16in to 1ft (1/192 scale) although some of the details and some of the smaller warships are drawn to the larger scale of 1/8in to 1ft (1/96 scale). In more recent years there have been some questions raised regarding the accuracy of Ough's plans and drawings, such as the lines plans of HMS *Hood*, but what has to be remembered is that Ough did not have the resources or the technology that we now take for granted in today's world. His plans included a huge amount of detail and they were mainly drawn using only photographs, measurements made by himself and a great deal of detective work. Yard or official drawings were difficult, if not impossible in some cases, to come by in the 1950s as many were still restricted under the Official Secrets Act. In a 1953 article on *Dido* class cruisers, published in *Model Ships and Power Boats*, Ough wrote:

One of the reasons why comparatively few models of ships of the Royal Navy are attempted by model makers is the fact that there are no detailed drawings of them. To my knowledge the plan reproduced here is the only one in existence of a modern cruiser available to the public.

In an earlier edition of that magazine, in an article about the destroyer HMS *Vega*, he said:

I have used no official information in making this plan, apart from that available to the public. It is based on my collection of photographs of HM ships gathered during the past thirty years and on experience gained in constructing detailed scale models for the Royal United Services Museum and the Imperial War Museum.

On a personal note, HMS *Dido* was the first plan of Ough's I ever purchased as my father had served on HMS *Hermione*, a *Dido* class cruiser, during the Second World War. Needless to say the small balsa wood model I made bore no resemblance to the standard of model that would have been produced by the draughtsman in question!

Ough's model making materials were very traditional for the time with (obviously) no use of modern epoxy resins, vacuum formed plastics, laser cut or acid etched parts. Although he has written very little about his techniques it appears that most of the ship's hulls he built were of American whitewood and it is known that he used veneers, 'Bristol board' and thin card for superstructures. Perspex was used for 'glass', and brass and steel wire were 'ground to appropriate taper' for mast structures and the like. Guns were turned on a lathe from duralumin, and strips of typewriter paper, painted with clear dope, were used to represent the strakes on plated hulls. We also know, from family correspondence, that he used his sister's hair for some of the rigging on his small-scale models depicting the British Grand Fleet at Jutland. He was a skilled metal worker and many of his later models, particularly working models, were fashioned out of tinplate; he wrote a series of articles entitled 'All Steel Construction' which have been included in this book.

His models varied in size and scale. The small waterline models, similar to 'recognition models' used by the Admiralty, were invariably to a scale of 1in to 100ft (1/1200 scale) or 1in to 50ft (1/600 scale) while most of his 'exhibition' models are 1/16in to 1ft (1/192 scale), the same scale as many of his plans, or sometimes half this size, that is, 1/32in to 1ft. The choice of size in this last category may have been simply that of convenience and/or display problems. If, for example, a model of the battle cruiser HMS *Hood* was being produced it would be 53in long at 1/192 scale but only 26.5in at half that scale – a big difference if the model were to be displayed. He also produced working models, some radio controlled. The largest model he is known to have made was a 3/8in to 1ft (1/32 scale) model of the aircraft carrier HMS *Ark Royal*, with a length of 25ft and capable of holding a 'crew' of two men, which he built for the film *Ships with Wings* in 1941.

It appears that Ough thrived on meticulous and thorough research, particularly when he had to depict a particular vessel at a specific time or period in history.

Model of HMS *Queen Elizabeth* that was presented to Admiral Beatty by Lord Howe. (Courtesy the Ough family)

Artist – Ough applying finishing touches to his model of HMS *Dorsetshire* in Dry Dock. (Courtesy the Ough family)

When he was commissioned to make a model for Admiral Lord Beatty of HMS *Queen Elizabeth* it had to be built exactly as she was on the day of the surrender of the German Fleet at Scapa Flow, including the precise signals she was flying at the time. This involved a tremendous amount of research, particularly as the model was made long after the time and the ship herself had gone through various modifications, for example from two funnels to one. At the presentation to Lord Beatty, he and quite a large number of the ship's company looked for faults: the only ones they could find were two oars too many in one of the Carley rafts, and one step too few in the companion-way!

Although Ough was a consummate draughtsman and craftsman we should remember that he originally trained as an artist and, perhaps, this is what makes his models unique. He looked upon his work as both a craft and an art. This was demonstrated

particularly when he was painting his models, as he was very much aware that the control of colour tone was critical to give the right 'feel' to the model, and such artistry is very much in evidence when examining his work.

This book is a tribute to Ough and a celebration of his work. It will bring back memories to some readers but also, hopefully, it will introduce a new generation to the skills of a model maker who knew nothing of computer-controlled robotic carving or Computer-aided Design (CAD) drawings. It is certainly not a definitive work on Ough – there are too many gaps, particularly in the identification and tracking down of all the 400+ models that Ough had supposedly made during his lifetime. During the course of research there have been some tantalising clues as to the whereabouts of some of his work but, unfortunately, not all have led to a successful outcome. All Ough's plans were drawn for model making purposes and many are still available through the ss Great Britain Trust. As far as his models are concerned, some are on display in private or public collections but the majority of those known by national museums are now held in storage at No. 1 The Smithery, Chatham Dockyard. Perhaps the current policy on the part of some of our museums of not displaying models such as Ough's should be questioned, as they are an important aid to the understanding of maritime history, ship building and naval architecture. One day they may be displayed more prominently so they can again 'appeal to the imagination and emotions' of those members of the public who want to gaze at them in wonder.

It has been said that ship modellers have always been a retiring breed, no matter which country they come from, and it is rare to be given a glimpse into a model maker's life, working conditions or personality. I would like to think that this book will remedy that omission and will give the reader an insight into the mind and work of one of the greatest warship model makers of the twentieth century.

Notes and Explanations
Ough's articles comprising 'Warship Detail', 'All Steel Construction' and various others have been reproduced with a minimum of editing. His written work, although it varies considerably throughout the years, is in itself an important archive which complements his models; no attempt has been made to alter it other than to remove references within the text which are irrelevant to the article in question. Some of his writing could be deemed tedious, even long-winded, in places but serendipity plays its part and there are often gems of information to be found within his work.

A number of pictures reproduced in this book have been 'enhanced' as they have come from family photographs or magazine articles, some a century old, and cannot therefore be compared with modern high resolution digital photographs. Hopefully

none of these 'alterations' will detract from the images illustrated or from the story being told about Ough and his work.

Those photographs which are shown with no attributions are those taken by the author or from his collection.

To make best use of available space it should be noted that the plans reproduced in the following chapters are not of a constant scale; rather, a dimensional scale is given in each drawing.

Equivalent Scales:

1in/100ft	=	1/1200
1/32in–1ft	=	1/384
1/16in–1ft	=	1/192
1/8in–1ft	=	1/96
3/16in–1ft	=	1/64
1/4in–1ft	=	1/48
3/8in–1ft	=	1/32
1/2in–1ft	=	1/24

Engineer – Ough lining up the trunnion blocks on the cradle of a model Mk XII 6in naval gun (1/24 scale). The barrel, correctly rifled, together with its pedestal can be seen in the foreground. (MyTimeMedia)

1
❖ BIOGRAPHY OF NORMAN OUGH ❖

Born at the family home at 5, Ashbridge Road, Leytonstone, London on 10 November 1898, Norman Arthur Ough was the eldest son of Arthur Henry Ough (1863–1946) and Annie Milburn (née Goldie). Arthur Ough was an architect, surveyor and civil engineer who worked for many years as architect for Hong Kong University and also the Kowloon–Canton Railway, while Annie had previously been a professional violin player. Norman, at the age of two, accompanied his parents to Hong Kong where he remained for four years, and it appears that it was at this early age that he made his first model boat or ship.

Like many middle-class children of that era Norman was sent to preparatory school; he went to Highfield School in Liphook, Hampshire. This was a small privately-run school that had been founded in Southampton in the summer term of 1892 and then in 1904 moved to a new 175-acre site in Liphook where it still remains. Little is known of Norman's education but it is known that he attended Bootham School (a Quaker Foundation) in York from 1913 until 1916. It appears he attended Bootham not because he was a Quaker – in fact the family were loyal Anglicans – but because the family home, during the First World War, was at Esk Hall in North Yorkshire, which is about forty miles from the school.

There are various records in the Bootham School archive which show his interests and achievements. His leaver's entry stated:

N. A. Ough leaves from Upper Senior. With pen and ink he could do marvels on paper, being an exceedingly clever draughtsman. As a metal worker he was well known, the Show never failing to contain some of his exhibits. He was also an archaeologist. Last term he obtained the Bronze Medallion.

Ough, age 2, with his parents. (Courtesy the Ough family)

Ough's drawing of his own hand, completed when at school in 1912 (note that he was left-handed). (Courtesy the Ough family)

The 1914 School Register gives his address as Esk Hall, Sleights, Yorkshire and it also states that he was placed 17th for his Archaeology Diary in the Inter-School Diary Competition in 1913. What is even more revealing is the entry in the 1935 Bootham School Register, which would have been compiled and submitted by Ough himself. He lists himself as Norman Arthur Ough, a 'Craftsman', and gives his address as 33, Greek Street, Shaftsbury Avenue, London W1. He then states he is a:

Specialist in Ship Models: Made series of historical models of ships from Roman times to present, now at Royal Albert Memorial Museum, Exeter: Models of historical ships in action during Great War (under supervision of Admiralty) for Imperial War Museum: Series of models of modern war ships for Royal United Service Museum, London: Model of Grand Fleet as organised at Battle of Jutland, for naval exhibit at HM Govt. Pavilion at British Exhibition, Wembley, 1925.

He goes on to say his hobbies are 'reading books on Socialism, interested in modern ideas generally, especially those concerned with eliminating the chance of war; sketching; furniture-making'.

Going back to 1916, when he left school during the First World War, it appears he received his conscription papers but refused to join up and instead became a conscientious objector. Although the records were destroyed in the Second World War it seems he was imprisoned in Dartmoor. The story goes that he escaped and went, during the night time, to his Aunt Eleanor, who lived with her parents in Torquay. At great risk she provided food and shelter to the young Norman. Apparently he was recaptured and returned to prison but it is unknown for how long.

After the war the family moved to Stanmore House, East Cliff Road, Dawlish in Devon. It was from here that Ough attended the Exeter School of Art where he started his modelling in earnest although, as was mentioned earlier, his interest in model ships dated back to when he was about three or four years old. It appears that Arthur Ough had invested well in the South American 'rubber boom', which enabled the

Bootham School photograph, circa 1916. Ough is second from the right in the back row. (Courtesy the Ough family)

family to live in Dawlish very comfortably. This is described in family papers that date from 1923:

The style of living was quite luxurious as the family were still very wealthy. The house was large and richly appointed. It consisted of basements, a ground floor with a huge lounge, hall and dining room with fine views on all sides, as the building together with its extensive grounds overlooked the sea. On the second floor were the bedrooms and beautifully appointed bathrooms. The numerous staff of maids, cook, butler and gardener, lived, with the exception of the gardener, on the uppermost floor of the house. In the grounds there was a fine tennis court and many lovely trees and flowering shrubs. There was also a conservatory in which luscious and enormous strawberries were grown … The family also owned a little sheltered corner of the beach …

Unfortunately Arthur lost the greater part of his fortune and Stanmore was sold, the family moving to a smaller property called St Cleer, also in Dawlish.

While at art school Ough built a working model of a sailing boat based on one he used to sail in Dawlish Bay. This model was displayed at the Exeter Museum and as a result he was commissioned by the then Curator to build a series of models depicting the development of ships through the ages (as mentioned in his School Register). Such

was Ough's enthusiasm that in the 1920s, when he was living in Dawlish, he would cycle to London and back in search of information – a round trip of over 360 miles!

Ough eventually moved to London and settled down to the job of completing the 1in to 100ft (1/1200 scale) model of the Grand Fleet at Jutland, comprising 151 waterline model ships, and simultaneously began work for the Imperial War Museum. He was also given various other commissions, such as a series of models for the Royal United Service Museum, a model of HMS *Queen Elizabeth*, that was presented by Lord Howe to Earl Beatty at a reunion dinner, and a larger version of the same ship for Lord Howe himself.

Having set up his main workshop at 98, Charing Cross Road, London WC2 during the mid-1930s, Ough remained there for the rest of his life. He produced many plans, articles and models over the years from this tiny top floor flat – part studio, part drawing office, part workshop and also living space. When Ough was working on the model of HMS *Glorious* in 1932 he was interviewed for *Ships and Ship Models* magazine by a reporter who stated that:

Mr Ough's workshop is so small that when he and I and the Glorious occupied the floor space, there seemed no room for a single thing more. But every inch of space is used, and every inch is crammed with tools, half finished models, books, files of drawings and photos, and stacks of material. In one corner is a small lathe, while the model on which Mr Ough is engaged occupies a special revolving stand in the centre. Under the window is a bench, littered with pieces of wood and metal which, under the magic touch of the craftsman, resolve themselves into delicate parts of a warship.

An intriguing story from the family papers reveals that when Ough was working on this model of HMS *Glorious* the only thing he could find that was fine enough to fabricate the ship's wireless aerials were strands of hair from his sister's head.

It was also said that Ough was so dedicated to his craft that he was hospitalised twice suffering from malnutrition, because

Self-portrait by Ough. (Courtesy the Ough family)

he considered that time spent eating was time that could be spent on his models! It appeared that he had the capacity for prolonged periods of concentration; among his interests, apart from model making, was philosophy (he was a Theosophist), which he thought promoted an analytic habit that was useful in any kind of work.

During the Second World War Ough remained a conscientious objector, albeit one who specialised in the study of warships, and it is believed that at this stage in his life he was employed by Lord Louis Mountbatten as a warship modeller. He also worked on ship models and special effects in the film industry during this time, producing propaganda and other films including: *Convoy* (1940); *Sailors Three* (1940); *Spare a Copper* (1940); *Ships with Wings* (1941); *Blockade* (1942); and *San Demetrio* (1943). Later, after the war, he worked on *Scott of the Antarctic* in 1948. Although not officially employed as a 'fire watcher' during the London Blitz it appears he used to climb up onto the roof of his flat in Charing Cross Road during air raids and watch the bombers disgorging their incendiary and high explosive bombs onto the city. Although a pacifist he was certainly not a coward.

To obtain an insight into the person Ough was is fairly difficult but I have been fortunate to have been lent a selection of letters between himself and his siblings. Ough had a younger brother Bernard (1907–1989), a younger sister Hilda (1900–1924) who died during the flu epidemic after the First World War, and another sister, Joan, who was born in 1916. He, Bernard and Joan frequently wrote to each other and

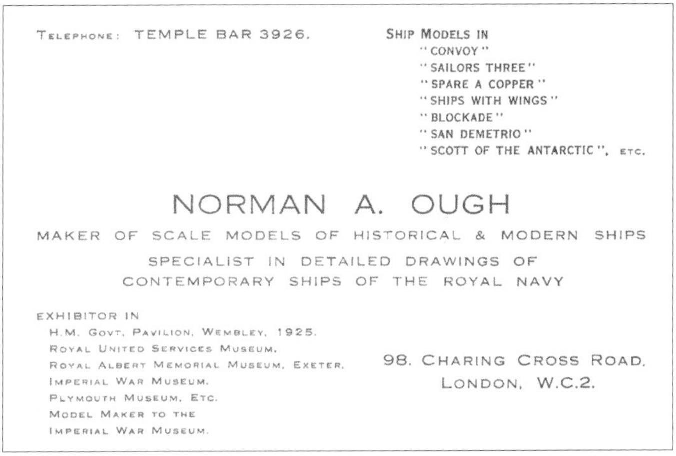

Telephone: TEMPLE BAR 3926.

Ship Models in
"CONVOY"
"SAILORS THREE"
"SPARE A COPPER"
"SHIPS WITH WINGS"
"BLOCKADE"
"SAN DEMETRIO"
"SCOTT OF THE ANTARCTIC", etc.

NORMAN A. OUGH

MAKER OF SCALE MODELS OF HISTORICAL & MODERN SHIPS

SPECIALIST IN DETAILED DRAWINGS OF CONTEMPORARY SHIPS OF THE ROYAL NAVY

EXHIBITOR IN
H.M. Govt. Pavilion, Wembley, 1925.
Royal United Services Museum.
Royal Albert Memorial Museum, Exeter.
Imperial War Museum.
Plymouth Museum, Etc.
Model Maker to the Imperial War Museum.

98. CHARING CROSS ROAD, LONDON, W.C.2.

Ough's business card. (Courtesy the Ough family)

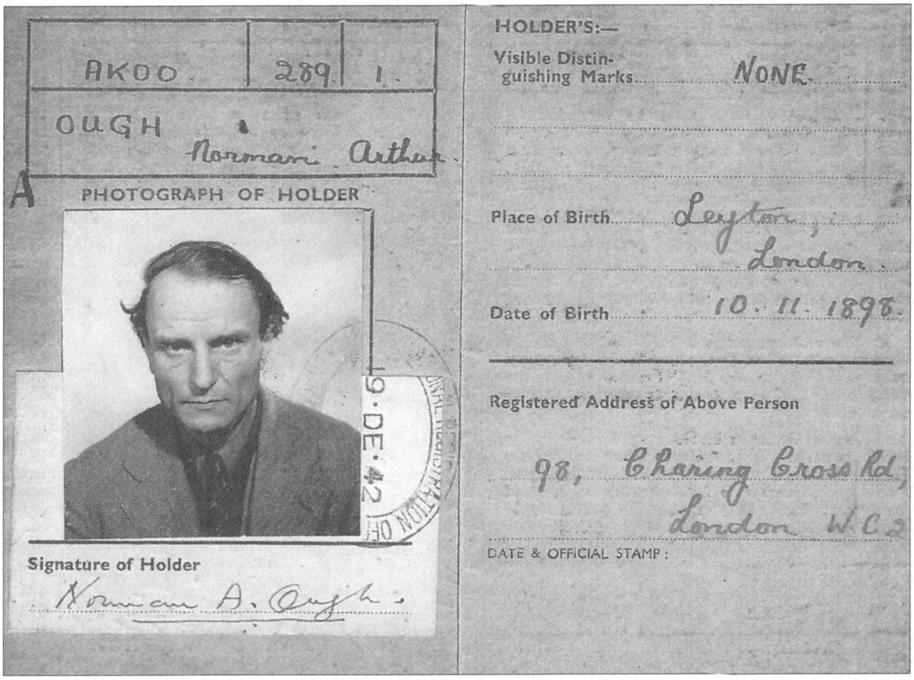

AKOO. 289 1.
OUGH Norman Arthur
A
PHOTOGRAPH OF HOLDER
Signature of Holder Norman A. Ough.

HOLDER'S:—
Visible Distin-guishing Marks NONE.
Place of Birth Leyton, London
Date of Birth 10. 11. 1898.
Registered Address of Above Person 98, Charing Cross Rd, London W.C.2
DATE & OFFICIAL STAMP:
9 DE 42

Ough's wartime Identity Card dated 1942. (Courtesy the Ough family) although much of the contents of the letters relate to family matters there are some intriguing facts which throw some light onto Ough's personality, his finances and the way he worked.

Why Ough moved to 98, Charing Cross Road we may never know but there is one connection, as far as location is concerned: his grandfather, Henry Ough (1836–1919), an architect, based his practice at 29, Charing Cross in 1868. The building which housed No. 98 has long gone and there is now a modern office block in its place. Where Ough lived was once described by one of his siblings as follows:

His environment gave no indication that he was the world's most famous ship model-maker. His one room was uncomfortable to say the least - brown linoleum floor, small window with a thin torn green curtain that dimmed the light to an eerie green. A cot under his beautiful hand-made lathe, a tiny round gas ring on the floor with a few pieces of asbestos balanced precariously over the flame to increase the heat. Two wooden chairs with split seats; a thin cushion on his was the only

Ough in his workshop/flat in Charing Cross Road, working on his model of HMS *Dorsetshire*. (Courtesy the Ough family)

concession to comfort. Books everywhere. And everything except his tools covered in thick dust. I doubt he ever made his bed. A modern eccentric genius. He lived on cheese rolls and tea from a small café downstairs. Yet he was lithe and seemingly healthy.

Ough's eccentricity became outwardly more obvious in later life as, due to a shortage of money, he would acquire 'new' items of clothing for himself from the cast-offs of various theatre company wardrobe departments, and perhaps 'accessorise' them with other pieces found in waste bins. Apparently he could be quite witty and could talk for hours – but he dried up if he became aware that he was the centre of attention as he was essentially a very shy man. Not only did he spend long hours at his workbench or drawing board producing models and plans but, having built up quite a reputation as a draughtsman, he had to spend a great deal of time answering enquiries and sending off samples and lists of what plans were available to buy. In one of his letters to his sister and brother-in-law, dated 6 March 1960, Ough wrote:

It has taken me 7 years to build up my plans service to an income of £6 a week and about £70 a year from articles, but it is growing slowly. I now have 2,000 letters of enquiry a year which I answer with the enclosed sample and price list. '*Model Maker*' wants me to turn the articles and plans into a book but it is too early yet as there is still a lot more of the subject 'British Warship Detail from 1890' still to be covered. I have sold £1,700 of plans since starting ...

It is uncertain how well off Ough was at this stage in his life. David Weller remembers that in the summer of 1960, when he was 16, he was taken by his father to see Ough at Charing Cross Road. Mr Weller and Ough were both members of the Naval Photograph Club and appear to have known each other for a number of years. David's memories of the occasion include the fact that Ough's flat was high up in one of the somewhat foreboding Victorian tenement buildings. It was rather dark inside and extremely cluttered. Ough appeared (from a 16-year-old's point of view) to be very old and a reclusive person, moving slowly but with an intense gaze. He was clearly immersed in his work, which at that time appeared to be concentrated on producing warship drawings rather than constructing ship models. David remembers that his father bought a large collection of drawings that afternoon, for which Ough appeared very grateful. David also had a distinct feeling that his father had spent considerably more than he had intended to. In retrospect he thinks that his father may have been acutely aware of Ough's lifestyle and circumstances and was motivated to help an old acquaintance in as unobtrusive a way as possible, and also without offending Ough's sense of dignity. At the time young David was just excited coming into contact with, and acquiring, so many stunning drawings of wonderful warships.

Later that same year, just after Christmas, Ough writes to his sister and brother-in-law again:

This is to thank you for 100 cigarettes – most enjoyable – a magnificent gift! I am not accustomed to smoking gentlemen's cigarettes and they are a distinguished change from 'Weights' [a very cheap cigarette of the time].

Everyone said I couldn't make a living by selling plans of RN ships – so I am making a living at it! Or rather, what I call a living, which means paying the rent, smoking a few fags and reading books about Flying Saucers and drawing most of the day. The rest of it is answering between 2,000 to 3,000 letters a year – about 4 or 5 times the Admiralty's pre-war figure for enquiries re. plans. Enclosed are a few samples of the latest. All this is OK by the Admiralty as all these ships have been scrapped or are obsolete anyway. It is almost impossible to imagine what the Navy's future will be apart from submarine classes and atomic submarines with atomic weapons ...

The rest of the letter is taken up with his thoughts and beliefs in flying saucers and alien life forms.

Some four years later, in December 1964, Ough writes again and it is apparent from this letter that his health is not as good as it was. He talks about shared friends using their nicknames such as 'Fount of all

Wisdom', 'Dirty Johnny', 'The Giant Sloth' and 'Lord Bountiful'! He mentions that for the past thirteen months he had been living on a £3 7s 6d a week retirement pension (equivalent to around £24.50 in 2015) but he was allowed to earn a further £5 before cuts were made. He complains that when 'he fell ill two and a half years ago' he had to hand over his plans service to 'his publishers' who took two-thirds of the takings. He doesn't state what his 'illness' was but mentions fibrositis (rheumatic inflammation) and having to take tablets to cut down on the pain, which had got worse over the past two months. It appears that every Sunday he walked to the Round Pond at Kensington Gardens, a return distance of about eight miles, to watch the model boating and yachting, and did this every week unless it was raining. He also complains that 'it is very cold at night in front of the little old gas fire'.

10 March 1960.

DRAWINGS OF WARSHIPS
(Whole hull and full detail)

All full scale Prints are sent rolled round a tube to save creasing.
PLEASE NOTE: Some of these plans have the "Lines" drawing separate.

BATTLESHIPS.

H.M.S. DUKE OF YORK. (Scale 1" = 16') 1941-58			
	PROFILE AND PLAN OF TOPSIDES	£1.	0. 0.
	LINES, BODY PLAN AND PLATING		10. 0.
H.M.S. WARSPITE (Scale 1" = 16') as in 1928 with		£1.	0. 0.
	trunked funnel		
	LINES PLAN FOR 1914 and 1930		10. 0.

BATTLE CRUISER

H.M.S. LION (Scale 1" = 16') as at Jutland ...	£1.	0. 0.
do. "Lines" only		10. 0.

CORVETTE

H.M.S. HEDINGHAM CASTLE (Scale 1" = 8') ...	£1.	0. 0.

CRUISERS

H.M.S. DIDO (Scale 1" = 16') 1939 to date ...	£1.	0. 0.
do. "Lines" only ...		10. 0.
H.M.S. CURACOA (Scale 1" = 16') 1916 - 42 ...	£1.	0. 0.
H.M.S. SHEFFIELD (Scale 1" = 16') as in 1954	£1.	0. 0.
do. "Lines" and "Detail"		
(2 drawings) together ...		10. 0.
H.M.S. PENELOPE (1936-44) (Scale 1" = 16', detail		
1" = 8')	£1.	0. 0.

DESTROYERS

			Class		
H.M.S. VEGA (Scale 1" = 16') 1916 - 45	"V"		12. 6.
H.M.S. DARING (Scale 1" = 16') 1934	"D"	£1.	0. 0.
H.M.S. MATABELE (Scale 1" = 16') 1936	"Tribal"	£1.	0. 0.
H.M.S. CADIZ (Scale 1" = 16')	"Battle"	£1.	0. 0.
H.M.S. KASHMIR (Scale 1" = 8') 1942	"K"	£1.	0. 0.
do. "Lines" only			10. 0.

OCEAN MINESWEEPER

H.M.S. MARVEL (Scale 1" = 8')	"Algerine"	10. 0.
do. "Lines", &c.		10. 0.

SUBMARINES

E. 29 (Scale 1" = 8')		10. 0.
L. 52 (Scale 1" = 8')		10. 0.
OLYMPUS (Scale 1" = 8')	"O"	10. 0.

ENLARGED DETAIL IS ON ALL 1/16" SCALE DRAWINGS AND IS TO THE SCALE
OF 1" = 8'

Model warship plans price list from 1960. (Courtesy the Ough family)

Ough's certificate of cremation after his death in 1965. (Courtesy the Ough family)

It must have been about this time that Ough was admitted to hospital as two months later, in February 1965, Ough's brother Bernard was sent a letter from the Royal Marsden Hospital, Fulham Road, London SW3. It informed him that Ough was unlikely to return home and that he was being transferred to the French Hospital, which had a number of beds belonging to the Marie Curie Memorial Hospital. Bernard was being told as next of kin. On the letter a scribbled note mentions a Mr Wallis, who was a consultant, and also 'carcinoma' (cancer). Ough was admitted to the Marie Curie Memorial Foundation Home, Edenhall, Lyndhurst Gardens, Hampstead, London NW3 on 8 June 1965 and he remained there until his death on 3 August. Two days later his funeral service was held at Golders Green Crematorium.

One story relating to Ough's stay in hospital was that as he was so used to sleeping under his workbench at Charing Cross Road, on occasions he would be found asleep under the hospital ward table, having moved his bedding there.

It is interesting to note that in his will Ough left a total of £931 19s 6d when he died – 20% of this he left to Joan Harris, his sister, 20% to the Theosophical Society and 60% to a Mrs Wyne Hunt, but nothing to his brother Bernard. From the family papers it appears that John and Wyne Hunt were Consultant Designers based at 26, Thurloe Street in Knightsbridge and Ough used their company to have his ship plans printed for customers. If Wyne Hunt had done most of this work for him this would have been reflected in his generous bequest.

Nothing is known of what happened to the personal effects, models and model making equipment that may have been left at his flat in Charing Cross Road. We do know, however, that David MacGregor (1925–2003), who was an eminent maritime historian and had his own plans service, apparently obtained the sole rights to Ough's plans, and marketed them from the 1960s onwards. This continued until MacGregor's own death in 2003 when he bequeathed his estate, including his and Ough's plans, to the ss Great Britain Trust. This bequest, and the handling of it, is discussed in the chapter on 'Drawings and Plans'.

2
❖ ORDNANCE ❖

The following articles, all depicting various forms of ordnance, were featured in the 'Warship Detail' series published by *Model Maker* magazine during the 1950s and '60s. They are an important archive of Ough's written work and were completed by him to describe the larger and more detailed scale drawings which he had produced to meet the demands of the really discerning modeller or collector. They have been edited to a minor degree to prevent any ambiguity or to make more sense in their present context, such as when Ough refers to other articles or pictures which have not been included. A list of the original publications can be found in the Bibliography at the end of this book.

4.7in Twin Quick Firing Guns

At a first glance this drawing may seem rather daunting to a model maker, and, if the whole mass as represented in the three general arrangement plans (2), (3) and (4) is considered it would be very difficult to make much sense of them without some acquaintance with the actual guns as mounted on a destroyer. If, however, the plan of the base plate of the mounting (7) is studied first, and after that the drawings of the right and left hand 'brackets' (9 and 10) and of the two cradles (6 and 8) it will be found that the rest of the complex detail will fit into place. The key to the understanding of an engineering drawing is to have some knowledge of how the machine it represents works, and it is hoped that this article will do something towards elucidation.

The 4.7in. twin guns were the main armament of many of the destroyers of the Second World War, including the 'Tribal' and the 'J', 'K' and 'N' class ships. The 'Tribal' class carried four mountings of two guns each and the 'J', 'K' and 'N' class three. In the 'Tribal' class the aftermost pair, 'Y' gun mounting (the others being 'A' and 'B' on the forecastle and 'X' on the after superstructure) was often found to be unworkable in heavy seas, and in the next class it was abolished, thus enabling these ships to carry a heavier torpedo armament.

The mounting consists of a circular base plate (7) with a central pivot about which it turns. The base plate runs on roller bearings situated beneath it and contained within the bearing ring, the latter having a broad flange pierced with holes through which pass massive bolts securing it to the deck. The base plate is held to the base ring by the four clips shown on the plan. On the base plate are built the two brackets (9 and 10) made of heavy steel plating stiffened with angle bars at the edges, which carry the bearings for the pivots or 'trunnions' of the gun cradles (6 and 8). At the side of each bracket is built a platform (4), covered with steel strips to prevent slipping, to accommodate the guns' crew. A shield of thin plating is built overall to keep rain and spray off the mounting and its fittings when the guns are not manned. In destroyers the plating of the shield is too thin to afford much protection against shell splinters but heavier plating would involve greater weight in positions high above the waterline, more than can be accepted in view of the stability of such ships.

The guns, one of which is shown in section in (1), consist of a single tube, the rifled barrel, and a reinforcing jacket which is shrunk over it. The jacket, which is partly tapered and partly made cylindrical to fit the cradle, is screwed into a massive steel forging called the 'breech ring' which carries the mechanism of the breech block. The rifled bore begins as a chamber of larger diameter to take the charge, and is partly formed in the breech ring and partly in the barrel of the gun. As may be seen in the drawing the chamber is long enough to accommodate the brass cartridge containing the charge and is of such a length that when the gun is loaded the copper 'driving band' of the shell just reaches the start of the rifling, against the grooves of which the driving band is rammed home. The band is fitted round the shell near its base and is of larger diameter than the bore so that, when the ridges of the rifling score into it on firing, a gas-tight joint results preventing the expanding gases of the charge from passing ahead of the shell. The grooves of the rifling, of which there are about 30, are, in effect, a very elongated multiple

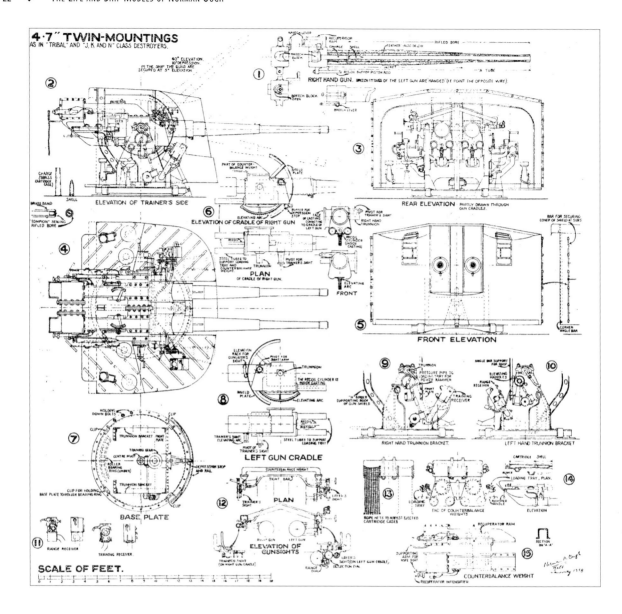

4.7in twin quick firing guns. (MyTimeMedia)

screw thread of a pitch equal to the length of the bore. This gives a rapid spin to the shell so ensuring that it will travel point forwards owing to gyroscopic action. The speed at which the shell leaves the muzzle of the gun, called the 'muzzle velocity', is more than half-a-mile a second. The shell weighs about 50lb, and there is about 12lb of cordite in the charge. The weight of each gun, without the breech mechanism, is about 3 tons.

The guns are mounted in a casting like a metal sleeve called the 'cradle' which fits over the cylindrical part of the jacket, the one for the right gun being shown in detail at (6) and for the left gun at (8). Into this casting the massive steel pins called trunnions are screwed and shrunk on opposite sides, their purpose being to serve as a pivot which the gun (or guns) elevate. The latter can move forwards and backwards freely in the cradle with an exact fit which is ensured by lining rings bearing on the jacket, and they are prevented from turning by steel 'feathers' which are hardened bars recessed into the jacket and running in a milled groove in the cradle. When the guns fire they recoil with immense force, over 2,000 foot tons for each, and the sudden shock to the mounting has to be damped down by converting it into a controlled lengthwise movement of declaration. This is effected partly by the recoil cylinder, which is fitted in the cradle casting below the gun, and partly by the recuperator, or return press, fitted above the cradle which runs the gun back to the loading position. The recoil cylinder consists of an accurately machined barrel carrying a piston, the rod of which is secured to a heavy steel lug on the breech ring. The cylinder is filled with oil at the breech end and when the gun recoils the oil passes through a reducing valve in the piston. This valve is arranged to require increasing pressure for the oil to pass through the piston in proportion to the length of the recoil, so bringing the movement to a standstill. In destroyers the guns are made to recoil over a longer distance than in cruisers to reduce the stress on their lighter decks and frames. Bolted to the top of the cradle is the counter-balance weight shown separately and in section at (15). This contains, at its rear end, the cylinder of the recuperator, the piston, or rather the ram, of which is secured to a steel lug on the top of the breech ring. When the gun recoils the ram, which is hollow, is thrust into the recuperator cylinder against the pressure of compressed air, thus helping the recoil cylinder below to damp down the thrust. At the end of its travel the air pressure is automatically increased in the recuperator balance weight and the ram is moved forward, returning the gun to the loading position. The rear end of the counter weight is supported below the gun by two steel tubes screwed into the lower part of the cradle. On one of these, at each gun, is fitted the loading tray, shown end on, and in plan and elevation at (14). This carries the shell, with its charge in a separate brass cartridge case, and the rammer for moving them into the breech when the tray is swung into line with the bore. An automatic mechanism prevents the tray from being in this position when the guns are loaded and the breech blocks are closed. The rammer is worked by a wire tackle the fall of which ends in a wood handle as shown.

All modern naval guns above 0.5in calibre are 'director controlled', that is the armament is directed and fired as a whole from the Director Control Tower (DCT) situated high up at the after end of the bridge. The information regarding the enemy's bearing, speed, etc., is gathered in the DCT and passed electrically to calculating machines situated deep in the ship in the Transmitting Station below the bridge. These make allowances for temperature, wind direction, drift of the shells after firing, differences of

angle of training owing to the spacing of the gun mountings, and many others, and pass the corrected information to the guns, which it reaches in the form of movements of pointers over the graduations on dials. The gun layer and trainer move their guns in accord with this information. The housing of the dials are shown in (11) and their position on the brackets of the mounting in (9) and (10). The guns are moved by the layer for elevation (range) by handles connected by reduction gearing to the elevating arc, a toothed segment bolted to the bottom of the cradle, and by the trainer who controls the bearing of the guns by similar handles geared to the bearing ring below the base plate. The layer and trainer have telescopic sights for use if the gunnery control system is damaged. These are very complex, but, in outline, they are kept visually on the enemy independently of the movement in elevation of the guns, and they are connected across together by a counter-balance weight and an adjustable arm. The sights are moved in elevation and deflection by the sight-setter on the layer's side, the connection to the cradle being by the toothed rack shown in (8). Doors in the shield allow space for the sights to obtain a clear view.

It would take many pages to describe all the details of these guns and mountings, but perhaps enough has been said to render the drawing a little more intelligible to model makers. It is not necessary to possess a lathe to make a model as nearly all the detail can be rendered in wood, wire and paper with tinfoil to represent the bright steelwork.

4in Twin High-Angle / Low-Angle (HA/LA) Guns
These are the guns carried by the majority of ships of the Royal Navy at the present day. Either as shown here, or in slightly modified forms, they are mounted in cruisers as long range high angle armament, or, used at low angles, as a secondary battery and as dual-purpose guns in frigates, sloops, in many destroyers and in ships converted from destroyers to fast anti-submarine escort vessels. The detail is even more crowded than in the 4.7in twin guns of which a drawing is shown above, but here again the bewildering complexities can be dealt with by considering the main items separately and afterwards combining them into a whole. The principal features are the guns, the recoil, the cradle, the carriage, the base plate, the training and elevating gear, the sights and the receivers for director control.

Model makers who attempt to show the detail of

a warship are nearly always defeated by the mechanism of the guns if they happen to be in open shields. Many photographs of them exist, usually taken with the guns' crew blocking the view, but what appears on a photograph is without meaning until some explanation of the significance of the various items is available. It is hoped that the principles involved, which are similar in most naval guns, will be made a little clearer in some of these articles, enough at least to enable a model maker to read photographs more easily. The gun detail, in its cold gleaming magnificence, is essential to the character of a model of a warship. It looks what it is, purposeful and deadly, like the ship herself. Incidentally, these

4in twin high-angle / low-angle guns. (MyTimeMedia)

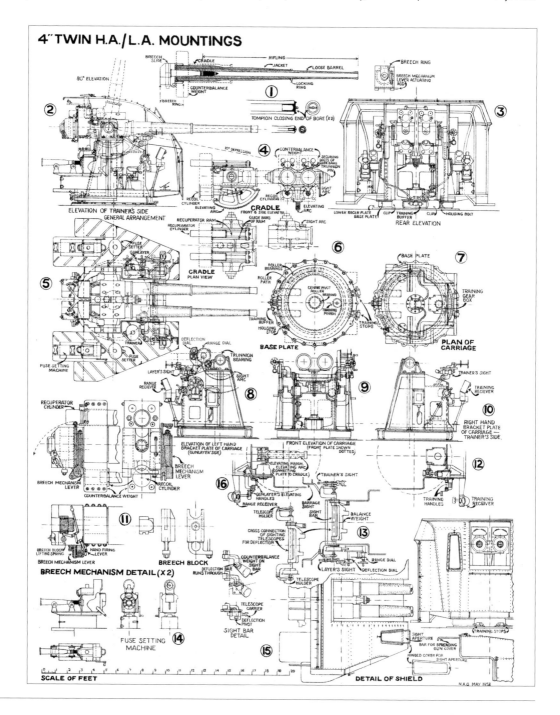

articles are the first anywhere to publish studies of this kind, based on serious research, of the detail of HM ships of today and of their equipment and armament for model makers.

The guns consist, as do the 4.7in previously described, of a rifled barrel, a jacket closely fitted over part of its length and secured by a collar, and a breech ring screwed to the end of the jacket. A chamber to take the cartridge carrying the charge and of larger diameter than the bore is formed partly in the breech ring and partly in the rifled barrel as shown in section in (1). The breech ring is, in spite of its name, a rectangular steel forging with a large space milled with parallel sides and in a vertical direction through it to take the sliding breech block. The latter carries, on a projection from its base, a heavy vertical rod round which a spiral spring is secured and housed in a circular space drilled into the breech ring, its purpose being to hold the block up to its highest point of travel when it is closed over the cartridge. The breech mechanism lever when pulled down horizontal – that is to the 'open' position – compresses this spring and draws the breech block clear of the bore and chamber, the down motion being arranged to bring the extractor levers into action so ejecting the used cartridge. The breech mechanism (BM) moves vertically to enable the guns to be mounted close together in the cradle thus saving space and weight, the arrangement for the right gun being shown enlarged in (11). The BM lever, etc., of the left gun is 'handed', that is reversed. The rifled barrel is given an increased diameter at the muzzle. The reason for this is that the tube can withstand the pressure of the expanding gas of the charge as it passes along the bore behind the shell since one part of the barrel supports the next, but, at the end where there is no further support, more metal is required to meet the stress. The pressure in the chamber when the charge is exploding is from 18 to 20 tons to the square inch. The rifling consists of about 30 grooves, the spiral making a single complete turn to the right.

The shell weighs about 35lb and the ammunition is fixed, that is, the shell is attached to the charge which is contained in a brass cartridge case as shown in (1) and in (2) and (14). It will be seen that the trunnions and cradle are placed far back along the length of the guns. This is to allow clearance below the breech when they are loaded at high elevation which, at maximum, is 80 degrees. Since the guns are pivoted so far back they would be out of balance,

or 'muzzle-heavy', so a massive counter-balance weight is built around the breech ring. This carries the recuperator, or running-out press above and the recoil cylinder below as in (4) and (11). The former is filled with air under high pressure and the latter with oil, a reserve supply of which is carried in containers on top and at the side of the counter-balance weight of each gun. On firing, the piston of the recoil cylinder is pulled forward by its attachment to a lug below the cradle. Oil flows from the forward side of the piston through a reducing valve converting the thrust of recoil into a lengthwise movement of deceleration. At the same time the ram of the recuperator, which is attached to the counter-balance weight of the gun as in (4), is thrust into its cylinder against air pressure, thus taking up part of the recoil. On the pressure being increased by the 'intensifier' the ram is pushed forward and carries the gun back to the loading position. The amount of force required to be damped down by the recoil mechanism is about 190 foot tons, the movement of which can vary between almost horizontal and almost vertical, so that the problem of mounting such guns in a lightly built ship involves many structural difficulties, one of which is to ensure that the 'racer' plate which carries the roller bearings of the mounting shall be, and remain, level and truly at right angles to its vertical axis. Errors in this respect are known as 'tilt' and have to be allowed for in trials of each mounting. Great accuracy is required in ordnance engineering. For example, in the final boring operation prior to the rifling of a 15in gun, the 'tolerance', or permitted error, is minus but not plus 0.001in. This amounts to the machining of a hole over 50 feet long and 15in in diameter not oversize at all, and undersize less than the thickness of a piece of cigarette paper!

The cradle is an intricate casting consisting of two cylindrical sleeves to hold the guns webbed together with their axes parallel and with projections below to receive the ends of the pistons of the recoil cylinders as shown in (4). Massive connections on top of each sleeve carry the recuperator cylinders. Along the centre line of the underside of the cradle is bolted the casting carrying the toothed rack of the elevating arc, and on each side of the main casting are screwed the heavy pins, or trunnions, which are the pivots about which the guns elevate. In the plan and elevation views in (4) the recuperator rams and draw bars are shown exposed. In (5) they are shown with the protective lagging with its access plates for

❖

lubrication fitted in place. When the guns recoil the draw rods, which are anchored in the upper part of the counter-balance weights, pull the rams into the recuperator cylinders against high pressure air. The intensifier steps up the pressure to return the guns to the loading position.

The carriage shown in (8), (9) and (10) consists of two heavy bracket plates reinforced by angle bars and a front plate connecting them. The left hand bracket plate (8) carries the elevating gearbox and a frame with bearings for the cranked handles which operate the elevating pinion through shafts and bevel and worm gears, and also the trunnion or bearing for the left hand or gun layer's end of the sight bar. It also carries a junction box for the many electrical connections. The right hand bracket plate is similar except that it carries the casting for the cranked handles for the training gear and the somewhat different bearing for the trainer's end of the sight bar. It also has a junction box. Projections from the forward end of the bracket plates act as supports for the range and training receivers. The front plate is shown dotted in (9), and on the base plate in the centre can be seen the box housing the large worm and pinion which trains the mounting. A plan view of the elevating gear is shown in (16).

The carriage as a whole rests on the base plate which is mainly circular with projections on the left and right. Under it is the 'racer plate' which is a machined casting bolted to the deck and which carries the track for the vertical roller bearings of the centre pivot and the path and guides for the horizontal roller bearings of the mounting. These are shown in (6) and (7) and, in the latter, the angle bar connections of the bracket plates with the base plate can be seen and also the toothed rack for the training pinion. A raised platform is built on each side to take the seats for the gun layer and trainer and the fuse setters. It is covered with footstrips to prevent the guns' crew from slipping on the steel plates in a seaway. The base ring has two massive stops bolted to it and a buffer on the revolving part of the base plate. These are placed so as to prevent the guns being trained into positions where they can hit part of the ship or cause damage by blast.

Nearly all modern naval guns are Director Controlled, that is they are given the range and bearing and can be fired in salvoes or as a full broadside from the Director Sight which is in the Director Control Tower high up at the after end of the bridge. Many corrections have to be applied to the information taken in by the Director Sight, such as allowance for wind direction, speed of own ship and that of the enemy, magazine temperature and others including an allowance for 'drift' or the tendency of the spinning shell to follow a curved path in the horizontal plane. The corrections are made in the Transmitting Station deep down in the ship and passed to the guns where they are accepted as pointer readings, by the receiver for range on the left of the mounting and for deflection on the right. This information is then applied to the sights. It is a paradox of artillery that a gun is never pointed at a target, but is laid and trained so as to hit the target which is not quite the same. It must be given the appropriate deflection to allow for drift at a given range, and must be elevated to allow the end of the curved path followed by the shell in the vertical plane to coincide with the target, or, more simply, to hit it!

The range and deflection angles having been applied to the sights, which are geared to the gun, the layer and trainer move the latter until the target appears in the centre of the sighting telescopes. The gun is then in the correct position for firing. The sights are carried on hinged plates at each end of a cross bar held in bearings on the carriage, the bar being fitted with a weight to counterbalance the sight carriers and telescopes as shown in (13). A toothed rack as in (4) connects the sight bar to the cradle of the gun and to the range dial. Through its centre runs the connecting bar for deflection which moves the sight carriers laterally and which is geared to the deflection dial. When the sights are set for range and deflection and brought on to the target, the gun is in position for firing. To describe the mechanism adequately would take a long time, but perhaps enough has been explained to make possible the fitting of the sights to a model of say 1/4in-1ft scale.

For high angle fire against aircraft, the shell has to be given a time fuse so that it will explode near them. The fuses are set to detonate the shell at the appropriate height by the fuse setter, who uses the machine shown in (14). This clamps and rotates the nose of the shell and sets the fuse, the required information being sent from the Director Sight via the Transmitting Station to the dial facing the fuse setter's seat.

The whole mounting is covered by a thin shield built of angle bar and 1/8in plating which is sometimes extended further to the rear than in the one shown in this drawing, which is of the most

A variety of guns on Ough's model of HMS *Barfleur*. (© National Maritime Museum, Greenwich, London – SLR 1576)

common type, details being shown in (14). The canvas cover is extended by bars projecting from the top of the shield and clamped into position by spikes projecting from clamping bars at the top and sides which pass through eyelet holes in the canvas. The small spikes on the shield, along the front opening are for securing the white canvas jackets of the guns which extend sometimes as far as the collar. All the parts of the breech, clear of the balance weight, are of polished bare steel, as are the parallel parts of the barrels of the guns where they project from the cradle. In peace time the muzzle ends have a brass band round them for securing the canvas cover, and from the band to the face of the gun the metal is bare and polished. The bore and rifling are protected by a brass plug called a 'tompion' as shown in (1), which has on its face a representation of the ship's badge cast in relief or, in its absence, a handle for drawing it out. As so much of the detail of the guns and mounting is visible within the shield, the 4in twins would be a fine subject for a model engineering study at 1/4in-1ft scale. The information in the drawing is hardly sufficient for a larger scale than this.

4in Mk XIX Gun

Continuing this series of drawings of the detail of ships of the Royal Navy of the present day, these are the guns carried in the 'Castle' class frigates, and by the 'River' and 'Flower' class corvettes. They were also fitted as anti-submarine defence in many merchant ships in the last war. Small warships of these classes

do not have director control for this one gun of their principal armament, and ranges are communicated to it presumably from a rangefinder or some other device by telephone or voice pipe.

The gun itself is very simple as it consists only of a barrel, all in one piece, and a breech ring screwed onto it. It is fired by percussion, that is, by a striking pin, or striker, which hits the centre of the base of the cartridge as in a rifle. The shell weighs about 35lb and the ammunition is 'fixed'. The rifling has 32 grooves giving a single complete turn to the right. The breech ring is shown enlarged in (1).

The breech block slides across from right to left on loading and is operated by a lever pivoted on its centre with a handle at each end. In (2) the breech mechanism (BM) lever is shown in the closed position as when the gun is loaded. In (4) it is shown in the open position. When it is swung to the right as in (4) a stud projecting from the face of the lever arm travels down a slot milled in the face of the breech ring. This forms the fulcrum for the lever to swing the block to the right. As it travels projections on the gun side of its face push the extractor lever into action thus throwing out the empty cartridge. When closed the vertical bar which can be seen in the recess at the right end of the breech block presses against the heels of the extractor and keeps it in place. As the BM lever is swung to the right to open the gun a cam path on the projection in its centre lifts the firing pin into the cocked position where it is held in place by a small steel pivoted support called the 'sear'. To fire

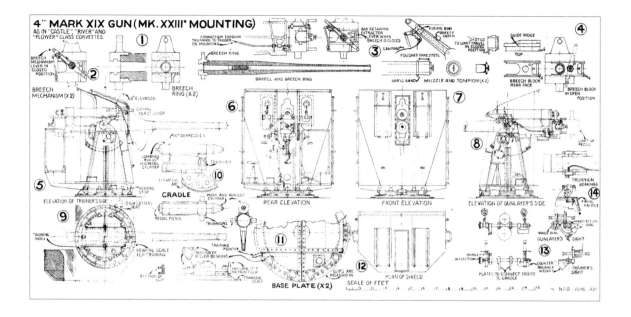

4in Mk XIX gun. (MyTime Media)

the gun the sear is given a sudden tilt by the firing bar which is housed on the rear face of the BM lever, thus allowing the striker to fall and hit the cartridge. The firing bar is operated by a series of rods and cranks, as shown in (2) and (3), which are moved by a flexible connection like those for the brakes of a bicycle and called an 'Arens Control', which passes through the centre of the left-hand trunnion and on through more rods to the pistol grip which can be seen in (8) and (14) on the layer's side of the mounting.

It seems rather roundabout but it is necessary, first, to place the firing handle in a convenient position for the gunner, and second, to make provision for the parting of the mechanical connection while the gun is recoiling. A lanyard may be used for firing as shown in the enlarged part of the BM lever in (3). The gun is mounted in a cast sleeve called the cradle which has projections on it, above, to take the combined recoil and run out cylinder, and, below, to take the elevating arc. The recoil piston is passed through the large lug (1) projecting from the top of the breech ring and anchored to it by heavy steel nuts on both sides. The square projection below the breech ring engages with the guides on the cradle which centre the gun when it is run back after recoil. All this area of the gun and breech mechanism is of polished bare steel. The cradle is painted ship grey but the inside of the shield is often white with the platforms and clips and the base plate black. The

barrel of the gun is often painted black with a high gloss and this is about the only part of a model warship that can legitimately be treated with shiny paint. The engraved bearing scale which surrounds the mounting on deck is of polished brass as are the bands round the barrel for securing the canvas covers at the opening in the shield and on the muzzle.

The gear teeth of the elevating arc are cut in a segment of a circle of which the radius originates in the centre of the trunnions which are the pivots on the cradle about which the gun elevates, and which are shown in plan and elevation in (10). At each end of the segment stops are fitted at positions corresponding to 60 degree elevation and 10 degree depression which strike against a buffer, just visible inside the mounting in (6), which prevents the gun passing these limits. A further stop, also visible in (6), is for setting the gun in the 'secure' position at 5 degree elevation. On the left side of the mounting in (8) can be seen the handwheel and gear box which operates the pinion engaging the elevating arc. A corresponding handwheel on the right shown in (5) operates the shaft which carries the pinion wheel that engages with the training rack below the base plate.

The 'carriage' consists of the base plate shown in (9) and enlarged in (11), and the two side or bracket plates that receive the trunnions as in (5) and (8). These are stiffened with heavy angle bars at the edges and connected across by a front plate and by a plate in the centre. They are riveted to the base plate by angle bar connections. Below the base plate is the 'racer' plate which is a machined casting bolted to the deck and surrounded by an engraved scale of 360 degrees showing the angle of training. The base plate turns on a centre pivot and on horizontal roller bearings and is kept in place by five clips recessed into its perimeter and which project into a groove turned in the racer plate. The roller bearings in this mounting are rather peculiar as they are contained in housings which look rather like thimbles on a triangular base. Below each of these the base plate is pierced to allow the roller bearing and its carriage to be dropped on to the machined surface of the racer, the casting like a thimble being the housing for a very heavy spring which holds down the carriage of the roller bearing. On the front clip of the mounting is a 'housing stop' which carries a steel rod that fits into a hole in the deck ring to secure the mounting in the fore and aft position.

On each side of the carriage are built platforms and steps of chequered steel plate for the gunlayer and trainer and the sight setter, for whom a seat is fitted. A shield of thin steel plating supported by angle bar stanchions is built over the mounting and provided with rails at the rear end of the top and sides for fastening the canvas cover. Openings are cut through the shield in front for the sights and these are closed by hinged steel doors stiffened by small angle bars. The opening for the gun is surrounded by a lining with a narrow plate and screws holding on the white canvas blast cover which is clamped on to the barrel or 'chase' of the gun by a polished brass band as shown in (5).

The sights are carried on the ends of a hollow cross bar which is clamped to the cradle and which passes under the recoil cylinder and over the chase of the gun. Through its centre runs the connecting bar which joins the trainer's and the layer's sights for deflection. The telescopes, and open, or 'barrage' sights are carried on hinged fittings on the ends of the cross bar and are provided with a counter-balance weight at the trainer's end. They are shown in plan and elevation and side views in (13).

An interesting point in regard to guns having sliding breech blocks (that is in all those below the calibre of 5.25in in recent times) the milled grooves that guide the block are not machined exactly at right angles to the bore, but at a slightly greater angle. The effect of this is that when the breech block begins to move on opening it is carried away from the base of the cartridge (or towards it in closing) instead of rubbing across it, thus reducing wear, and, in the closing motion, pressing the cartridge firmly into the chamber. The gun here is able to fire 2,000 rounds at full charge before the barrel is required to be replaced. The wear on the block would be considerable in this number were it to slide across the base of each cartridge and in contact surface to surface.

20mm Single & Twin Oerlikon Guns

Continuing this series of studies of the detail of contemporary ships of the Royal Navy, many builders of models of fast naval motor boats, MTBs, and coastal craft may find this drawing useful as the Oerlikon gun is their usual armament and it is also carried in cruisers of the 'Dido' class and in some destroyers.

The Oerlikon is an automatic gun of 20mm calibre designed for close range anti-aircraft fire and is effective up to about 1,000 yards. It is supported on a single shoulder-controlled mounting as shown in (1) and (2) or on a twin power-operated mounting as shown in (7), (8) and (9). There are many modifications of the cradle and mounting (Mark I, II, III, etc.) but these two examples are typical.

The gun is operated by the pressure set up by the explosion of the round. The cartridge case is blown back against the breech face, marked by the arrow in (5), which moves away from the fixed barrel against the pull of the barrel springs, also shown in (5) which return it and its complex moving parts, including the automatic loading mechanism, to the firing position. The barrel and its casing do not recoil, the whole force of the explosion being used to propel the projectile and to operate the moving parts. The explosion ejects the used cartridge, forcing the breech and loading mechanism to the rear; on returning these pick up the next round, pushing it into the chamber and releasing the firing pin, the next explosion causing the cycle of operations to be repeated, so that the gun is entirely automatic and, so long as the trigger is pressed, will continue firing until the 60 rounds of ammunition contained in the drum are used. Six drums, containing a total of 360 rounds, are placed in a locker near each gun. The used cartridges fall through an opening in the floor of the cradle and are collected in the bag underneath. In the single mounting, and in the twin mountings, if they are not power-driven as in the one shown in (7), (8) and (9), the gunner's shoulders fit into the two curved

20mm single and twin
Oerlikon guns. (ss Great
Britain Trust)

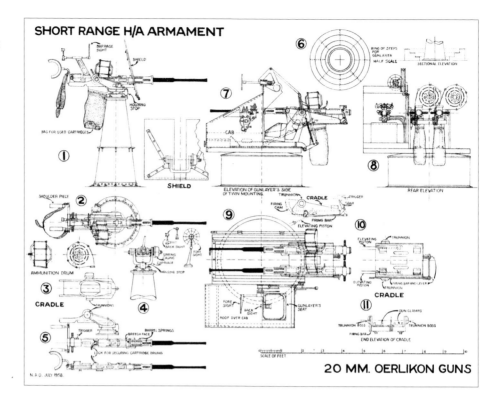

projections at the rear of the cradle, his back being
supported by the broad strap shown in (1) and (2).
Efficiency in the use of the Oerlikon gun depends a
great deal on good footwork, and this is usually
assisted by a ring of steps surrounding each
mounting as shown in (6).

In the power mounting the gunner sits in a steel
plated cab with his hands on the control levers which
operate training, elevating and firing from one
position through hydraulic power led to and from the
levers along a bundle of pipes shown in the end
elevation in (8). The cradle is elevated and depressed
by the two hydraulic pistons shown beneath it in (10)
and (7). The cradle and the open, or 'barrage' sights,
are connected by levers so that the sights follow it in
elevation. In the single mounting it is assisted in
elevation by a spiral spring contained in the circular
box on the left-hand trunnion (4). Oerlikon guns fire
'tracer' bullets at intervals to enable the gunner to
follow the direction of fire. The ammunition drums
are locked on to the breech mass by the lever shown
in the plan and elevation of the gun in (5) and this
also shows the two handles, or handgrips for the
gunlayer, the trigger being close to the one on the
left near the cross bar that supports the shoulder

pieces. If not power mounted, the single and twin
guns usually have a flat shield plate, about 1/4in
thick, bolted to projections fixed to the sides of the
carriage, which is provided with a housing stop to
make it fast to the pedestal when secured and not in
use. The cradle of the twin mounting, (10) and (11),
is broader and is built of flat steel plate pivoted on
the trunnion projections. At its rear end is a cross
connecting rod carrying the firing levers that bear
against the trigger of each gun; clamps on the floor
of the cradle hold the two guns in position exactly
parallel. The carriage is mounted on a steel platform
built of plate and angle bar which revolves under
power about a pivot in the centre of the mounting.

40mm Twin Bofors Guns
Continuing the study of ordnance in this series on the
detail of the ships of the Royal Navy of today these,
the 40mm Bofors guns, constitute the medium range
high angle armament of the majority of vessels in
commission now. The twin mounting is a prominent
feature of the 'Southampton' and 'Colony' class
cruisers, in the *Achilles* (now *Delhi*) of the 'Leander'
class, in most of the 'Battle', 'Weapon' and 'Daring'
class destroyers (with radar controlled mountings), in

destroyers converted to fast anti-submarine frigates, in some corvettes, and (single mounted) in the 'Algerine' class minesweepers. They are also part of the armament (in single and twin mountings) in aircraft carriers. The single guns will be described in a later article.

The twin Bofors mounting is very complicated as it is fitted for three kinds of control, (1) by hand, (2) by power and (3) by remote control from the director tower. This involves much machinery being crammed below the platforms, including a water tank and rotary pump for circulating cooling water to the jackets of the guns. The drawing shows the arrangement in detail in (1) from the trainer's side and in (2) from the gunlayer's position, (3) showing the arrangement in plan and (4) the front aspect.

The mounting consists of a heavy circular base plate pivoted at the centre which rides on roller bearings in the base casting which has the teeth of the training rack machined on it internally. The base plate is almost entirely covered by the carriage and by the stepped platform on which are placed the seats for the layer and trainer. The sides of the base casting are housed in by guard plates (6) so that none of the detail of its construction would show on a model. The guard plates are divided horizontally, the upper being fixed to the base plate and revolving with it, while the lower is bolted to the base ring, so that the holding down bolts that secure the ring to the deck are not visible. All the working parts of the mounting round the platform are enclosed at the front with 1/2in steel plate and at the sides and back by 1/4in, an access door being fitted at each side as shown in (13). At the back are openings for the insertion of the ready use ammunition racks, each of the six shelves of which holds a clip of four rounds. Openings in the front plate are cut to allow clearance for the guns and sights, the maximum elevation of which is 90 degrees with 15 degrees depression.

The guns are machined from a single block of high grade steel and bored to a calibre of 40mm or 1.5748in. There are 16 grooves in the rifling and the projectile weighs just over 2lb. The effective range is about 2,500 yards, the number of rounds per minute fired being about 120 or one every half second. Unlike the Oerlikon guns, in these the barrel recoils on firing the blow being absorbed by the barrel springs and by the buffer shown underneath in (11), the latter assisting the springs to return the gun to the firing position. The two guns are bolted together

parallel by means of the housing over the breech mechanism, trunnions being fitted outside each for pivoting them on the carriage. There is no cradle and the elevating arc is bolted to the underside of the housing of the left gun. The recoil thrust operates the breech block and loading mechanism, and, so long as the trigger is pressed, the sequence of recoil, ejection of cartridge, ramming of next round and the run out follows automatically so long as the loader keeps the ammunition flowing down the guides on top of the jacket. The rounds of cartridge combined with projectile are fixed together in batches of four by a metal clip holding their bases in line, the clip being ejected down an opening in the side of the jacket below the rear guide as the rounds fall into the mechanism. The empty cartridge cases are thrown out to the rear into U section guides which pass in two long curves down into the trough below the guns and forward to fall from the ends of the two tubes passing through the front plate as may be seen in (4). In most cases the guns are placed centrally in the water jacket, although in some they appear to be slightly below the axial line.

The two guns are pivoted in trunnion bearings on the arms of the carriage which is bolted to the revolving base plate as shown in (8), (9) and (10). The casting is lightened by a rectangular opening in front. On its left side are the gear box and training handles with a shaft leading to the worm drive that operates a large gear wheel engaging with the training rack in the lower base plate, but most of this is out of sight below the platform. On the right side are the elevating handles and the gear box and shaft to the

4in gun and 40mm Bofors guns on Ough's model of HMS *Barfleur*. (© National Maritime Museum, Greenwich, London – SLR 1576)

MEDIUM RANGE H/A ARMAMENT

40mm twin Bofors guns.
(MyTimeMedia)

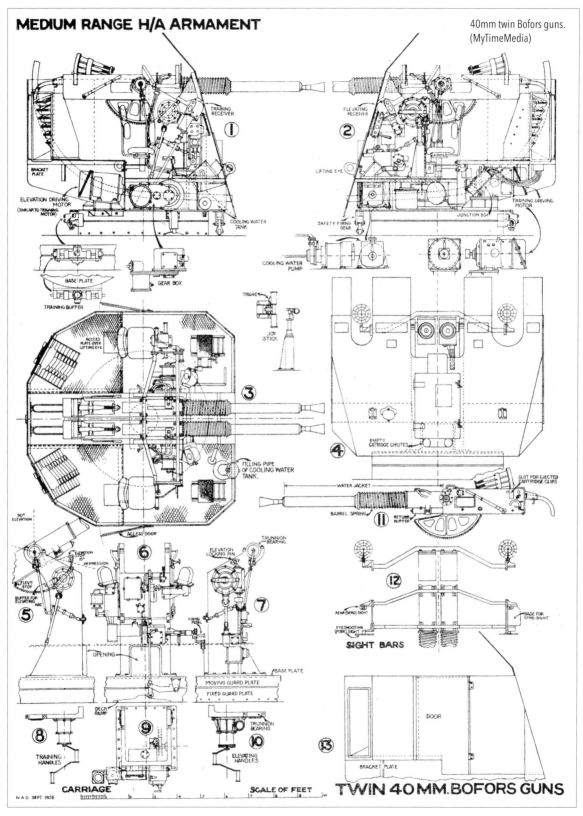

TWIN 40 MM. BOFORS GUNS

toothed wheel that operates the elevating arc. The shafts that appear to end in the centre of the trunnions are the firing rods that connect at one end with the firing pedal shown in (6) and at the other with a rod passing through the trunnions to the trigger. Above the firing pedal is the elevation receiver which is electrically connected to the high angle control tower, and in the corresponding position on the left is the training receiver which is similarly connected.

In front of the carriage are electrical junction boxes and covers over the mechanism of the safety firing gear. A ramp on the deck is placed in line with a wheel and shaft which is raised and lowered by passing over it thus interrupting the firing circuits, the ramp being located so as to prevent the guns from firing at parts of the ship. A housing stop for securing the mounting when it is not manned is fitted on the trainer's side of the base as may be seen in (1). It consists of a square steel pin which slides into a hole in a stop block bolted to the deck and placed so as to lock the mounting in a fore and aft position or on the beam. A training buffer at the rear of the base is fitted to prevent the mounting being brought to the limit stop for training with a violent blow which could cause much damage.

The platform, which is shown dotted in (4), (5), (6) and (7), is in two steps, and beneath it are housed the training and elevating motors for power operation, junction boxes and the tank and circulating pump for the cooling water. Seats are fitted for the trainer on the right and for the gunlayer on the left with footrests in front of them. Near the layer's footrests is the firing pedal. The guns can be fired from a trigger on the joystick as well, the latter being used in conjunction with a gyro sight. When the joystick is used the gunlayer trains the mounting by turning the handles in the horizontal plane to right or left, and elevates by twisting them upwards. Laying and training can also be done by hand, and 'eyeshooting' sights, shown in (12), are provided if damage occurs to the director control system. The layer's and trainer's sights are connected across by the sight bars shown in (12) which are rigidly fastened to the casings of the two guns. The connections for the cooling water supply to the gun jackets are made of flexible wire-wound hose pipe joined to square-ended connections on top, the flexible pipes being long enough to allow full movement in elevation and depression. A profile of the outside plating that encloses the whole is

shown in (13). The clips of ammunition are slid into the racks at the rear from the ammunition lockers outside, and they are held in place by springs until required to be taken out and fed into the guides on the guns by the loader who stands inside the plating in rear of each gun.

It is unlikely that many models of warships will be made to a scale larger than 3/16in-1ft, or, at the most 1/4in-1ft, and it is hoped that this drawing and description will contain enough for an adequately detailed model to be made to the latter scale. For a larger scale than this, say, 1/2in-1ft, a much more detailed drawing would be required. The author's aim in these articles on detail is to show enough to give the character of the intricacies of naval ordnance, which is the impression required from a good model, rather than to make large scale work feasible as this would require extensive study of the official manuals and would be too specialised for general interest. Even in a 1/4in scale model some of the detail shown in (6) of the front of the carriage would be difficult to see as the front plate hides most of it, and the platform covers most of it below. At the scale of 1/8in-1ft it is interesting to note that a model of this mounting (and the model of the ship that carries it) would be 884,736 times smaller than reality. At 1/4in-1ft it would be 110,592 times smaller.

40mm Single Bofors (Mk VII) Gun

These are the medium range anti-aircraft guns which are carried in the majority of ships of the Royal Navy today. They are to be seen in aircraft carriers, sloops, frigates and corvettes, in the 'Algerine' class minesweepers, in most destroyers, and in the few remaining cruisers. It is very difficult to make out the proportions and arrangements of these guns from photographs, which is not surprising, as this drawing shows how complex they are, even more so than the twin mounted version of them. At first glance the drawing seems very confused but, if one ignores detail and considers only the main features, comprehension may result. The scale of the original is 1/2in-1ft which, on reproduction, becomes about 1/4in-1ft. This is a large scale for warship models, most of which are near 1/8in scale.

The mounting consists of a circular conical base casting held to the deck by 12 hexagon bolts. This, in warships, replaces the wheeled army gun carriage. On top of it is a casting containing the ball-bearing races of the circular base plate shown in (2). On the

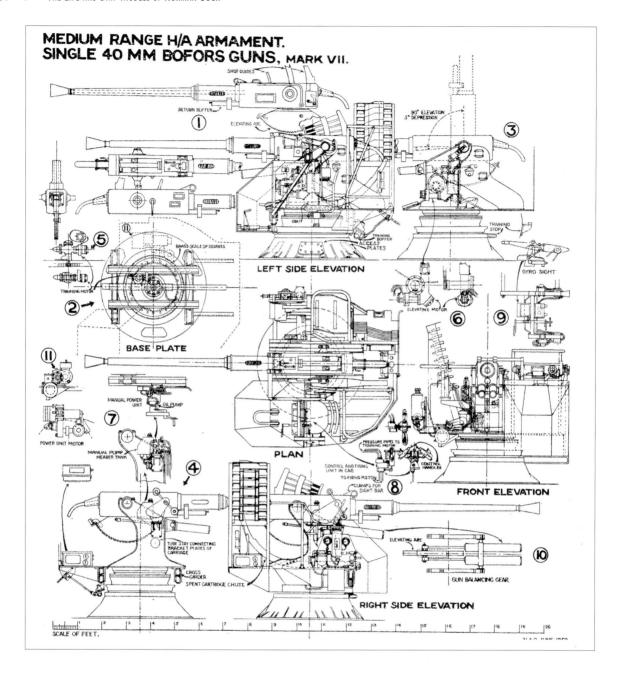

MEDIUM RANGE H/A ARMAMENT.
SINGLE 40 MM BOFORS GUNS, MARK VII.

40mm single Bofors (Mk VII) gun. (MyTimeMedia)

latter are mounted the two bracket plates or sides of the carriage as in (3) and (4). Around the base plate is a brass circle engraved in 360 degrees, which would show in places on a model, and on the right and left are platforms, very much cut up to accommodate fittings, for the ammunition rack and for the loading members of the gun's crew. On the left is a cab for the gun layer who is also the trainer, the control handles which operate the valves that

regulate the flow of hydraulic pressure to the elevating and training motors being placed in front of him. The gun is the same as those of the twin mounting except that it is air-cooled, that is, without the water jacket. It is able to fire 120 rounds a minute, the projectile weighing just over 2lb and of 40mm or 1.5748in in diameter. Unlike Oerlikon guns, in these the barrel recoils on firing, the blow being absorbed by the barrel springs and by the buffer shown underneath the spring casing which assists the springs to return the gun to the firing position. The recoil thrust operates the breech block and loading mechanism, but all the intricacies of these are enclosed in the rectangular housing on which the trunnion pins and the guides for the ammunition are placed and could not be seen on a model. The rounds of cartridge combined with projectile are fixed together in batches of four by a metal clip holding their bases in line, the clip being ejected down an opening on the side of the casing on the left of and below the rear guide as the rounds fall into the firing mechanism. The spent cartridge cases are thrown out into the U section guide which passes down and forward through the mounting along its centre line. There is no cradle for the gun and the elevating arc is bolted direct to the casing. The latter, which is built of two plates with the toothed segment between them, is fitted with a stop at each end of the rack to limit depression to 5 degrees and elevation to 90 degrees. The gun is pivoted in trunnion bearings fitted to the arms of the carriage. As these are not at the point of balance the overweight of the barrel is compensated by the two spring-loaded pistons of the gun-balancing gear, which are pivoted on the front of the carriage with their ends in bearings on each side of the elevating arc as shown in (10). The springs are at their greatest compression when the elevation is least, and least when the elevation is greatest.

At the fore end of the breech casing are the two clamps for the sight bar which is shown in (9) and also in the front elevation. The sights are pivoted in trunnion bearings on the top of the cab and are raised and lowered by the sight bar as the gun is moved in elevation or depression. The guns are trained by a gear wheel engaging with a circular toothed rack situated below the base plate and shown dotted in (2). The gear wheel is driven through reduction bevel gears by the hydraulic training motor which is controlled by the hand levers in the cab as detailed in (8), the motor and gear casing being shown in (5). Pressure pipes lead from the valves controlled by these handles to the driving motor. A similar hydraulic motor, also controlled by these handles, operates through reduction pinions, a gear engaging with the elevating arc, the movement being assisted by the spring-loaded rods of the gun-balancing gear, the casing of the elevating mechanism being shown in (6). In addition to the power drive an arrangement for hand operation is fitted in case of failure of electric power, the pump motor or the main motor, the latter being shown in (11), its position being partly above and partly below the platform on the right side of the mounting. On the left side of the carriage is a flat plate which carries electrical junction boxes. This is bolted to the platform and to the left bracket plate of the carriage. Another plate, also carrying electrical fittings, is placed across the space between the bracket plates in the rear of the cartridge chute. A stand with eight racks for clips of cartridges constituting 32 rounds is placed at the right rear of the platform.

In the Mark VII mounting, as shown here, the pressure pipes leading over the front of the right bracket of the carriage from the manual power gear are a prominent feature. In some earlier versions, as in those in the 'Algerine' class minesweepers, they are not fitted. The one shown is characteristic of 'Battle' class destroyers and of many other ships.

15in Mk I & Mk I (N) Guns

Continuing this series on the detail of HM ships for model makers, here are some of the big guns of the main armament of the majority of battleships and battle cruisers of the most recent times. These are the guns that were fought in capital ship and fleet actions in the two World Wars, and the 15in particularly may be said to have decided the fate of nations at the Battle of Jutland. Had the German High Seas Fleet prevailed that afternoon and evening of the 31st of May in 1916 their surface fleet would have achieved command of the sea which would have enabled them to escort their raiding cruisers out into the Atlantic to attack the convoys upon which our existence depended. It was the 15in guns of the fast manoeuvring wing of the British fleet, the four battleships *Barham*, *Valiant*, *Warspite* and *Malaya* that inflicted much of the damage to the van of the German fleet up to the time when the main body of our capital ships could deploy into action. Jutland was a gunners' battle and all the world knows now that it was the turning point in the war at sea in the 1914–18 conflict. The then new 15in guns could outrange any the enemy could bring to bear and the ships that carried them could outspeed him. And perhaps no big warships of modern times could equal those so armed in splendour of appearance. It will be seen from the plan and profile of the twin guns of the *Queen Elizabeth* and *Royal Sovereign* how elegant and well-proportioned was the design of the

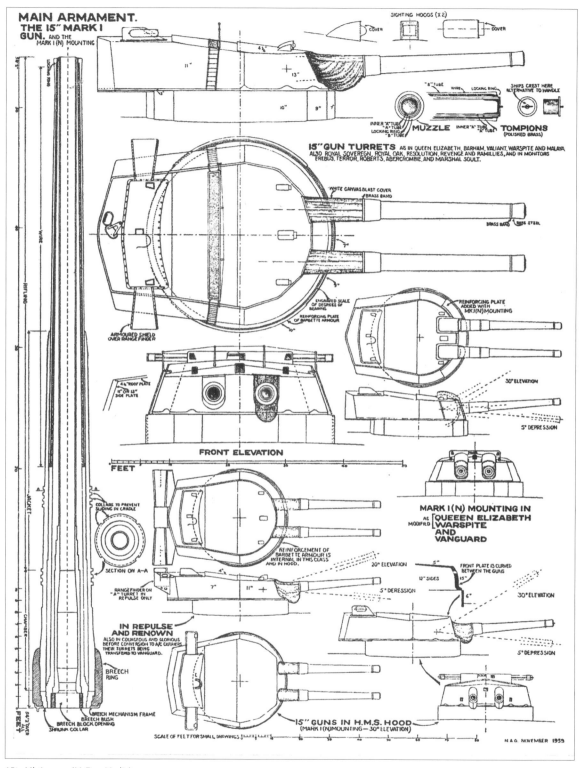

15in Mk 1 guns. (MyTimeMedia)

turrets and barbettes. Seen from forward the superimposed mass of 'A' and 'B' turrets made a magnificent perspective.

The 15in gun weighed, without the breech mechanism, just one hundred tons. The rifled bore, of 76 grooves, ran a length of 42 calibres, or 42 times the bore or the diameter of the shell, making one complete turn to the right in a distance of 30 calibres, the overall length of the gun being 54ft 2in from breech to muzzle. The construction consisted of the inner 'A' tube or rifled barrel, which included the chamber for the cordite charges, over which was shrunk the outer 'A' tube ending at the 'breech bush' into which the interrupted threads of the breech block recess were machined. Over this again, as will be seen in the sectional drawings on the left, was shrunk the 'B' tube for part of its length, the chase of the gun as far as the locking ring at the muzzle being bound round with about 120 miles of flat steel wire of high tensile strength, the many turns of which were locked into position by this ring. Over the wire of the chase was shrunk the outer part of 'B' tube going back as far as the ring locking the commencement of the wire. Again, over 'B' tube was shrunk the jacket on which were machined the seven collars whose function was to engage with corresponding recesses on the gun cradle of the mounting, the huge breech ring being finally screwed and shrunk on over all at the loading end bringing the outside diameter here up to six feet. In the original mounting (Mark I) the guns were given a maximum elevation of 20 degrees with 5 degrees depression, but this was modified in the Mark I (N) mounting as in *Queen Elizabeth* and *Warspite* in their final reconstructions, to give an elevation of 30 degrees with the same angle of depression, and also in the turrets of *Courageous* and *Glorious* on their conversion to aircraft carriers, these being transferred to *Vanguard*. The higher elevation required the roof plates of the turrets to be cut back and the opening covered by armoured hoods, the front openings being protected by heavy 'mantlet' plates attached to the cradle. Seen from the outside these plates are markedly convex in the cross direction but are circles concentric to the point of pivot of the trunnions vertically. At the same time the fronts of the turrets were reinforced with an extra thickness of armour as shown in the small drawings of those in *Vanguard*, *Queen Elizabeth* and *Warspite*. In HMS *Hood* the turret roofs were higher, thus avoiding cutting into the plates, but the turrets are,

in consequence, less shapely. The muzzle velocity of a 15in gun was 2,640 feet per second and its maximum range, with a supercharge of 490lbs of cordite, was 28,700 yards. The shell, which was 5ft 7in long, weighed 1,920lbs and each gun could fire two rounds a minute. The normal full charge was 428 lbs of cordite giving a range of 23,400 yards. The rifled lining, or inner 'A' tube, was condemned after 350 full charge rounds had been fired. It could be taken out and a new one substituted.

The turrets revolved on circular armoured platforms called barbettes, the armour of which extended downwards into the ship to include the working chamber and the trunking containing the shell and cordite hoists, the turrets themselves revolving on massive roller bearings carried in a complete circle round inside the rim of the barbette armour. In the *Queen Elizabeth* and 'R' class battleships the latter was a smooth vertical cylinder the walls of which were 7in thick, but it was increased at the sides by an additional segment 2in thick extending round most of the circumference, and with another segment 1in thick covering about 90 degrees of the circle on each side. In other ships this reinforcement was internal. In all, on top of the barbette outside the turret, was an engraved brass scale of degrees of bearing as shown in the plan view of the twin guns and turrets. This is an important feature in a model as the brass scale was polished brightly; it is hardly ever shown in builders' models. The roofs of the turrets were bolted into a rebate worked in the thickness of the side plates as shown in the section on the left of the large front view. They were usually painted black or dark grey, the sides and fronts being ship colour which was carried over as far as the edge of the roof plates thus forming a narrow grey border, the rangefinder casing and sighting hoods being ship grey, the track way across the roof of 'Corticene' being its own colour, about that of milk chocolate. The blast covers that closed the gun ports were of white canvas secured to the jackets of the guns by a polished brass band, another at the muzzle acting as a stop for securing a white canvas cover over the bright ends of the guns. An invariable rule in the Service was that the guns of the main armament should be secured in the true fore and aft position (zero training) and always at 5 degrees elevation, never horizontal. This slight elevation gave them their challenging look.

It will be noticed, in the sectional drawing, how

surprisingly slender the barrels of the guns are away from the massive breech end. This was mainly due to the wire winding which gave immense lateral strength, but it was partly due to the fact that the cordite which propelled the shell out of the rifling was designed to be 'slow' burning, so spreading the thrust of the expanding gases of the explosion rather than producing a shattering effect. As the shell moved along the rifling the parts of the barrel in front of it supported some of the lateral stress of expansion but when it was at the point of leaving there was no more support so 'B' tube is increased in diameter at the muzzle. The form of the slight curve, leading to this, is very subtle and it is worth taking some trouble to get it right in a model as it is very characteristic of British naval guns. In the model of the *Vanguard* in the Science Museum this point is entirely missed as the 15in guns are represented with no swell at the ends. If they were like this in the actual ship the barrels would crack after a few rounds had been fired. The straight end is characteristic of German guns which have to be longer to compensate for the absence at the swell ends. The pressure in the chamber when the charge was fired was about 19 tons to the square inch!

The construction of a heavy gun took as long as the building of the ship designed to carry it. It was a major feat of mechanical engineering and the machining of all the parts to be shrunk together required great precision. For example in the final boring operation that finished the interior of the inner 'A' tube the permitted tolerance, or error, was minus but not plus 0.002in. That is that it might be finished two thousandths of an inch under the required 15in diameter, but on no account over that size. This was in the final machining of a hole 50 feet long and large enough to pull a man through! After this operation had been gauged and passed the cutting of the 76 spiral grooves of the rifling began, and simultaneously the whole length of the outer 'A' tube had to be machined and stepped inside and outside to such a size as, when heated, it would slide easily over the inner tube but also allowing for the fit not being too tight when it was chilled or it might crack in contracting, and so on till 'B' tube, the wire, the jacket and the breech ring were all shrunk together with the right amount of tension in each.

It is most likely that builders of working models will avoid capital ships, as, at 1/8in-1ft scale, which is about the smallest for showing detail satisfactorily,

the displacement of true to scale models becomes very large – from 70 to 100lbs, which is a heavy weight to carry to a pond even if the necessary ballast is transported separately, so the information in this article and drawing is more for the 'glass case' model maker, but, in either type, the big guns are best represented by turning them from duralumin which gives a fine untarnishing surface for the bright ends.

21in Quadruple Torpedo Tubes

This drawing shows the detail of the torpedo tubes of the 'Tribal' class destroyers of from 1935 onwards. In these ships, which carried a very heavy gun armament, there were only four torpedo tubes on the single power-driven mounting shown, but in the following 'J', 'K' and 'N' classes the ratio of guns to torpedo tubes was very much altered in favour of the latter – six 4.7in guns in three twin mountings and ten tubes on two 'pentad' or five-fold mountings.

The torpedo was the deadliest weapon of the two World Wars and its advent towards the end of the nineteenth century profoundly modified both the strategy and the tactics of war at sea – strategically because of the disposition of escorts for the Fleet and for convoys, and, tactically, because of changes in the handling of the Fleet in action and of devising means of countering the menace during its approach and withdrawal from the scene of battle.

The self propelled or 'mobile' torpedo was invented in the 1860s and it superseded the 'spar' torpedo carried by a small steam boat at the end of a long boom over the bows and exploded against a ship's side under water. The earliest craft to carry and launch the 'fish' torpedo were quite small and only intended to be used in the defence of harbours and of the nearby coast, but, as the torpedo grew in accuracy and speed and range it was carried in tubes on the decks of larger vessels that had considerable radius of action, being boats of 250–300 tons displacement and of about 26 knots in speed. These became sufficiently formidable to require to be countered by ships of even greater speed and equipped with a gun armament in addition to the lighter guns and deck tubes of their adversaries. Their office was to chase and destroy the torpedo boats hence the name 'torpedo boat destroyer' or 'TBD' which became shortened to the familiar 'destroyer' of today. But as the destroyers grew larger they became a menace to ships at sea so that it was necessary to build them of such dimensions as would enable them

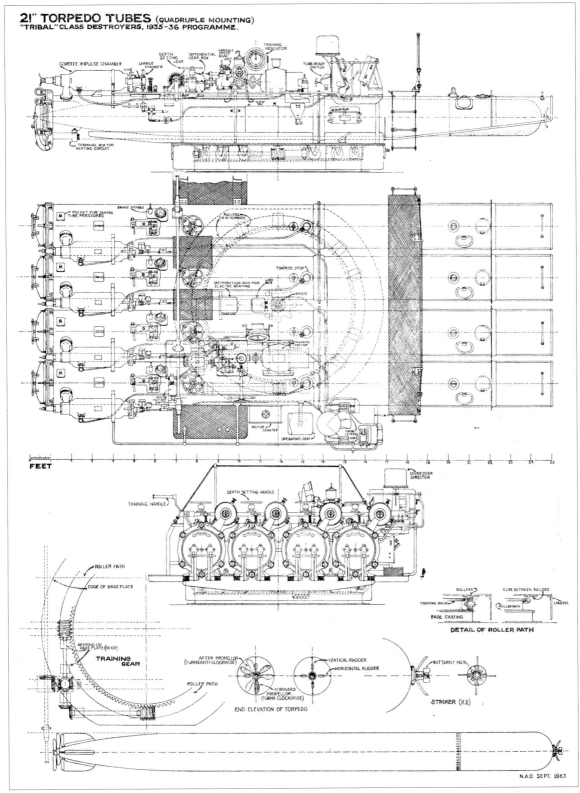

21in quadruple torpedo tubes. (MyTimeMedia)

to keep with the Fleet in all weathers, acting as escorts and yet with a gun armament equal to engaging corresponding destroyers of the enemy's fleet. From this followed the development of their tactical role of screening the battle fleet and also of attacking the opposing fleet with torpedoes.

A destroyer can cripple a battleship, not necessarily so as to sink her, but to cause a rent so large below water, partly flooding the hull and reducing her speed, that she can no longer keep station in the line and it becomes an objective for the destroyers to race ahead and fire torpedoes across the opposing line in the hope of causing some of the enemy's ships to withdraw. Increased chances of hitting occur if the attack can be made from the cover of a smoke screen from which the destroyers can dash at high speed, fire their torpedoes, and retreat into the smoke, but while they are exposed they run the fearful hazard of being shot to pieces by the secondary armament of the enemy's battleships. This manoeuvre may be attempted by both sides, in which case the destroyers are involved in a gunnery duel of their own between the lines of the opposing fleets, the heavy ships firing their big guns over them.

Destroyers have another function, the escorting of convoys of merchant ships. Their great speed and weather endurance enable them to circle the convoy thus keeping hostile submarines below periscope depth to prevent them from getting a bearing sight for using their torpedoes. Also they carry 'Asdic' or echo-sounding gear and depth charges so that they can find and sink submarines.

In most surface ships torpedoes are fired from tubes on deck, although in most capital ships they were launched from submerged tubes in flats below the waterline, and driven from the tubes by compressed air as in submarines. In above-water tubes, as in the type shown here, they were fired by the expanding gases of a cordite charge although compressed air was used in earlier deck tubes such as those of the 'V' and 'W' class destroyers of from 1918 onwards.

The torpedo itself is a marvel of mechanical engineering and before 1938 each cost about £2,000. It consists of a warhead containing 500lb of high explosive, a body containing a long vessel filled with air under a pressure of 2,500lb to the square inch, and a tail section consisting of an engine and two hollow propeller shafts, one within the other, the two propellers, and the horizontal and vertical fins

and rudders, the length overall being 24ft with a diameter of 21in. The warhead is fitted with a striker, the steel arms of which, projecting at right angles to each other, are intended to ensure its explosion even if it strikes a ship with a glancing blow. All four arms pass through the firing rod which is threaded at its outer end to take a four-bladed 'butterfly' nut, the blades of which are inclined so as to make it rotate like a propeller when the torpedo strikes the water, the friction of which causes it to run up the thread and fall off, thus 'arming' the torpedo. If it fails to hit the target it is designed to sink at the end of its run to prevent it becoming a free floating mine.

It will be seen from the drawing that the launch of torpedoes requires complicated machinery as they have to be set on a course so as to bring them to the anticipated position of the target when they reach it and they have also to be adjusted for depth and gyro angle before firing. The gyro, which retains a constant position in space once started, controlling the vertical rudders to keep them on course.

The four tubes are mounted on a circular base platform which revolves on a cast steel base plate secured to the deck. It is held down by a central pivot and by a number of clips which engage below the toothed rack by which the tubes are turned by two worm wheels and shafts. The clips are to prevent tilting and damage to the mounting due to the great stresses set up when the torpedoes are fired. The worm shafts are operated by a vertical shaft connected to them by bevel gears which are duplicated at the upper end to connect it with the hand-turning shaft. This latter can be disconnected and engaged with the variable speed electric motor for turning by power.

Each tube has a rear door hinged vertically to admit the torpedo which is loaded into the tube by the torpedo davit near the ship's side. A destroyer carries only the torpedoes in the tubes and there is no magazine of spares as in larger ships or in submarines, hence the large number of tubes in the 'J', 'K' and 'N' classes and 'Battles', and in earlier destroyers. In this respect the 'Tribals' had only four as they were designed more to fight with a large gun armament.

The torpedo is placed in the tube in such a position as to bring the openings in its hull directly below the gear for depth-setting, gyro adjustment and range-setting which are outside on top of the tube and from which rods can be passed down and withdrawn after the adjustments have been made. The angle of bearing is transmitted from the bridge to the training indicator on the operator's left on the tubes, also the orders for firing. A seat on the right in front of the director accommodates the operator who has the four firing levers within reach to left and right of the director. When the firing contact is made cordite is exploded in the charge chamber and the expanding gases enter the cordite impulse chamber whence they pass into the rear end of the tube, filling all the available space and driving the torpedo out and overboard. As it passes out of the tube a trigger on the hull is tripped to start the engine.

The original of this drawing is to the scale of 1/2in-1ft but the reproduction this time is not exactly to half the scale so that, for a model, the measurements need to be taken from the scale of feet.

21in Five Fold (Pentad) Torpedo Tubes

These were the torpedo tubes of the 'J', 'K' and 'N' classes of destroyers of 1939. The mounting was five-fold and was known as the 'pentad' mounting.

Following the 'Tribal' class of 1936 in which the torpedo armament took second place to gun power these ships reverted to the ten-tube design of the 'I' class of 1934. Their gun armament was less than in the 'Tribal' to allow for the additional group of tubes which were shown here, the after set having a circular enclosed spray shield to protect the operator from heavy seas coming on board at this position, the forward set having an open rectangular shield. The dimensions of the ships of this class were: Length over all 355ft, beam 35ft, and draught 9–10ft with a standard displacement of 1,760 tons, shaft horse power 40,000 giving a speed of 36 knots, their peacetime complement being 183 officers and men.

Owing to their having been built so soon before the outbreak of the war in 1939 these ships were less photographed than earlier destroyers but a few clear pictures of them are obtainable from Messrs. Wright and Logan, Albert Road, Southsea, Hants. This firm is probably the best in the world for fine detail in warship pictures, few others being comparable for quality of contrast and sharpness of definition. At present their post card size photographs cost 2/- each.

The arrangement for loading and firing the torpedoes is much the same as in the quadruple mounting in the 'Tribal' class but the mounting is different. In this case the training drive is by direct gearing to a toothed rack in the base ring, the driving shaft being turned by a worm wheel on the training shaft which is worked by hand from both ends from the platforms shown on the right and left sides of the base plate which is rectangular. It revolves about a central pivot on a roller path and is carried on 18 small trucks holding the roller bearings and which are bolted to the underside of the base plate. Next to each of these roller carriages is a holding down clip which takes under a rim machined on the outside of the base ring on a level flush with the toothed rack as shown in the sectional detail on the right of the end elevation. The worm and gear wheel which move all this are housed under a metal lagging to protect them from the weather as shown dotted on the drawing. The long platform going over the tubes is to allow passage across the deck since, when trained to the fore and aft position, they prevent this. It is not clear from such information that is available to the writer where the stop is placed which locks the tubes in this, the 'secure', position, but it is probably on a bracket projecting from the mounting. A steel peg falls into a hole in the stop, the peg being raised or lowered by a cam on the cross bar at the after end of the base plate. The lever rotating this bar can be seen on the elevation, and it is known as the 'training stop lever'.

The torpedoes are fired by moving the five levers which can be seen on each side of the director platform inside the spray screen. These are known as 'Arens Controls' and they work in much the same way as the levers and wires running through a tube which operate the brakes of a bicycle. The leading tubes pass along the right upper side of the torpedo tubes to a bell crank which, on being moved, fires the cordite charge in the breech block at the end of the cordite impulse chamber. The block is tilted sideways and downwards by the breech lever for loading. At the opposite end of the chamber is a spring loaded valve for regulating the pressure generated by the charge. Part of this pressure is let out of the chamber through a tube which leads to the torpedo stop which, when lifted, frees the torpedo. The latter is normally held locked in the tube in case it should move with the rolling of the ship. At the loading end of the tube on top is a massive eyeplate. This is for the block and tackle used for moving the torpedo into the tube when it has been introduced into the loading end by the slings of the torpedo davit. To effect this a rod is inserted in the hollow propeller shaft having an arm at right angles, the upper end of which takes the outer end of the tackle. By hauling on the rope the

21in five fold (Pentad) torpedo tubes. (ss Great Britain Trust)

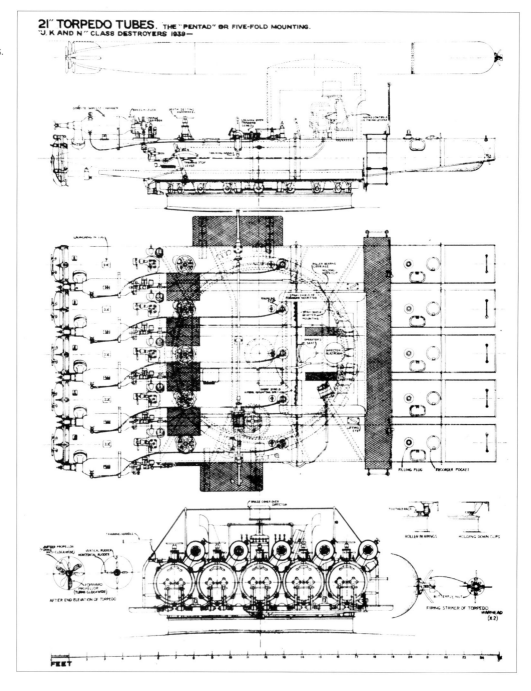

distance between the end of the arm and the loading lug is diminished till the torpedo is completely housed in the tube. The loading doors hinge downwards and they are made pressure tight by six massive clips securing each against the seating. There are four heavy lifting eyes in the base plate for shackling on the sling wires for lifting the whole

mounting in or out of the ship. It will be seen from the drawing that the base plate is stiffened by four angle bar frames. These are placed so as to lie clear of the carriages for the roller bearings of the racer of the turntable. In the housed, or secure position, the tubes are always trained with the loading ends forwards and the 'lip' ends aft.

As fittings on a model of a 'J' class destroyer, with all the detail shown here the two sets of tubes would make a very impressive array as they take up most of the waist of the vessel. They are a principal feature since the whole ship was designed to be able to deliver her 10 torpedoes across the line of battle of the enemy's fleet at the right tactical moment for they were her main offensive armament. Such an attack from a flotilla of destroyers so armed could cripple any ships that were hit effectively and it could thus influence the course of a war at sea and hence the fate of a nation.

The scale of the original of this drawing is 1/2in to 1ft but a reduction has to be made, therefore in making a model the scale needs to be read off the scale of feet shown at the foot of the drawing.

3 Pounder Mk I Saluting Gun

Since the 1890s this gun has been mounted in nearly all of HM ships above the destroyer category in size and it was also, in a modified form as a 6 pounder, mounted in torpedo craft. It began its long career in the Service by being fitted in large numbers in nearly all ships as a defence against close range attack by such vessels. With the advent of heavier guns in the secondary armament of battleships and cruisers, owing to the development of torpedo boats into ocean-going destroyers, it was reduced mainly to the role of a saluting gun, firing blank charges of gunpowder for ceremonial purposes, four guns being the usual number carried in the majority of ships. The 3 pounder, however, could be shipped in the 42ft launch and the 50ft steam picket boats on a mounting in the bows and it was so used in harbour defence in the 1914–18 war. In its earliest days it was mounted in the fighting tops on the masts of battleships and cruisers, hence the large angle of 15 degrees of depression provided. The invention of the 3pdr and 6pdr guns in about 1885 was due to Nordenfelt and Hotchkiss, the type developed by the latter being the one that became universal in the Royal Navy.

As the drawing shows the 3 pounder gun consists of a barrel and a jacket, the barrel being screwed and shrunk into the latter which is enlarged to a square section at the breech end to allow for the machining of the mortise for the breech block which passes right through. The trunnions at the centre of gravity of the gun are formed on the single piece of steel which constitutes the jacket. The bore of the gun is 1.85in and there are 20 grooves in the rifling.

The breech block belongs to what is known as the wedge system and it is worked vertically by the two-handed lever on the right of the breech. It runs in a mortise, the rear face of which is slightly inclined forward to cause the breech block to wedge tightly against the front face when closed, thus ensuring that the base of the brass cartridge that contains the charge is pressed home in the chamber. The block is hollow and contains the mechanism of the firing pin and ejector which jerks out the empty case when the breech is opened. The breech mechanism lever moves the block up and down by means of a cam projecting from its shaft, the cam moving a stud which travels in a slot in the right side of the block, which is prevented from falling out of the mortise by a bolt, called the breech block stud, which projects into a groove in the block on the left side. A secondary action of part of the breech mechanism lever sets the firing pin and operates the ejector when the breech is opened.

The upper face of the block is formed into a semi-circular trough which, when the block is lowered, uncovers the chamber and serves as a guide to lead the shell and cartridge case into it when the gun is being loaded. About 15 aimed rounds a minute could be fired. The firing and ejector mechanism is inside the block and so is not visible. Attached to the lower end of the breech face is the pistol grip for the trigger with a rod to enable it to be pulled from a point nearer the shoulder piece. A graduated sight bar moving over a scale is fitted as a backsight above the pistol grip, the foresight being on a projection at the fore end of the jacket. The gun is sighted up to 3,400 yards.

As in all naval ordnance the gun is mounted in a cradle which carries the recoil mechanism and which enables the gun to be elevated, and on a revolving carriage which enables the gun to be 'laid' or turned to a bearing required by the target. The cradle is a single casting formed on each side into two cylinders, the forward pair being oil-filled with a piston action to damp down the recoil and the after pair containing the running-out or return springs. The interior of the recoil cylinders is machined to a taper into which the piston only fits at the end point of recoil. In moving backwards the piston in its oil bath encounters increasing resistance which decelerates its travel till it is stopped by the compressed oil. The gun is then returned to the loading position by the springs. The part of the cradle where the trunnion blocks travel is cut away and is open at the top so that the block, part

3 pounder Mk 1
saluting gun.
(MyTimeMedia)

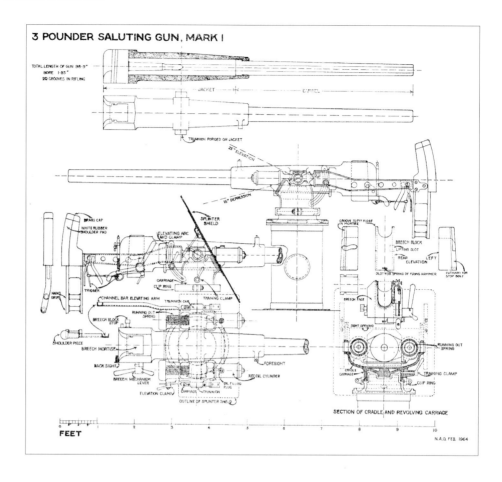

of the piston rods and part of the springs are visible. It is unusual for a naval gun to have trunnions formed on the jacket but this was due to the 3 pounder having been designed for a land mounting as well, in which the carriage would be the gun limber. The pistons are continued part way into the return springs through blocks which take the trunnions of the gun. These are repeated on the outside of the cradle where they fit into the bearings on the cheeks of the carriage. The latter is again a single casting provided with a massive central pivot about which it revolves on a turntable machined on the base casting as shown in the sectional drawing. The two parts are connected by a clip ring which is housed over them in two halves joined together by horizontal bolts, passing through joining lugs. The elevating and training arm with its shoulder piece is bolted to the spring casing on the left side of the cradle. It is formed of channel bar section and has lightening holes cut through it. The vertical shoulder piece is

padded with white rubber and is topped by a polished brass cap. Hand grips are provided at its lower end for the gunner who stands behind the backsight with his left shoulder against the pad and his right hand on the trigger. The rectangular splinter shield shown on the drawing was only fitted in early days.

The 3pdr guns were carried on the shelter deck in capital ships near 'B' turret or on the superstructure in ships with only two turrets, and on the after superstructure in most cruisers after about 1920, and there were usually four of them. Before 1914 they were mounted all along the berthing of the waist in cruisers and in large numbers on the superstructure and even on the masts of heavy ships.

Used in ceremonial, they make large puffs of blue-white smoke and sound of great resonance. In a 21-gun salute the whole fleet was wreathed in smoke on a calm day, its colour being the same as that in the sea battles of the old wooden walls.

3
❖ CAPITAL SHIPS ❖

The main purpose of those chapters that highlight different types of warships, and that are interspersed between those on warship details, is not to look at the actual ships themselves as they are more than adequately covered in other publications. The focus is to try to identify the models within each category that Ough actually built and to provide as much background as possible on every model that has been discovered. Although the whereabouts of some of these models are known, others will have to be deemed 'lost' or 'missing' as no trace has been found of them during the course of research. In some cases it is believed they may well still exist, having been handed down through the generations, but their importance has not yet been recognised by their owners nor have they been identified for what they are.

HMS *Queen Elizabeth* (1913)

It appears that Ough may have made at least two or even three different models of this vessel. Although the ship herself was launched in 1913 she was rebuilt twice during her lifetime – once in 1926–7 and again in 1937–41. During these rebuilds her appearance was altered considerably: for example, her original two funnels were 'trunked' into one, four 4in guns were added and a new foretop was installed.

The first evidence we have of an Ough model of *Queen Elizabeth* is one that was commissioned by Lord Howe and presented by him to Earl Beatty. This was mentioned earlier in the Introduction with the story of Beatty and a number of the ship's company looking for faults – the only ones they could find were two oars too many in one of the Carley rafts, and one step too few in the

companion way! This particular model was to a scale of 1in-32ft and, according to Ough's own notes, made from 'Admiralty sketches published by the Institute of Naval Architects and from photographs'. She is depicted as a waterline model and as Grand Fleet Flagship in 1918. It is believed that the Beatty family are still in possession of this model.

Lord Howe was apparently so impressed by the presentation model that he commissioned another one for himself but to be built on a larger scale. This was also made as a waterline model, with a drifter alongside, all to a scale of 1in-16ft, using Admiralty 'as fitted' drawings and depicting the ship showing her appearance on the day of the surrender of the German Fleet on 25 November 1918. It is also known that Ough charged Lord Howe £200 for the model, as

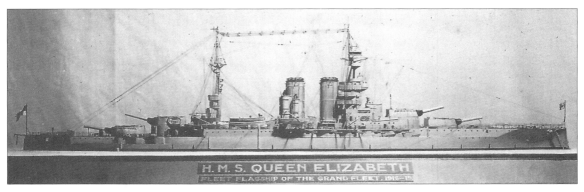

Model of HMS *Queen Elizabeth* (1/384 scale) presented to Earl Beatty. (Courtesy the Ough family)

A larger model (1/192 scale) of *Queen Elizabeth* commissioned by Lord Howe. (Courtesy the Ough family)

'Rebuilt' model of HMS *Queen Elizabeth*, completed in 1935, and now set in a diorama with HMS *Cygnet* and drifter HMS *Crescent Moon*. (© National Maritime Museum, Greenwich, London - SLR 1414)

he was quoted in the May 1932 edition of *Ships and Ship Models* magazine as saying:

Just to show you how it is the labour and not the material which is the main expense in producing ship models, I may say that the *Queen Elizabeth* I built for Lord Howe, which I sold complete for £200, cost only 2s 5d for materials – all the rest was time and labour at only two shillings an hour.

It may be of interest to the reader that £200 in 1932 equates to approximately £12,150 in present-day values and 2 shillings an hour works out at £12.15p.

This model does not appear to be in the possession of the family any longer but there is a possibility that it was returned to Ough for a 'rebuild'. There is photographic evidence from the family archive that Ough 'modernised' a waterline 1in–16ft model of *Queen Elizabeth* in September 1935, depicting her as the 1929 Mediterranean Fleet Flagship. She is also shown with a drifter alongside and Ough names this drifter as HMS *Crescent Moon*. It appears that

this 'modernised' version is the same one that was displayed by the Royal United Service Museum (RUSM) in Whitehall before being acquired in the 1960s by the National Maritime Museum (Collection No. SLR1414).

HMS *Nelson* (1925)

Ough was commissioned to build a waterline model of *Nelson* for the 'Procession of Ships' for the then Department of Overseas Trade as part of the exhibit to be displayed at the International Exhibition at Antwerp in 1930. He referred to it as a 'sketch model' and it is unusual in that it was built to a scale of 1in–14ft. After the Exhibition was over the model was acquired by the RUSM. The intriguing thing is that this model now appears to be in the possession of the Howe family but nobody knows why. Although conjectural, there may be a possibility that the 'Howe' model of *Queen Elizabeth* was modernised by Ough to be

Ough working on his model of HMS *Nelson* for the International Exhibition at Antwerp in 1930. (MyTimeMedia)

Model of HMS *Nelson* in Ough's workshop with pocket watch to show scale. (Courtesy the Ough family)

A rather indistinct picture of the cased model of HMS *Lion* built for Admiral Drax. (Courtesy the Ough family)

displayed at the RUSM. When that museum was closed in the 1960s the family may have been given *Nelson* in lieu of *Queen Elizabeth* that, in turn, went to the National Maritime Museum.

HMS *Lion* (1910)

This waterline model was commissioned by the Imperial War Museum (IWM) and was built to a scale of 1in-32ft. She was rigged 'approximately as at the date of the Battle of Jutland' but Ough mentions in his notes that he wasn't certain as to the correctness of the net defences displayed. Made from Admiralty 'as fitted' drawings she was completed in May 1929 and handed over to the IWM, where she still remains (Catalogue No. MOD 143).

A second waterline model of *Lion* was made by Ough in 1934–5, built to the same scale of 1in-32ft and depicting her at Jutland in 1916. She was commissioned by the then Commander in Chief, Devonport – Vice Admiral the Hon. Sir Reginald Aylmer Ranfurly Plunket-Ernle-Erie-Drax. The Drax family do not know where the model is or even if it still exists.

HMS *Revenge* (1915)

A waterline model of *Revenge* built to the scale of 1in-32ft, depicting her as Fleet Flagship Atlantic Fleet 1924–7 and with a drifter alongside, was made by Ough in 1927. She became part of the Exeter Museum Loan Collection before being acquired by the IWM, where she still remains (Catalogue No. MOD 123).

HMS *Iron Duke* (1912)

It appears that there could have been at least two models of *Iron Duke* made by Ough. One was definitely commissioned by the IWM and made for them in 1928. A waterline model, with accompanying drifter, to a scale of 1in-32ft and with post-war (First World War) rig, she was built from sketches and general arrangements published by the Institute of Naval Architects. The model is still held by the IWM (Catalogue No. MOD 127).

There is an intriguing puzzle in photographs from the Ough archive which show parts of the main superstructure and main armament. These photographs, which are dated 1926, clearly show 'B' turret with 'bearing markings' or 'deflection scales'. These markings were adopted by the Grand Fleet to assist other ships within the fleet take bearings on an enemy ship even if she couldn't be seen due to smoke or to being masked by other ships. The markings are not shown on the IWM model which, according to another set of photographs, was made in 1928. Whether there were two *Iron*

Duke models or whether there was only one and Ough changed the 1926 version we shall probably never know.

HMS *Repulse* (1916)

This particular model came to light in 2005 when a person using the name 'Robbie' sought advice on the internet as he had just inherited two of Ough's models, namely *Repulse* and the destroyer HMS *Nestor* (which is discussed in the chapter on 'Destroyers'). Most replies advised 'Robbie' to seek professional advice or to go to an auction house if he wished to sell them.

In May 2006 both models were sold by Christie's at their South Kensington Maritime Auction. They appeared as one lot, Lot No. 250, and the hammer price reached was £3,840. Adding the buyer's premium and VAT (15% at that time) brought the total sale price up to £4,723.20p.

Unfortunately, it has not been possible to ascertain who bought these models or where they are now.

The *Repulse* model was built to a scale of 1in-100ft and depicted the ship flying the flag of Vice Admiral Sir Lionel Halsey conveying HRH the Prince of Wales to Africa and South America in 1925. It was mounted as a waterline model in a glass case, and the base was inscribed by Ough. He wrote: 'This model was made at Dawlish Down in 1925. It was exhibited at HM Govt. Pavilion at the British Empire Exhibition, 1925 and was for 28 years at the Royal Albert Memorial Museum, Exeter. Norman A. Ough, maker 1925.' It would appear that the model was removed from the Exeter Museum loan collection in 1953 but it is not known whether it was sold by them or by Ough, or 'acquired' by another person.

Model of HMS *Iron Duke*, made in 1926, showing 'deflection scales' marked on 'B' turret. (Courtesy the Ough family)

1/1200 scale model of HMS *Repulse*. (Bridgeman Images - CH2644967)

HMS *Hood* (1918)

Ough appears to have made at least two models of *Hood*. It is known that while at Exeter Art School he began a model of the Grand Fleet, to a scale of 1in–100ft, and applied to the chief of the Naval Section of the British Government Pavilion asking whether it could be displayed at the 1925 Wembley Exhibition. As an example of his work he showed a 1in–100ft waterline model of HMS *Hood* to the adjudicator and was told that if he finished his model of the fleet (151 ships) in time he could show it at the exhibition. He did finish the model in time and it was exhibited, after which he sold it to the Royal United Service Institution who displayed it in their museum at Whitehall. (This miniature fleet is discussed in more detail in the chapter on 'Other Collections'.) The fate of this small-scale model of *Hood*, that Ough had presented as an example of his work, is unknown.

The other version of *Hood* that we know Ough made was built as a full hull model, as opposed to a waterline version, to a larger scale of 1in–32ft. A photograph from the

Model of HMS *Hood* (1/1200 scale) used by Ough as an example of his work for the 1925 Wembley Exhibition. (Courtesy the Ough Family)

family archive depicts the model; on the reverse is written 'Dr Worthington Collection. Exon. 1927'. It appears she was part of a loan collection at the Royal Albert Memorial Museum, Exeter. Today she forms part of the Harmsworth Collection at Plymouth City Museum and is on display there. Ough's name and address are written on the base of the mount and it also states that she was made between July and October 1927.

Ough made a number of plans for *Hood* and he also started to write a series in *Model Maker* magazine for those wishing to make a model of the ship. He only managed to write five parts in all, from July 1964 until January 1965, before illness got the better of him and he was unable to complete the series before he died. In effect this was his last work.

HMS *Duke of York* (1940)

Although Ough drew up plans for the *Duke of York* there appears to be no known model.

The article he wrote for *Model Maker* magazine in April 1960 now follows.

Ough's plan of the battleship HMS *Duke of York*.
(MyTimeMedia)

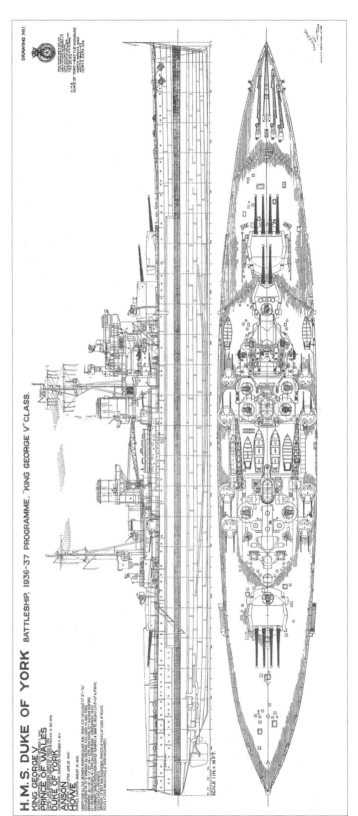

The drawing included with this article gives some idea of the characteristic detail of a battleship, the primary unit of a fleet until very recent times. Apart from HMS *Vanguard*, the last British battleship, the five ships *King George V*, *Prince of Wales*, *Anson*, *Howe* and *Duke of York* were the last in the history of the Royal Navy to be built as a class in the three centuries long tradition as ships-of-the-line, and with their passing ended the long era of the line-of-battle in warfare at sea. HMS *Duke of York*, the subject of this drawing, was laid down at Clydebank in May 1937, launched in February 1940 and completed in November 1941. On her first commission she joined the Home Fleet and took part in many sweeps in northern waters covering the Murmansk convoys; in December 1943, as Flagship of Admiral Sir Bruce Frazer, she intercepted the *Scharnhorst* which was being engaged by the cruisers *Belfast*, *Jamaica* and *Norfolk* and escorting destroyers. During the night action the *Scharnhorst* received at least four torpedo hits from the destroyers while under fire of the guns of the *Duke of York* and was sunk. After the capitulation of Germany the ship sailed for Japan and was flagship of Admiral Frazer in Tokio Bay on the surrender of that country. In 1946 she returned to the Home Fleet and, after some service, was placed in reserve, being sold to the shipbreakers in 1957. The drawing shows her as in her last commission as Flagship of The Commander-in-Chief of the Home Fleet. At this time, and until her end, she was painted the very light violet-grey of the Mediterranean Fleet, a colour that enhanced her apparent size and added greatly to her magnificent appearance.

The ships of the 'King George V' Class were the first in the Royal Navy since HMS *Canada*, which was present at the Battle of Jutland, to carry 14 inch guns. As originally designed they were to have had three turrets with four guns in each, but later, when tests on the firing range with improved shells had shown the need for greater magazine protection, it was decided to allow for the weight of the additional heavy armour required by altering 'B' turret to a twin. As built each quadruple turret weighed 1,550 tons and the twin 900 tons. The weight of the broadside was 15,900lbs. reaching 36,000yds with a penetration at 15,000yds of 13 inches of armour. Much discussion arose concerning the secondary armament, for there were those who advised separation of the anti-destroyer from the anti-aircraft batteries. This would have meant overcrowded topsides, with much interference from blast, more fire control positions, complication of ammunition supply arrangements, and larger complement. Eventually a HA/LA battery of sixteen 5.25 inch guns was accepted as firing shells heavy enough to disable a destroyer and the heaviest that could be handled fast enough to deal with attacking aircraft at long range. The guns were carried in eight round turrets, each weighing 80 tons and had a range of 22,500 yards. But for the amidships catapult which was fitted in earlier commissions there would have been room for four more of these turrets. The drawing shows the ship with the area where the catapult formerly was plated up and the space used for accommodation under a boat deck between the funnels. The decision to carry aircraft, for which hangars for four were provided, involved much controversy, and, in the case of these, and other recent capital ships, finding deck space for the athwartship catapult must have been a troublesome problem for the constructors. Those against aircraft being carried objected to the inevitable highly inflammable petrol supply and they pointed to the weakness of the contemporary Walrus amphibian compared to carrier-borne planes, and also to the risk to the ship from submarine attack as she slowed down to recover them. In favour it was argued that without aircraft the area of vision for long range gunnery would often be limited, as fire control would be less effective since aircraft-carrier attendance would

not be available at all times. Such are examples of the many contradictory requirements involved in the design of a great warship, the resulting vessel being always a compromise, a complex balance of mutually excluding factors. The ships of the class were designed under Sir Arthur Johns when Director of Naval Construction, and completed under Sir Stanley Goodall, those in charge of production being W. G. Sanders and H. S. Pengelly of the Royal Corps of Naval Constructors at the Admiralty.

It will be seen from the body plan, and which shows the view of the plating, that a large area of the bottom of the ship amidships is flat, a feature that is common to all large warships as it facilitates docking on three rows of keel blocks without requiring shores to support the bilges in this area. The armour extends, though with reduced thickness, right forward to the stem forging and nearly as far aft as the contour plate of the stern, the plating of the armour being flush jointed vertically as in the shell plating, but with no laps. The individual slabs of armour, which are 15 inches thick amidships, can sometimes be seen defined by a thin vertical line at each butt. The plating above waterline is quite straightforward, the end laps showing clearly in the drawing of the profile. Below armour and round the bilges it is more complicated as the immense girth of the hull required an increase in the number of strakes, the additional ones ending in 'stealer' plates at which a single strake is converted into two.

It is most likely that this drawing will make more appeal to the miniaturist and the 'glass case' model

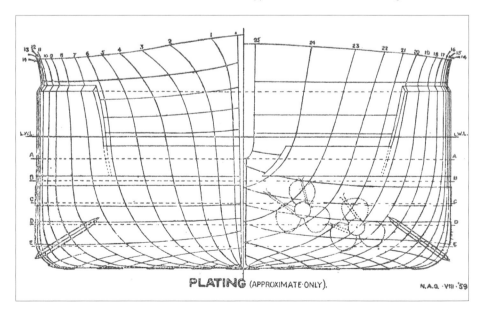

'Body Plan', showing plating, of HMS *Duke of York*. (MyTimeMedia)

PLATING (APPROXIMATE·ONLY).

N.A.O. ·VIII·'59

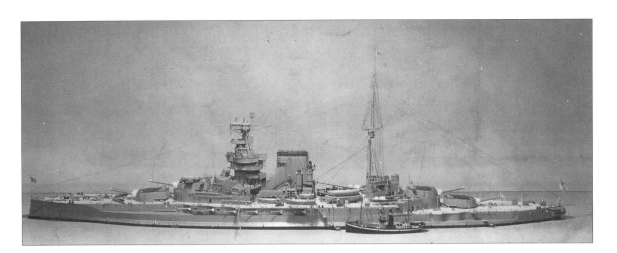

maker than to those who want to build a power job, as the latter, if they work to 1/8in-1ft scale, would at once encounter the problem of size and heavy displacement. At this scale the length overall would be 7ft 9 1/8in with a beam of 12 7/8in and draught of 4in and at this load the displacement would be about 94lbs. All the same, if such a model could be transported and successfully launched she would be a fine sight on the water and could easily be powered to cross the Channel under radio control, the scale speed for full power being three knots. The large displacement would give great scope for long range power plant, either steam or electric, the turrets could be made to train and fire and the model could be fitted with radio-controlled searchlights! If the scale was halved to 1/16in-1ft, the length would be 3ft 7 3/4in, beam 6 7/16in and draught 2in and the displacement would be about 12lbs. This is a manageable size but the detail, if shown, would be rather fragile.

Since the model and machinery, with radio, could probably be constructed at 1/8in scale to weigh about 35lbs which could be carried on a cradle on top of a car, the rest of the necessary 60lbs of ballast could be kept separate and those parts of it which were not accumulators could be cast into lead blocks fitting into spaces arranged at appropriate places in the hull. The shell plating would need to be about 0.01in or 0.012in tinplate which is about the thickness of the metal in Huntley and Palmer's large cubical biscuit tins, four or five of which would be needed to build the hull, the armour being built out so as to appear to have the required thickness. All of the upper deck of these ships was planked which would give the builder plenty of scope for making a fine quarter deck and forecastle. The decks of the superstructure were of steel. Owing to her low freeboard forward the model would tend to take in heavy seas over her bows as she would only pitch slightly on account of her fine entry under water.

'Modernised' model of HMS *Queen Elizabeth* in Ough's workshop. (Courtesy the Ough family)

4
✤ RN Service Boats ✤

The following articles are, as in the chapter on 'Ordnance', reproductions of Ough's original work that was published in *Model Maker* magazine during the 1950s and '60s as part of his 'Warship Detail' series. These plans of ships' boats are invaluable not only for the warship modeller who wishes to incorporate them into a larger model but also for modellers who wish to build larger versions of the actual boats themselves.

50ft Steam Picket Boat

The slight hope that information for this series of articles would be preserved and made available is now fading. After 18 months of endeavour to get the situation clarified and after further letters to those concerned in the Admiralty the author was invited recently to visit the Ship Department (formerly Department of Naval Construction) at Bath, and in the course of wandering round the establishment for most of an afternoon seeing various offices, including the Curator of Drawings, it became abundantly clear that

the bulk of the priceless historical material that is needed for this record has been destroyed. Apparently it has never been officially recognised that the nation has any rights in this, its own, property. One might think that the specification books of the Service boats, the gunnery manuals, the tracings from the small scale design drawings and the 'as fitted' drawings and a host of other non-security items could have been sent to some convenient place of safety or to the libraries of the National Maritime Museum or the Imperial War Museum. As things stand now it is going to be more

50ft steam picket boat. (MyTimeMedia)

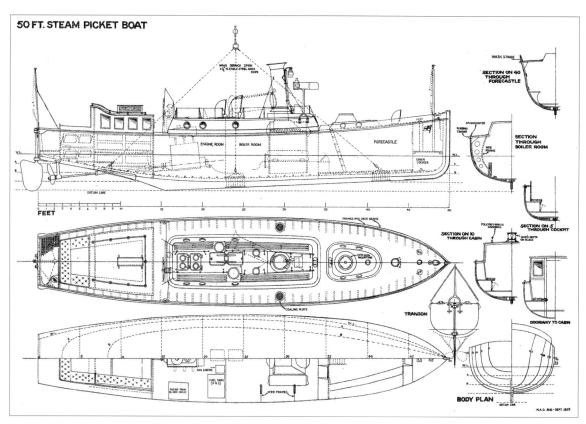

difficult to find details of ships of the Royal Navy of the past 50 years than to find those of vessels of the Trafalgar period, especially as the amount of information required is vastly greater. A simple way out of the difficulty had been urged by the author for a long time at every meeting as a member of the Council of the Society for Nautical Research, and that was to try to persuade them to use their influence with the Admiralty to have photographs taken of a representative ship of each class before her disposal to the shipbreakers. With a 35mm camera in half an hour on a fine day a set of 72 pictures could be taken all over the decks and topsides of a ship at a cost of seven and sixpence. These photographs would equal the value of many drawings, the negatives could be preserved in a matchbox, and a considerable fortune could be made from the sale of prints from them. One of the most important parts of any warship is the bridge, a place where, not infrequently, decisions have been taken that have affected the fate of nations, but, as far as can be discovered, no detailed drawings of this in any ship have been kept. A few photographs would have preserved the record once and for all if taken there. However, the author's attempts to move the Council in this matter led nowhere.

It amounts to this, that a comprehensive book of reference on the detail of ships of the Royal Navy of this century cannot be produced for the thousands all over the world who are interested, as the sources of information have been destroyed. Only a nationwide advertising campaign, or an intensive search, by one armed with plenary powers, through every Admiralty establishment might recover some of it. This series in *Model Maker* was intended, in the course of about 100 items, to be such a comprehensive work, but, as things now stand, it can at best only be a scrapbook compiled from such items as the one here which was obtained for the author by a senior draughtsman and his colleagues at Bath after much searching along with a few other plans. The specification book for the 50ft steam boats which would be needed for a proper description to go with this drawing has been destroyed with the rest. It is sad to feel compelled to say all this, for, in all the author's long and very interesting association with the Admiralty, amounting to 34 years now, the constructors and draughtsmen whom it has been his privilege to know have been endlessly kind and helpful with these researches, although their just responsibility is towards the operational Navy. But the above remarks are in no way a criticism of individuals,

but concern a defect, perhaps a 'blind spot', in the system that might be remedied in the future.

Here is one of the items salvaged. The official drawing is of a 50ft steam boat used for harbour service, but the corrections for a capital ship's picket boat have been added from the author's collection of photographs. For more than half a century battleships carried two of them, and, in the case of a flagship, a third 45ft long, with a counter stern as the admiral's barge. As the specification book is gone it is not possible to state the power developed by the twin-cylinder compound reciprocating engine or what speed it gave, but the picket boats always produced an impression of power and speed on their journeys in charge of a midshipman among the anchored battleships and to the shore. Before about 1908 they were of similar form but of a length of 56ft with twin funnels, and a drawing of them ought to be included in this series as they were also carried in the large cruisers at the turn of the century, and in battleships up to the 'King Edward VII' class, but the specification of these is another item that has been destroyed as of no value!

The hull is quite smooth, being built of double diagonal planking with a massive keel and a steep sheer up to the bows and with a slightly raked flat transom stern. There were slight differences in detail of fittings introduced from time to time. In some the funnel was more upright, being perpendicular to the casing, and the bar funnel stays led direct to its sides instead of being crossed on top as shown. In some the whole of the brass funnel was polished bright, in others only the bell top was polished, the rest being painted black, and, in some, the raised after part of the cabin roof is longer than the one shown in the drawing. The decks were usually covered with 'Corticene', which is a plain brown linoleum the colour of milk chocolate, with the 'round-up' grating across the stern of bare wood. This, which was usually of teak or Borneo whitewood, made a small deck over the tiller and its steering wires. On the cabin top, which was also covered in 'Corticene' and with polished brass hand rails, was a long box of varnished teak with glass sides and ends and with electric lights inside. On the side glasses the name of the ship to which the picket boat belonged was shown in plain block capitals, white on a black ground with the initial letter of her name on the ends. The design of these name boxes varied slightly and they may have been made and fitted by the ship's carpenter. The ensign and jackstaff shown in the drawing were usually only shipped for ceremonial purposes, and the stanchions and brackets for the port and starboard bow lights were kept below until required after sunset. It will be seen that the funnel was hinged. This was in order to get it clear of the heavy main derrick span of 4 1/2in flexible steel wire rope, the three legs of which were secured to shackle plates in the bottom of the boat for hoisting her inboard. The boiler and engine casings, which were continuous, with three glazed portholes on each side and one 10in and a 14in cowl ventilator on top, were built of metal and painted all over ship's grey. Bare wood slats were laid along the top for seats for the liberty men who were taken ashore on board with a low guard rail to serve as a handhold in rough weather. At the after end of the casing was a metal screen, or, in earlier types, one of canvas stretched over stanchions to shelter the helmsman, the steering wheel being placed to starboard with a binnacle to port. The tiller wires led down from the hub of the wheel through leading sheaves, across the deck through other sheaves and along the spurn-water to another pair of sheaves which led them to the tiller. It will be seen that the command flag of a vice-admiral is painted on the bows. This was sometimes raised, the flag being carved with its staff and truck, in low relief. Above the forecastle is a metal casing with an access hatch in its after end on top of which is the securing ring for the 3 pounder gun mounting, as the picket boats were often used as small warships.

25ft Motor Boat

At the present time the 25ft motor boat is the most widely distributed of all the power boats supplied to HM ships, as it is found in all the 'Algerine' class mine-sweepers, in most frigates and in all destroyers including the 'Weapon' and 'Daring' class ships. For a Service boat it is remarkably ugly especially in the form of the hull where the planking, at the place where it meets the deadwood of the keel under the stern, has a sudden bend upwards leading into a straight line up to the transom as will be seen in the profile, and it is said that if the draining plug, which is situated aft of this bend, is taken out when the boat is going at speed no water enters on account of the eddy that forms there. Even the rudder, the tiller and the propeller opening in the deadwood are rather shapeless, and the cabin tops, with their straight upper edges, do not appear to 'marry' satisfactorily with the hull. It is a large heavy boat and requires radial davits and massive falls to hoist and lower it. Nevertheless it is so common in

the Service that few models of present day warships would be complete without it.

The hull is built clinker fashion, that is, with the planks overlapping as in the 27ft whaler. There are 15 strakes of planking each side if only one rubbing timber is fitted, or 14 if a second one is riveted near the lower edge of an extra wide plank below the gunwale strake, but the former arrangement is most common, the latter being shown in the sections to the right of the drawing. As in the whaler the overlapping of the planks is made to die away flush as shown in the drawings of that boat. There is a short planked deck forward with a chain pipe, bollard, fairleads and a step for the jackstaff, and a narrow deck with a grating in it across the stern. The cabin tops have rounded edges in some varieties of this boat but in some they have sharp edges as shown in the sections. The square hatch in the forward canopy is placed so as to allow the falls to be passed down and hooked on for hoisting and lowering, the after falls passing clear of the stern canopy and being hooked on to the shackle by lifting the floor of the cockpit. The ensign and jackstaffs are not shipped when the boat is secured in the davits. On top of the after canopy, on the centre line, is the usual illuminated name box. This has the ship's name in white block capitals on a black ground on the glass panels at each side. The number of windows in it varies, in some there are three, as shown, and in some four and often the ends are semicircular with a 3/4in flat chromium-plated rim round their edges. The colour is varnished teak but they are sometimes painted white, those with sharp edges being covered with 'Corticene' on top. A grass rope fender is lashed along the sides of the boat, under the rubbing strake, passing round the bows where it is increased in diameter by a rope 'pudding' covered with canvas painted white, and tapered off on the transom and secured to eyebolts as shown in the detail of the stern at the foot of the drawing. The plan view of the hull shows the timbering which is visible where it rises above the thwarts and side benches so it is worth showing in models of 1/8th scale and upwards. In most Service boats the floors of the cockpit and in other places are fitted with gratings over the central area but in these boats they are just planked over, sections being made portable.

It is quite easy to make the boats of a warship model, including a working model, from paper in the form of 'gumstrip'. It is necessary to make a solid model of the hull first to act as a former and it is better if this is painted and rubbed over with some candle grease

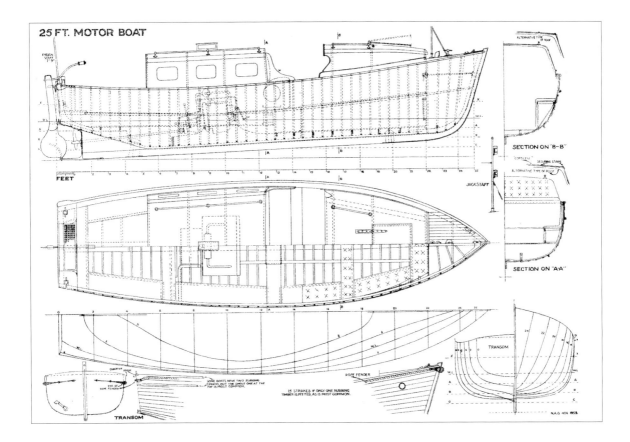

25 FT. MOTOR BOAT

25ft motor boat.
(MyTimeMedia)

before use. Broad bands of wet tissue paper are laid on the former and carried up to just above the gunwale. These are followed by bands of gumstrip to strap them on, these also being stuck to the deck of the former. More are added till the surfaces are covered, and a second and third layer to build up the required thickness. The strakes can be formed by narrow bands of gumstrip laid fore and aft, the edges towards the keel being spaced correctly but it is of little consequence what becomes of their opposite edges as these will be covered by the over-lap of the next strake. When the planking is finished the shell can be taken off the former by cutting along the gunwale, a cut with a razor blade down the stem assisting its removal and allowing a piece of card to be stuck in the resulting opening to form the stem. If the shell is difficult to get off it is probably because the first layer of gumstrip has been put on too wet and the gum has run into the tissue paper. When the shell is completed and dry the rising and gunwale timbers, keel and ribs can be added with strips of card and the whole made waterproof with model aircraft clear dope with some thinners in it. This will work right into the fibres of the

paper better than paint which can be put on after. It is not advisable to use shellac as this is rather heavy and it is doubtful if it is truly waterproof. Anyone who has tried this method will be convinced that it is a most valuable technique. It gives a boat hull that is of scale thickness but very strong in a fraction of the time needed to carve one, and the same former can be used again and again for repeats. It is also useful in making cowl ventilators. In fact, as a method in ship model making it has nearly as many possibilities as shown in the 'All-Steel Construction' series.

32ft Cutter & 32ft Motor Cutter

The 32ft rowing and sailing cutters were used as sea boats in all capital ships, including aircraft carriers, and in most large cruisers, although in recent times they have been replaced by the 27ft whaler in cruisers below 10,000 tons displacement. They were always clinker built boats with a drop keel fitted for rowing by 12 or 14 oars, and were hoisted on radial davits and secured against a griping spar as shown in the drawing of davits [see 'General Details' chapter]. As the sea boats in a warship model are a fairly prominent feature this

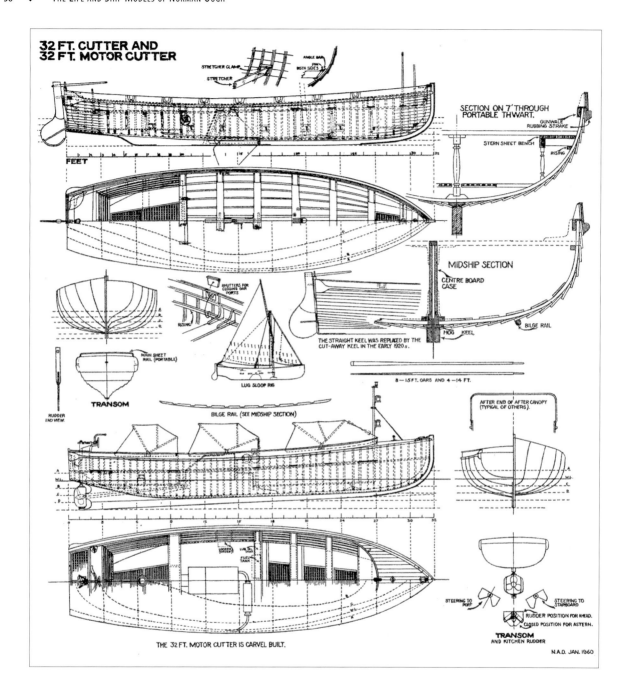

32 FT. CUTTER AND 32 FT. MOTOR CUTTER

THE 32 FT. MOTOR CUTTER IS CARVEL BUILT.

N.A.O. JAN. 1960

32ft cutter and motor cutter. (MyTimeMedia)

drawing is of some importance as even in builders' models, they are nearly always shown incorrectly. When they are turned outboard in harbour there is always a long line of heavy rope, called the boat rope, leading from the bows of the cutters to bollards far up on the forecastle to which they are led through small fairleads. The boats are painted all over ship grey externally with the rubbing timber and its quarter

badges at the corners of the stern left bare scrubbed teak. The interior is painted white down to the upper edges of the bottom boards, below which it was usually painted dark grey or sometimes sky blue, the boards, thwarts and gratings being of bare wood. The hull consists of 17 strakes of planking if the washstrake or gunwale is included, and, up to about the end of the 1914-18 war, had a straight keel running right aft to the transom as shown in the sketch of the stern near the enlarged midship section. This type was replaced gradually by boats with the cut away keel as shown in the profile. The gunwale was formed by a thicker plank slotted with 14 slightly wedge-shaped openings for the oars, these being closed by 14 similarly shaped pieces called poppets or shutters, with slightly bevelled edges to prevent them falling outboard, and secured by a rope lanyard to the rising as shown in the perspective sketch to the left of the small drawing of the sail plan. Inside the gunwale were riveted wooden doublings lined with bronze castings to take the friction of the oars. Of these there were eight of 15 feet and four of 14 feet. Unlike those of the whaler illustrated elsewhere, a cutter's oars had straight blades, and when stowed, were placed with the blade pointing forwards. There were six rowing thwarts and an additional one with corresponding oar ports could be shipped across the stern sheet benches and this is shown dotted on the plan. Underneath the aftermost fixed or 'stroke' thwart was a cordage reel on which was rolled the boat's cable consisting of 25 fathoms (150 feet) of 3in manila rope, as measured by circumference. Modern sailing cutters have a single mast and two sails as storm canvas which are shown dotted. The construction of the boat is similar to that of the whaler with like floorboards, and gratings. The metal fittings that hold the ends of the stretchers for the oarsmen are shown in the perspective sketch at the top of the drawing. Most capital ships also carried a 30ft cutter of the same design and, in some, a motorised version, the canopies of which were similar to those shown on the 32ft motor cutter. This latter was a carvel built boat with a shell of double diagonal planking, presenting a smooth exterior, and was carried in many cruisers. A feature in some was the 'Kitchin' rudder which consisted of a hollow bronze shell including the propeller and divided in half vertically, the after edge being slightly lipped inwards. By means of a handwheel on the tiller casting the two halves of the shell could be closed behind the propeller thus forming a column of water moving forwards and driving the boat astern when required. In either position the whole shell could be turned to port or starboard for steering either ahead or astern, as shown near the drawing of the transom of the boat. As the specification books of both these boats have been lost or destroyed by the Admiralty along with many others it is not possible for the author to give any more detail such as the type of engine and the speed of the motor cutter.

30ft Captain's Gig

Gigs and galleys were perhaps the most elegant and graceful of all the Service boats. The former were carried in most large warships and were in the jealous care of the captain's coxswain who usually went with him from ship to ship. In a flagship a galley, for the sole use of the admiral, was carried as well. This was two feet longer than the gig and was usually clinker built whereas most gigs were almost always carvel built like the one shown in the drawing which gives enlarged half sections contrasting the two methods. The gig was generally called the 'blue boat' as it was painted dark blue in the Home Fleet and pale blue in the Mediterranean Fleet, and it was kept in a condition of extreme smartness, even more so than the rest of those carried, which were also maintained at a high standard, for it is an old saying in the Royal Navy that 'a ship is known by her boats' and when away from the ship her boats' crews carry the credit of the ship with them.

Apart from the historical record, this series on boats may be of value to modelmakers as most of those who try warships generally get the boats wrong, and the makers of the great builders' models are no exception. Most of those shown on the model of the *Vanguard* in the Science Museum, and on others elsewhere, are incorrect in detail and are wrong in form and proportion and miss most of the points that make a warship's boats one of the most impressive parts of her equipment. Also a detailed model of a Service boat made to say, 1/4in-1 ft. scale is a very pretty thing in itself and it would be a fine mantelpiece ornament.

The drawing shows a typical 30ft carvel-built gig with two masts carrying dipping lugsails. An alternative arrangement is for the mast to be stepped just forward of amidships and carrying the mainsail only. The masts are stepped through the sailing thwart or footboard, also called the mast caning, through holes surrounded by flat brass rims and stepped into heel sockets fastened to the hog of the keel. The sails are hoisted by a wire halliard attached to a tackle which joins a wire pendant shackled to an eyebolt on the keel, and the yards are slung from a hook on a leather covered metal traveller attached to the halliard. The tacks are bowsed down by a tackle shackled to an eyebolt below the sailing thwart. The main sheet rides on a brass horse on the transom of the stern, the fore sheet reeving through blocks attached to wire pendants slung on slip hooks below the gunwale. The sails are laced to the yards with spiral lashings and they have two rows of reef points. Below the level of the gunwale the masts

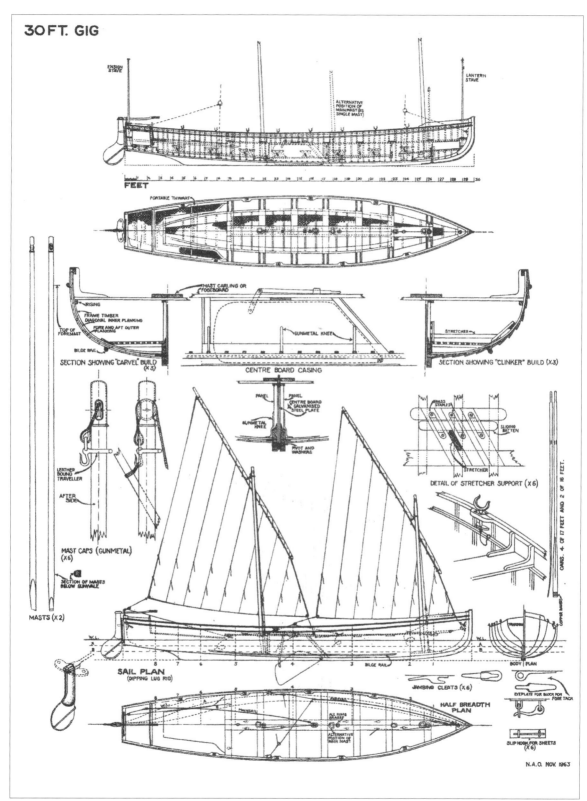

30ft gig. (MyTimeMedia)

are made flat on the fore side and of half round section on the after side. They have caps of gunmetal which contain the sheaves for the halliards.

A carvel-built gig has a double shell, the outer being built of fore and aft planks as in clinker build but with flush edges, the inner being of planks laid within this at an angle of 45 degrees to the keel and sloping aft, the frame timbers being worked on the flush surface of the inner shell. The lowermost plank, or garboard strake, of the outer hull is fastened to the 'hog' or inner keel but the diagonal planks are butted against it with the ends of the frames spiked to its upper surface. Riding on the frames along the bilges is the 'skirting', or boundary plank, which holds the gratings of the floor in position, while above these, running most of the length of the boat, is the 'rising' which carries the thwarts, the latter being fixed to the sides by grown timbers called 'knees'. The gunwale is strengthened along the whole of its upper edge by a timber of rectangular section and this is covered by a flat plank over both called the 'capping'. Along the lower edge of the gunwale strake is the half round rubbing strake which is always left unpainted and this is repeated along the bilges for half the boat's length as similar timbers called the bilge rails. These help to reinforce and to protect the bottom planks. Amidships is the centreboard casing containing the drop keel. The casing is built on the hog of the keel and it consists of a frame reaching as high as the lower side of the thwarts, and of side panels. It is connected to the frame timbers by very strong gunmetal knees. The drop keel pivots round a pin going through the outer keel which is fixed by riveting to square iron plates at each end.

Stretchers are fitted for the heels of the rowers for use when the boat is not under sail. These run across the bottom just above the floor except in way of the centreboard casing which divides two of them. They are supported at each end by chocks screwed to the frame timbers as shown in the enlarged sketch of this detail. A sliding batten running under brass staples prevents them from lifting.

The usual painting for ships' boats is grey outside and white inside, although the area within the skirting and all over under the floor gratings is sometimes dark grey or pale blue. The capping and rubbing strake are left bare and frequently scrubbed. The masts and yards are varnished. The framing of the gratings of the floor is of teak, all the gratings being of Canada rock elm as are all the thwarts, pillars, backboard, yoke and tiller and the mast carling, and they are all unpainted, as are

also the oars. There are four sling plates for lifting the boat, two on the hog of the keel, one on the stem timber and one on the sternpost. The boat is rowed by the oars pivoting in gunmetal crutches as shown in the perspective sketch.

The builders' models of warships show the woodwork of the boats as if it were of some dark wood like mahogany which they make darker still with varnish. This is quite out of character since in the real boats it is of elm or ash and this requires a light coloured wood such as lime or American whitewood to represent it. They also give the decks of their models a polish like the floor of a ballroom which, in real life, would cause a good many casualties.

42ft Launch & 36ft Pinnace

The 42ft launch and the 36ft pinnace were carried in most large warships from about 1890 onwards, in large cruisers up to 1914 and in all capital ships. They were stowed, one inside the other and usually with a 22ft or 27ft whaler inside the pinnace, next to the steam picket boats, and the Admiral's barge in a flagship and always within reach of the main derrick. They were large heavy boats, carvel built with a double diagonal shell and were strong enough to carry a 3pdr gun or, alternatively a Maxim gun, the mountings for which were fitted to a heavy wide thwart in the bows. They could be used to cover landings of seamen and marines and for detached service against pirates. Before the use of steam drifters for that purpose they also carried the 'liberty men' ashore when the ship was not alongside a wharf.

Like the gigs and galleys, cutters and dinghies, the launch and pinnace were sailing boats, but with only a single mast carrying a jib, or foresail, and a mainsail, an arrangement known in the Service as the 'De Horsey' rig, both being identical apart from the difference in size. In fine weather they could be sailed by a crew of six men and a coxswain. A motorised version of the pinnace is shown in the lower half of the drawing, and the fitting of a propeller involves modifications of rudder and stern-post, but, as a sailing boat, the stern would be the same as that of the 42ft launch.

The mast is set up by a wire forestay passing over a roller fairlead on top of the stem, and a preventer stay, also of wire, which carries the jib. This goes over a second roller in the same fitting. Both are set up by tackles secured to eyebolts low down in the hull near the foot of the mast.

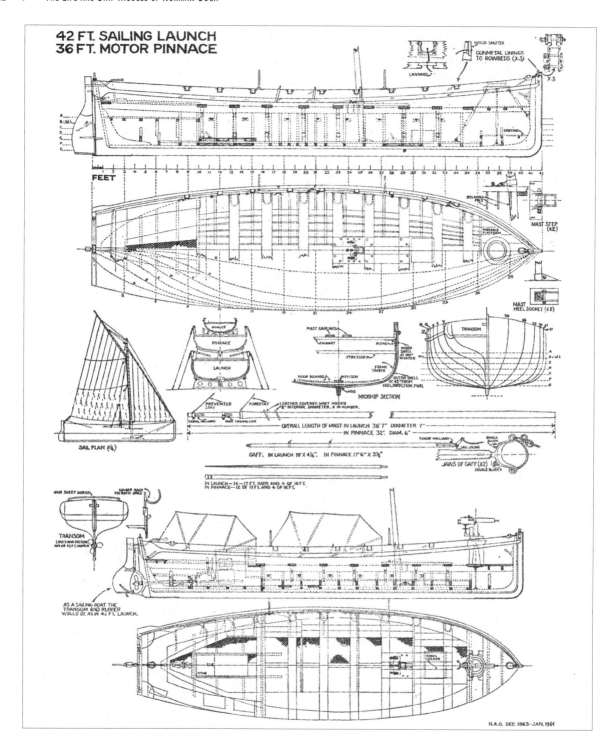

42ft launch and 36ft
pinnace. (MyTimeMedia)

The drawing shows the details of the mast and gaff.
The former is of square section where it passes through
the step on the mast caning and is tapered slightly on
the fore side where it goes into the heel socket. It is

36ft 7in long in the launch and 32ft in the pinnace, the
respective diameters being 7in and 6in. The gaff has
metal jaws and is secured to the mast by a rope
lashing. An eyebolt at the end takes the throat halliard

27 FT. WHALER

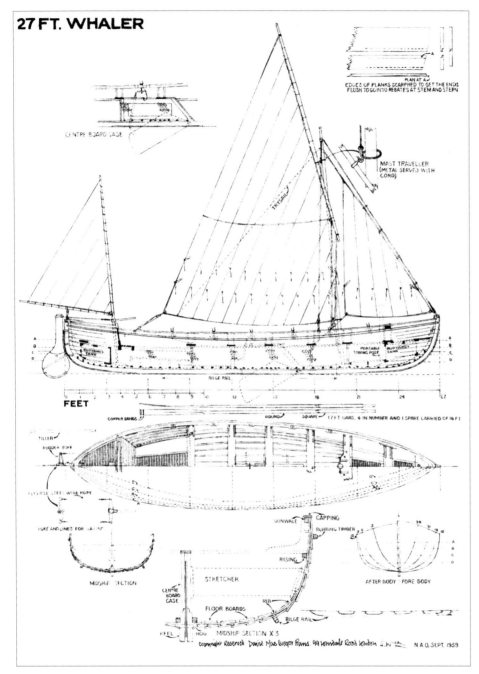

PLAN AT A
EDGES OF PLANKS SCARPHED TO GET THE ENDS
FLUSH TO GO INTO REBATES AT STEM AND STERN

CENTRE BOARD CASE

TRYSAIL

MAST TRAVELLER
(METAL SERVED WITH CORD)

BUOYANT TANK

PORTABLE TOWING POST

BUOYANT TANK

BILGE RAIL

FEET

COPPER BANDS   ROUND   SQUARE   17 FT OARS, 4 IN NUMBER AND 1 SPARE CARRIED OF 16 FT

TILLER
RUDDER YOKE

FLEXIBLE STEEL WIRE ROPE

YOKE AND LINES FOR SAILING

GUNWALE   CAPPING
RUBBING TIMBER

RISING

MIDSHIP SECTION   AFTER BODY   FORE BODY

CENTRE BOARD CASE   STRETCHER

FLOOR BOARDS   RIB
BILGE RAIL

KEEL   HOG   MIDSHIP SECTION X 3

Copyright Reserved David MacGregor Plans. 99 Lonsdale Road London   N.A.O. SEPT. 1959

This 27ft whaler plan was drawn by Ough although he never wrote an article on it. (ss Great Britain Trust)

block and two further along, formed on iron bands, take the two blocks for the peak halliards. The mast is set up by wire shrouds with rope lanyards and by a flying backstay as shown in the small sail plan. The mainsail is triced up by brails when not in use instead of being lowered. The lower part of the luff of the sail is secured to the mast by a lacing and the upper part by mast hoops of iron covered with leather. The brails are shortened in by single and double block tackles shackled to eyebolts on the mast carling, the brailing lines leading through blocks shackled to the jaws of the gaff. The falls of the halliards and brails are made fast to the belaying pins projecting below the mast carling. When the boats are 'nested', or stowed one

Ship's boats shown on Ough's HMS *Queen Elizabeth* (© National Maritime Museum, Greenwich, London - SLR1414)

inside the other, as shown in the sectional sketch, the mast, sails and oars of the launch are stowed in the iron fittings called 'lumber racks' to allow room for the pinnace, and, likewise, those of the latter are stowed to clear the way for the whaler. The boats are secured to the upper deck of the ship by clamps fitted over the gunwale connected to wire pendants boused down to eyebolts in the deck by rope lanyards.

The frame timbers of the hull are more massive and more widely and irregularly spaced than in other Service boats, and the pinnace has a flat floor filled with gratings, the launch having bottom boards. The thwarts in both are peculiar as they are not connected to the hull by the usual wood knees but are slid into position on the rising and fixed by metal fittings with spikes projecting downwards and held by iron castings on the hull which receive them. They are thus made portable and, on their removal, the pinnace or whaler can be lowered deep in for close stowage. There is no centre board casing. These boats are heavy enough to be used for laying out the ship's stream anchor and a roller fairlead is fitted in the transom to guide the wire cable attached to it.

The launch is pulled by 18 oars and the sailing

pinnace by 16. The oars that are one foot shorter are for use from the bow thwarts. They are worked in gunmetal-lined rowbeds fitted in the washstrake above the gunwale as shown in the sketch of this detail at the top of the drawing. The ports are filled when sailing by wood shutters, called 'poppets', fitted into the woodwork and secured to the boat inboard by rope lanyards. The outside of the hull has a massive rubbing strake which ends in a large shapely wood boss called the 'quarter badge' which protects the stern.

As a motor boat the pinnace has a 20hp engine which gives a speed of 7 1/2 knots. She has a 90lb Admiralty pattern anchor and 40 fathoms of 3/8in chain cable. Her weight, empty of crew, is 5 1/2 tons and she has a life-saving capacity of 86.

The launch weighs 6 1/2 tons and has a life-saving capacity of 130. She also has 40 fathoms of the same size cable but with an anchor of 120lb.

The details of these two boats are important for models of all capital ships of the past sixty years and for those of the majority of large cruisers up to 1914. They are a prominent feature on the upper deck near the main derrick, or, in the 'King George V' class, near the cranes.

Waterline model of HMS *Iron Duke*, with
accompanying drifter, built to a scale of
1in–32ft with post First World War rig.
(Imperial War Museum – MOD127)

A 1in–32ft model of HMS *Revenge*,
depicted as Fleet Flagship Atlantic
Fleet 1924-7, made by Ough in 1927.
(Imperial War Museum – MOD123)

A 1in–16ft scale model 'County' class cruiser
HMS *London*, originally commissioned by the
Royal United Service Museum and acquired
by the Imperial War Museum in the 1960s.
(Imperial War Museum – MOD563)

A 1in–16ft model of the modified 'Arrogant' class cruiser HMS
Vindictive depicted as she appeared in April 1918 when used
in the Zeebrugge raid. (Imperial War
Museum – MOD352)

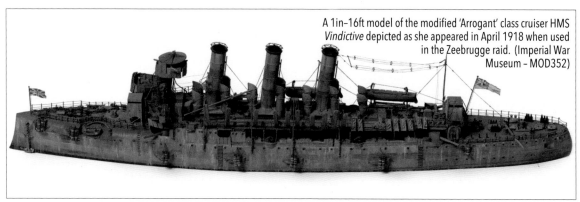

Waterline model of HMS *Illustrious* built to a scale of 1in–16ft. Commissioned by the Royal United Service Museum in 1949 and was featured in their special exhibition for the 'Festival of Britain' in 1951. The model is now part of the National Maritime Museum collection. (© National Maritime Museum, Greenwich, London – SLR1544)

This class of carrier was the first with fully armoured hangers to be built by any navy. After the end of the Second World War *Illustrious* acted as a trials carrier for pilots of various aircraft such as Seafires, Sea Furies and Supermarine Attackers – a jet fighter of the day. Ough's model originally depicted these 'modern' aircraft but then it was altered to show her at the end of the war with ten Swordfish aircraft on the flight deck.

Above: Waterline model of HMS *Hawkins* built by Ough to a scale of 1in–32ft in 1926 and displayed in what appears to be its original glass case with contemporary label. This model was sold privately at auction in May 2016. (Courtesy Charles Miller Ltd)

Below: Details of Ough's model aircraft carrier HMS *Glorious*. Built to a scale of 1in–16ft and now displayed in the 'Carrier Experience' area of the Fleet Air Arm Museum, Yeovilton. (Author's photo.)

Right: The midship section of Ough's 1in–16ft model battleship HMS *Queen Elizabeth*. A steam drifter and the destroyer HMS *Cygnet* can be seen in the background. (© National Maritime Museum, Greenwich, London – SLR1414)

Right: Ough's 1in–16ft model of HMS *Queen Elizabeth* with a steam drifter and picket boat in the foreground. (© National Maritime Museum, Greenwich, London – SLR1414)

Below: Waterline model of the destroyer HMS *Cygnet* built by Ough in 1933 to a scale of 1in–16ft. The 15in guns of 'X' and 'Y' turrets from the model *Queen Elizabeth* are depicted in the foreground and the steam drifter HMS *Crescent Moon* is shown to the left. (© National Maritime Museum, Greenwich, London – SLR1500)

This diorama of waterline ships, built by Ough to a scale of 1in–16ft, depicts the battleship HMS *Queen Elizabeth* and the 'C' class destroyer HMS *Cygnet* both secured fore and aft to buoys, which represent permanent moorings. It also shows two ancillary vessels, HMS *Crescent Moon* – an Admiralty drifter – and a small steam picket boat busying themselves around the larger ships. (© National Maritime Museum, Greenwich, London – SLR1414 and SLR1500)

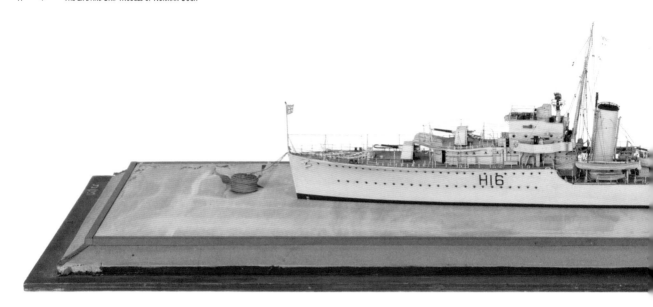

This model of the 'D' class destroyer HMS *Daring* is one of two larger scale models of this ship known to have been built by Ough. The first was a private commission for Lord Mountbatten to a scale of 1in–12ft whilst this version was built to a scale of 1in–16ft and is part of the National Maritime Museum collection. It depicts the ship when she was part of the First Destroyer Flotilla Mediterranean Fleet in 1934. (© National Maritime Museum, Greenwich, London - SLR1504)

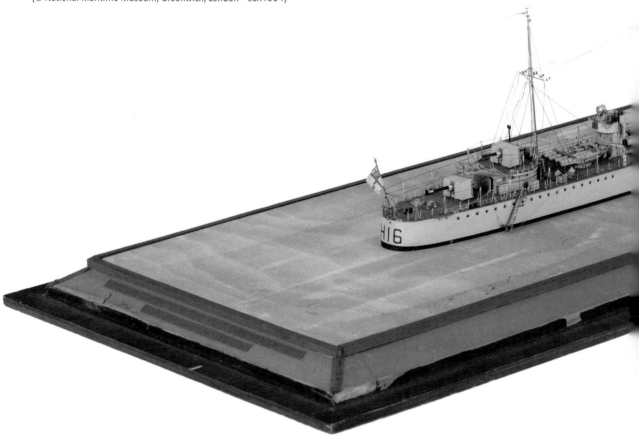

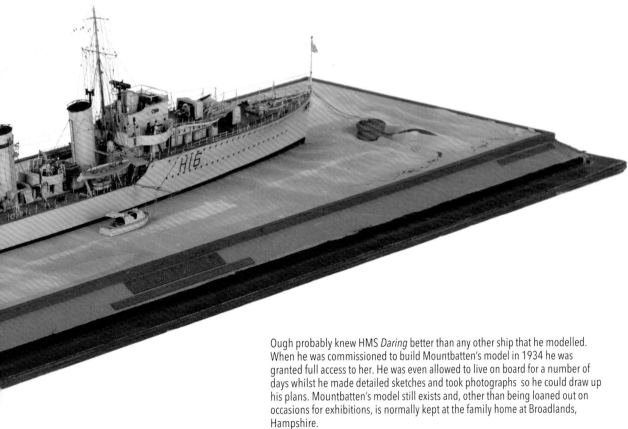

Ough probably knew HMS *Daring* better than any other ship that he modelled. When he was commissioned to build Mountbatten's model in 1934 he was granted full access to her. He was even allowed to live on board for a number of days whilst he made detailed sketches and took photographs so he could draw up his plans. Mountbatten's model still exists and, other than being loaned out on occasions for exhibitions, is normally kept at the family home at Broadlands, Hampshire.

This 1in–16ft waterline model of the destroyer HMS *Warwick* was originally built by Ough for the Royal United Services Museum and depicted her in her original configuration as a minelayer bearing the pennant number D25.

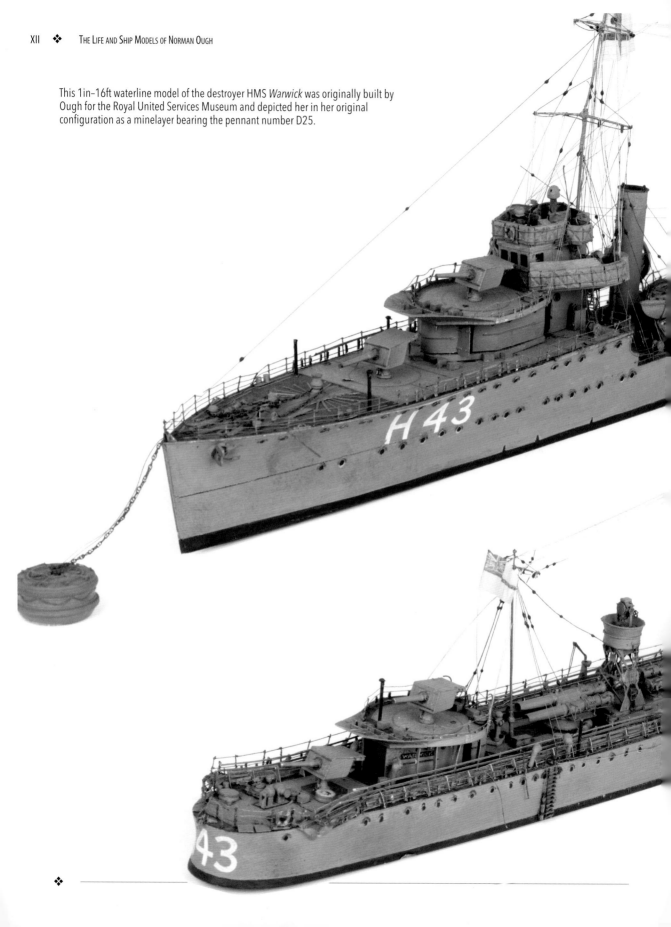

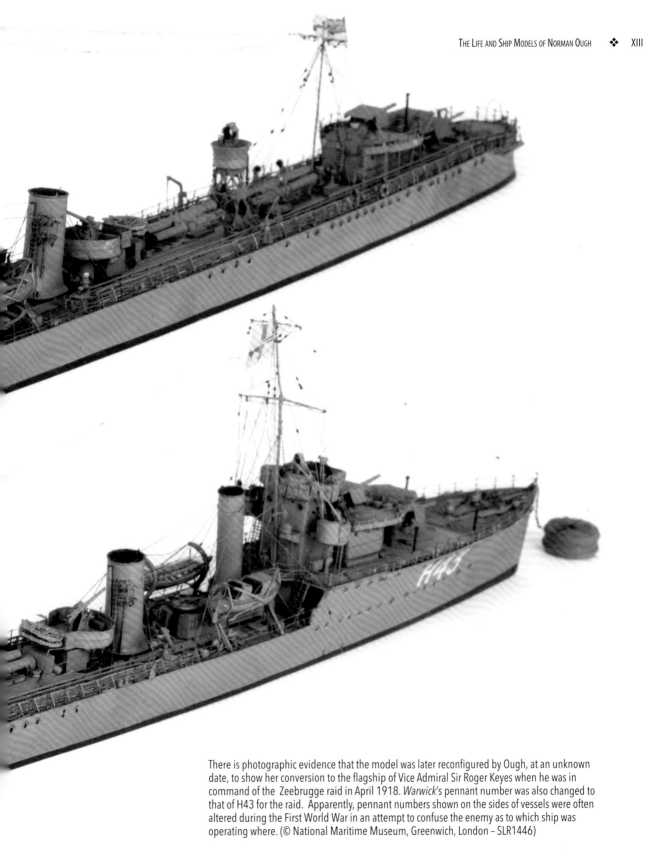

There is photographic evidence that the model was later reconfigured by Ough, at an unknown
date, to show her conversion to the flagship of Vice Admiral Sir Roger Keyes when he was in
command of the Zeebrugge raid in April 1918. *Warwick*'s pennant number was also changed to
that of H43 for the raid. Apparently, pennant numbers shown on the sides of vessels were often
altered during the First World War in an attempt to confuse the enemy as to which ship was
operating where. (© National Maritime Museum, Greenwich, London – SLR1446)

❖

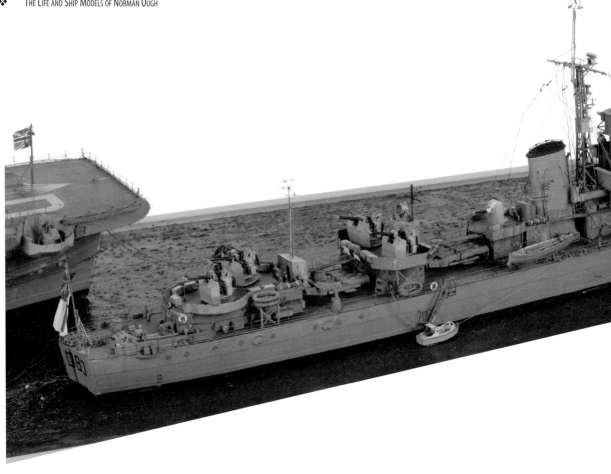

When commissioned by the Royal United Service Museum the model *Barfleur* was to depict a 'modern' destroyer of that era. This class of ship was built larger than previous destroyers, to give them the capabilities of a longer range, and were intended originally for operations in the Pacific.

This waterline model of the 'Battle' class destroyer HMS *Barfleur* was originally commissioned by the Royal United Service Museum. Built by Ough to a scale of 1in–16ft she was later displayed on a scenic base with his model aircraft carrier HMS *Illustrious* and acquired by the National Maritime Museum. (© National Maritime Museum – SLR1576)

Left: A 1in–16ft model of HMS *Dorsetshire* in No.14 Dry Dock, Portsmouth, commissioned by the Imperial War Museum. (Imperial War Museum – MOD269)

Above: Ough's model of HMS *Dorsetshire* showing her bow section and the inner part of the Dry Dock. (Imperial War Museum – MOD269)

Right: A 1in–8ft (1/96) scale model of a 32ft naval cutter. Built by Ough out of card, note paper and tissue paper and displayed in his own handmade case (now broken). (© National Maritime Museum, Greenwich, London – SLR1819)

5

❖ AIRCRAFT CARRIERS ❖

I t appears that Ough made at least three models of aircraft carriers throughout his life although none of his original drawings or plans for these ships appear to have survived.

HMS *Ark Royal* (1937)

This was to be one of Ough's largest models. During the Second World War Ough was engaged in special effects for film work. His model of the *Ark Royal* was built for the Ealing Studios picture *Ships with Wings* in 1941 and was made to a scale of 3/8in-1ft, giving an overall length of 25ft. The guns fired, aerial masts were functional, aircraft lifts worked and there was a smoke generator fitted in the funnel. Two 'crew' could be accommodated in the hull to make all the special effects work while she was operated in the 'infinity' pool at the studios. It is presumed that the studios dismantled or scrapped the model after filming was completed.

HMS *Glorious* (1916, converted 1930)

This model was commissioned for the Royal United Service Museum (RUSM) in 1931 and took over a year to build. Ough wrote an article about his work for the August 1932 edition of *Ships and Ship Models* magazine: it is reprinted below.

Built to a scale of 1in-16ft on a waterline configuration, *Glorious* was said to have been very complex to build and took Ough about three times longer than typical work on a model battleship. When the RUSM was disbanded in the 1960s it appears she was acquired by the Imperial War Museum (Catalogue No. MOD172) but is now displayed in the 'Carrier Experience' area of the Fleet Air Arm Museum, Yeovilton in Somerset.

It is interesting to note that Ough mentions RAF personnel and boats when referring to *Glorious* – it is sometimes forgotten that in these inter-war years the Fleet Air Arm was an organisational unit of the Royal Air Force and did not return to Admiralty control until 1939.

A depiction of the 1/32 scale (25ft) model built by Ough for the film *Ships with Wings*.

Model of HMS *Glorious* in Ough's workshop before being delivered to the Royal United Service Museum. (Courtesy the Ough family)

HMS *Illustrious* (1939)

Commissioned by the RUSM in 1949 as a continuation of the series of warship models that Ough had been building for them for a quarter of a century, *Illustrious* also featured in their special exhibition for the 1951 Festival of Britain. This waterline model was made to their uniform scale of 1in-16ft, and Ough wrote an article in the May 1951 edition of *The Model Engineer*, describing the ship and his model of her. *Illustrious* is now part of the National Maritime Museum collection (Ref. No. SLR1544) but is displayed differently than when originally built. At some stage Ough altered her to appear in a diorama alongside the destroyer

The flight deck of the model HMS *Illustrious* depicting 1949 'modern' aircraft. (MyTimeMedia)

HMS *Barfleur* (Ref. No. SLR1576), both displayed on a 'sea' baseboard with ancillary vessels. She is also now depicted as she was at the end of the Second World War with ten Swordfish aircraft on deck, but when first exhibited by the RUSM she displayed 1949 'modern' aircraft, such as Seafires, Sea Furies and even a Supermarine Attacker – a single-seater naval jet fighter of the day.

The article written by Ough on the *Glorious* is featured below.

HMS *Glorious* (1916, converted 1930)

When I was asked by the Secretary of the Royal United Service Institution in 1931 to make a model of the Navy's most recent aircraft-carrier, HMS *Glorious*, for their Museum, I realised that the task would be formidable.

Of all warships, an aircraft carrier is, from a model maker's point of view, the most complex. The great height and freeboard of the hangar means greater weight above the water-line, so that in order to preserve stability the structure must be as light as possible and large sections of the ship's side outboard of the hangar left unplated. The effect is to leave much of the interior visible, and modelling such a vessel, one is, in a sense, working in four dimensions - length, breadth, height and 'inside'. Previous experience with more normal ships, such as battleships and cruisers, was found to count for little, and it was only after about a month's work on drawing out the

necessary details of the ship deck by deck that I understood enough of the arrangements to be sure of success. I would like to pay tribute to the members of the Admiralty Staff in the aircraft carrier section for their great help in explaining things to me. Without their assistance I should have been lost in the maze of unfamiliar and uncomprehended detail.

The Hangars

The *Glorious* and her sister ship, the *Courageous*, were originally built, in 1916, as large light cruisers, and had an armament of four 15in guns. She was converted to an aircraft carrier in 1930. The *Glorious* has two hangars and two flight decks, one above the hangars which occupy about three quarters of the length and a shorter one on the level of the upper hangar deck over the forecastle. Aircraft can take off from either, but can land only on the upper flight deck. The hangars occupy most of the internal space on and above what was the forecastle deck of the original ship, and consequently all the ventilation trunks from below, the boats and boat-hoisting gear and guns are crowded to the ship's side clear of them. The hangars run fore and aft, one above the other, the upper being about 80ft longer than the lower, and approximately 56ft wide, the lower being about 49ft in width through most of its length. Two lifts, large enough to take an aeroplane, with wings spread, carry aircraft from both hangars to the flight deck. The funnel uptakes are trunked round underneath the lower hangar and up the starboard side to the funnel round which are situated the navigating and signal bridges, chart and plotting rooms, RAF control

Model of HMS *Glorious* in Ough's workshop. (Courtesy the Ough family)

❖

Model of HMS *Glorious* under construction in Ough's workshop. (Courtesy the Ough family)

position, and the sea cabins of the captain and navigating officer.

The Flight Deck

The flight deck proper is about 60ft above the water line: it is 100ft wide and about 600ft long overall, although not the whole of this length is available as landing space. It is ramped up over part of its length to 4ft higher forward than aft. It has to be very strong yet very light, and its construction is one of the many marvels in this wonderful ship. Along each side are nets to accommodate the crews engaged in landing aircraft, while palisades are rigged over part of the length to prevent an aeroplane from pitching overboard in case of a bad landing.

Both upper and lower flight decks carry windscreens to protect aircraft while they are stationary. These are cleared away for flying by lowering them flush with the deck. On the lower flight deck are two large derricks for embarking seaplanes, which stow against the ship's side when not in use.

Immediately below the flight deck is the upper gallery deck, about halfway down the upper hangar. This, on the port side, is open for much of its length and the internal arrangements of the ship at this level can be seen, among them being the large air trunks that

ventilate the boiler rooms and the second wireless office. The marines' mess deck is also situated on it, and recreation and lecture rooms. The deck is extended outboard on the starboard side as a walking platform, to allow a passage fore and aft round the funnel uptakes – a unique feature in a warship.

The Upper Hangar Deck

The upper hangar deck, below the upper gallery deck, is continuous with the flight deck over the forecastle, on to which it gives through great doors, wide enough to pass aircraft with wings spread. These doors, when closed, form an angle projecting forward which helps to lessen the wind resistance made by the ship when under way. Aircraft, when in the hangar, are parked along both sides with their wings folded back, and the hangar itself is divided at intervals transversely by fireproof curtains. On this level, externally, are two 35ft RAF motor boats with their hoisting gear, on shelves on the ship's quarters opposite the after lift, where they are in a convenient position for lowering into the water in an emergency. Below the upper hangar deck is the lower gallery deck, which carries the boats and winches for running them out and lowering them over the side. Each boat has three winches, one for hoisting, and two for traversing outboard along beams (instead of davits)

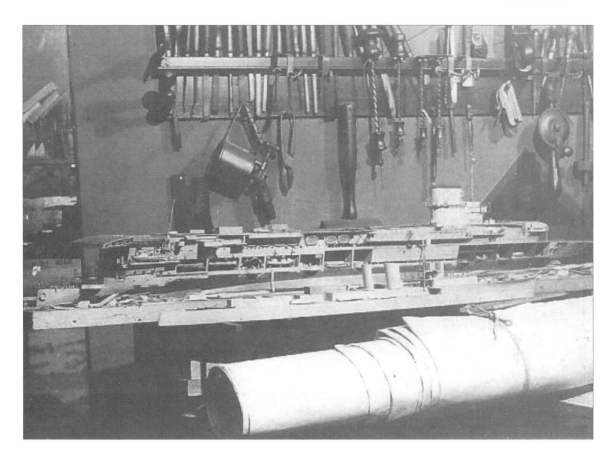

under the upper hangar deck, which latter support the lifting tackle. There are 16 boats, the largest being the two 35ft motor pinnaces, and the smallest the 16ft skiff dinghys. The lower gallery deck is not continuous, except through the RAF mess spaces which are part of it, but consists mainly of small winch platforms and frames for the boat chocks. Below it is the deck of the original ship, now called the lower hangar deck, and this, for modelling, is the most complex of all. Forward it carries the anchors and cables, capstans, paravane gear and winches, while along both sides are scores of hatches leading below, ventilation trunks leading from the flats and cabins on the upper and main decks through it and up the hangar bulkheads, gun sponsons and 4.7in AA guns and mountings, ammunition lockers and hoists, funnel uptakes and boiler room vents, and the transverse bulkheads, most of them covered with ladders and ventilation pipes, which divide the guns and boats from each other. Being a 'weather deck' it is planked from end to end, and extends from the extreme bow to about 30ft from the stern, where it ends in a projection giving on to a ladder-way leading to the upper deck. The latter is a small part of the original quarter deck, and is still so used.

At the present moment the aircraft carried in the *Glorious* consist of flights of torpedo bombers, fighters and reconnaissance machines. The torpedo bombers are of the Blackburn 'Ripon' type and carry an 18in torpedo. The fighters are, at present, of the single-seater 'Flycatcher' type, while the reconnaissance machines are Fairey III F, 570hp three-seaters.

In spite of unusual features, the design of the ship is, from the point of view of appearance, exceedingly impressive. The vast bulk is so well proportioned that it does not overshadow the lines of power and speed, which are greatly enhanced by the superb 'flare' of the bows, and the towering mass of superstructure and funnel.

Building the Model
The model was built to templates taken off the drawing of the transverse sections, the hull being carved first from the joined planks of American whitewood, and the superimposed hangars and flight decks added afterwards in convenient sections. The flight deck itself

Unfinished models of HMS *Glorious* and HMS *Curacoa* in Ough's workshop. (Courtesy the Ough family)

Ough's notes on reverse of his photograph of HMS *Glorious*. The stick-on note referring to the use of his sister's hair to make aerials has been added later by a member of the family - J.G.O is Ough's sister Joan. (Courtesy the Ough family)

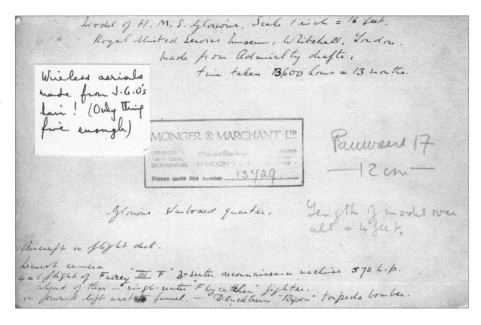

is made of veneer laid over beams in the upper hangar. This deck, with its nets and palisades and windscreens, was one of the most complicated parts to make, the overhanging portion at the after end alone requiring over 400 pieces in its construction. The after lift is shown part way down, which renders some of the hoisting gear visible, and also the structural detail underneath the lift itself, and the well into which it houses on reaching the lower hangar deck.

The main armament of 4.7in AA guns in this model proved a formidable item, as there are 16 of them. The Mark XII guns carried in the *Glorious* and *Courageous* are very complicated weapons, since nearly all the elevating, training and director gear is exposed to view. In order to work out an effective convention to show the principal features, I made a detailed model to the scale of 1/8in to 1ft from a 3/4in scale drawing, and afterwards repeated it on the scale of the model of the ship (1/16in-1ft), leaving out such detail as would disappear on approaching the limit of visibility of ordinary eyesight.

The model was made to be uniform with the rest of the series in the Royal United Service Museum, of which it now forms part, and which includes a battleship, the *Queen Elizabeth*, a 10,000 ton cruiser, the *London*; a destroyer, a minesweeper, and one of the 'O' class submarines. Like all the others, the ship is represented at anchor, with lower booms out, accommodation ladders down, and the attached drifter alongside to give an idea of her huge proportions.

The time taken in building was about 3,600 hours (approximately 13 months), or nearly three times as long as the battleship in the same series. There is more work in one side of an aircraft carrier of this size than in a whole battleship model, and the work is much more troublesome owing to the inaccessibility of many parts of the structure. But, although modelling such a vessel is both difficult and tedious in places, it is also of enthralling interest, and one has always the satisfaction of knowing that every stroke of work done will produce a visible result, and that it will record for the student of the future the details of one of the most important ships of the present day.

6

❖ GENERAL DETAILS ❖

These articles are, like those in the 'Ordnance' chapter, taken from Ough's 'Warship Detail' series of articles that were published in *Model Maker* magazine. It shows Ough's great eye for detail and also his consummate knowledge of the minutiae of Royal Naval warships. It is understood that he visited ships whenever possible, armed with camera and notebooks, taking photographs and measuring details at every opportunity. It is a pity that the original descriptive archives have apparently been lost over the years although, fortunately, these articles, which are based on the original documents, are still available to the researcher.

Anchors and Cables

Anchors and cables are rather a large subject to cover in one article so this is an outline.

There are three ways of securing a ship in harbour or in an open roadstead or alongside a wharf, when her engines are stopped or her sails are furled. They are either (1) by anchoring, or (2) by mooring or (3) by berthing. These three terms have distinct meanings in the Navy and are not really interchangeable although they are often used in writings about the sea as if they were. Some knowledge of what is involved can be of value to makers of ship models as this great hobby is increasing in scope year by year, especially among those interested in miniatures, who often attempt scenic subjects to scales of 50ft or 100ft to the inch, a size that allows more than one ship or even part of a fleet to be represented, or one ship with others alongside or secured to a wharf.

Anchoring, in its simplest form, consists in bringing a ship to a required position and 'letting go' one anchor. The cable is then 'veered', or run out, until four or five times more chain is in the water than its depth at that point. As the ship takes up her position under the influence of wind and tide, or both, she will draw the chain along the bottom until it makes a straight line to the anchor. As the anchor is moved along with the ship its blades tilt and dig into the mud or sand and hold. The anchor alone does not hold the ship but its grip on the sea bed combined with the weight and friction of the many fathoms of chain laid out along the bottom do the work. In the days of rope cables this friction was not available as they were of little weight in the water, and sailing ships as a consequence required, relatively, much larger anchors. If some of the cable is 'shortened in' the hold

of both anchor and cable is lessened; when still more cable is brought in the ship is said to be 'hove short' and there is very little hold; a few more links and the cable is said to be 'up and down'. Immediately after this the anchor is 'broken out' and 'weighed' into the hawse pipe. In the Navy, all the time the cable is being brought in it is sprayed with salt water under considerable pressure from a hose pointed down the hawse pipe, to remove the mud, before it goes down the deck pipe into the cable locker. It is also scrubbed and hosed as it moves along the deck.

Since the anchors of even the smallest warships weigh about half-a-ton and those of a capital ship as much as nine tons, the expression 'cast anchor', so often used, is hardly descriptive. Apart from those of small boats, a ship's anchor is not a thing that can be picked up and 'cast' over the side! The correct expression is to 'let go an anchor' or simply 'to anchor'. In a battleship, when the order to 'let go' is given from the bridge, the shipwright, who is a member of the 'cable party' on the forecastle, knocks open the jaws of the Blake slip and the cable runs out with a roar through the hawse pipe, echoed by the same sound from the other ships of the squadron. When one has heard this one can no longer think in terms of 'cast anchor'!

A warship is usually a unit in a squadron or a flotilla, and frequently a whole fleet is required to take up positions in harbour according to a pre-arranged plan laid down by the Master of the Fleet, a senior navigating officer in the flagship. For many reasons the ships will be disposed as near together as is consistent with safety, so their movements under the influence of wind and tide need to be controlled more closely than would be possible if each were to ride to

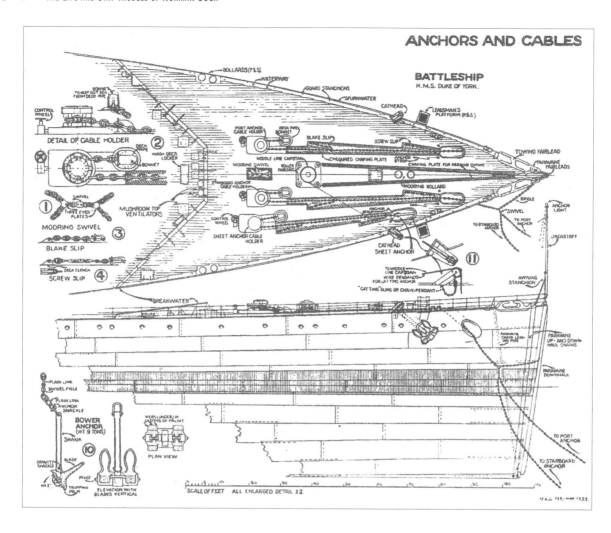

Anchors and cables.
(MyTimeMedia)

a single anchor. For this reason two anchors are let go at some distance apart, their cables being brought together and attached to a 'mooring swivel' so as to confine the ship's movement mainly to this point, and to the circle she can make between the two anchors when the tide sets the opposite way. In the drawing of the cable arrangements of a battleship, the position of the mooring swivel, the junction of the two cables, is shown; it is inserted at this point to prevent the cables from twisting together as the ship swings round, since, if this were to happen it would require a long and difficult process of manoeuvring to take out the turns. The bight of cable from the port anchor can be seen in the drawing coming round the bows to the swivel, and in this relation it is known as the 'bridle'. From the point of view of a maker of a waterline model it is a very characteristic feature of an anchored warship and it should be shown. The whole operation

is known as 'mooring'. An alternative use of the term 'mooring' is when a warship is secured to one of the buoys in a long line of permanent moorings allotted to the squadron or flotilla to which she belongs. The details of the swivel and its connection to the 'three eyed plates' above and below are shown in (1). It is always hauled into a position above the water where it can be seen from the deck.

In the drawings the anchor and cable arrangements are shown for three typical warships – a battleship, a cruiser and a destroyer. In a battleship three anchors are carried, the third, for an emergency, being known as the 'sheet' anchor. This term comes from the days of sail when the spare bower anchor was stowed at the foot of the rigging of the foremast at the point where the 'sheet' or holding rope of the lowest sail on that mast, the foresail or fore 'course', was led inboard, so that in time, the spare became known as 'the sheet anchor', the term surviving, like so many terms of the sea, into modern times. The cable holder for the sheet anchor is different from the others as it is fitted only for 'veering', or running out cable and, if the cable is let go, it has to be weighed by the middle line capstan. The cable holders are shown in detail in (2) for a capital ship and in (6) for destroyers, those for a cruiser being the same as for a battleship but smaller. The middle line capstan is shown, both as a warping drum and as a cable holder in (5). Typical anchors for the three types of ship are shown in (8), (9) and (10).

A cable holder works rather like the sprocket wheel of a bicycle chain except that it grips a different kind of chain and from the outside. It is similar to a very large gear wheel of very few teeth, each upright link of the chain lying in the space between the teeth and each horizontal link lying in a deep slot cast in the teeth as shown in (2) and (5), the teeth in a cable holder being known as 'snugs'. The holder is driven by a vertical spindle operated by the capstan engine on the deck below the forecastle. It can be disengaged from the spindle by a dog clutch, which is operated by the control wheel on top, to allow the cable to run out free. The handwheels near the cable holders are for working friction brakes to control the amount of cable to be run out and also its speed.

When the anchors are 'weighed' the cables lie fore and aft along the deck on steel 'chafing' plates which protect the planking or the steel deck plating. The screw slips (4) are hooked on to the chain and tightened so as to bring the anchors firmly home into the hawse pipes, where they are secured by strops of flexible steel wire rope rove through the shackles. The 'Blake slip' (3) is put on when an anchor is prepared for letting go. Its function is to hold the cable, when the screw slip and strops have been taken off and everything cleared away, until the order 'let go' is given, when the blacksmith or the shipwright knocks open the jaws of the hook and the cable 'runs'. The ship rides on the Blake slip and on the brake of the cable holder, or, in destroyers, on the Blake slip and the compressor (7) which is incorporated in the cover, or 'bonnet', over the deck pipe leading to the cable locker.

Situated on each bow in battleships and cruisers are the 'catheads' (11) pointing towards the middle line capstan. These are for 'catting' or slinging an anchor should it be necessary to unshackle the cable and use it for making fast to a buoy. In this case a wire hawser is shackled to the anchor and taken over the sheave in the cathead and to the capstan, the anchor being hove in and slung from the chain pendant or 'catting sling'.

Up in the bows of the ship are the towing fairleads which are also used for the berthing wires, and the paravane fairleads through which the small chains run down to the lowest point of the stem and up on the other side. Shackles on these take the ends of the towing wires of the paravanes down to the 'point of tow' which is kept as low as possible. The paravanes resemble kites with a torpedo-shaped body and vanes at the fore end which cause them to stream away from the ship underwater, thus making a 'V' of wire which cuts across the mooring wires of mines, pushing them away and eventually cutting them. On the drawing of the battleship an alternative single wire towing chain is shown.

This leads through the 'bullring' fairlead at the head of the stem down to the forefoot and back into a pipe which leads it back to the deck. On either side of the bows, just before the catheads, are the leadsman's platforms used for taking soundings. In a cruiser these are further aft. In the cruiser and destroyer the forecastle deck is of bare steel which can be very slippery. For this reason it is crossed by a pattern of 'footstrips' which are flat steel bars about 1/4in thick and about 1 1/2in wide welded or riveted to the plates. The breakwater which bounds the forecastle aft is to check some of the water coming over the bows in heavy weather.

The method of 'berthing' a ship is shown in (12). In the Navy 'catamarans' are used to fend her off the wharf. These are heavy wooden pontoons surrounded by thick rope fenders. The bow and stern are made fast by the head and stern ropes, the ship is kept close in by the 'breast ropes', and prevented from 'surging' fore and aft by the 'springs'. For big ships, especially aircraft carriers, these ropes, which are heavy flexible steel wire hawsers and belong to the ship, are often doubled, or even trebled. They have an eye spliced in the ends to go over the single bollards on the wharf.

The anchors and cables – 'the ground tackle' – of a large warship are of a great size and weight, and of immense length. A battleship of the size and displacement of HMS *Duke of York*, the forecastle of which is shown on the drawing, would carry about 35 shackles of cable totalling about 500 fathoms or 3,000 feet, a shackle being a length of 15 fathoms. If an anchor could tell of what happens down there at the end of ten shackles of cable perhaps it could say that

Funnels. (MyTimeMedia)

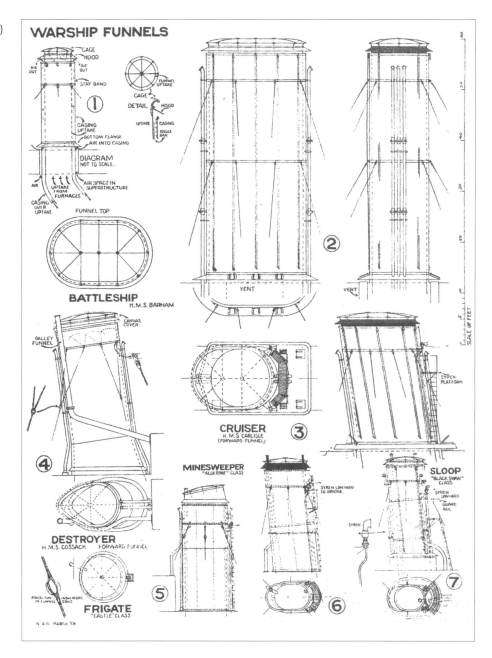

it had, on occasion, put a massive steel claw into one of the lost cities of Atlantis.

Funnels

The funnels of warships are rather different in appearance from those of merchant ships as the former are often 'paid off into dockyard control' for long periods of re-fitting, or into the Reserve Fleet. For this reason the hood and cage are fitted to the top of the funnel in HM Ships to prevent rain getting down into the interior when the furnaces are out and there is no updraught to check it. The function of the cage is to spread a painted canvas cover over the uptake. It is made convex so that the canvas will not sag downwards and allow rain to collect in the trough of its folds. It is shown dotted in the drawing of the forward funnel of a destroyer in (4). It is sometimes laced on as shown, sometimes it is pulled tight and lashed under the flange, and is a characteristic feature of a ship under refit. The hood and the cage are essential parts of the character of the funnels of all British warships from about 1890 till now, the few exceptions being that in the earliest destroyers and torpedo craft the cage consisted of only two curved frames at right angles to spread the canvas cover, no hood being fitted, and it does not appear on the funnels of some very recent ships, such as the latest frigates, and on HMS *Vanguard*. Details of its construction are shown in (1). The angle of the bevel of the hood varies from class to class.

A funnel consists of an uptake through which flow the hot gases from the furnaces and a casing concentric to and separated by a few inches from the uptake to keep rain and spray out of the air space. Air flows upwards through this space being admitted through holes in the casing under the bottom flange and discharged under the hood, or upper flange, which is riveted to the top of the uptake to keep rain and spray out of the air space. The gases from the boiler room render the uptake too hot for it to be painted, and it would rust away if it were not protected by the comparatively cool outer casing.

The Navy has sometimes been called 'The Grey Funnel Line' but the funnels are not entirely grey as the hood and cage are invariably painted black. Destroyers have, on the after funnel, black bands with narrow white borders to denote the flotilla to which they belong, and frigates and minesweepers usually have numbers, sometimes in red with a white border, painted on the sides of the funnel. A flotilla leader of destroyers has a 4ft deep black band at the top of the forward funnel. In the days of the dark grey Home Fleet colour the markings were white, and earlier, in cruisers, occasionally red. In these ships the bands were used for identification at a distance when a number of the same class formed a squadron, each ship bearing a different combination of them.

The shape of the bottom flange varies greatly as it is sometimes spread wide enough to cover the vent trunks which bring air from the boiler room up through the superstructure, in which case hinged plates are fitted on the flange to give access to the vents from above as shown in (2) and (3). In some ships such as the 'Algerine' class ocean minesweepers, and in the 'Castle' class frigates, there is no bottom flange, the outer casing being carried down through the deck below and into the boiler room.

In the drawing examples are shown, to the same scale, of the funnels of a battleship, a cruiser, a destroyer, a minesweeper, a frigate and a sloop. These are fairly representative although they do not cover all types, as some that have appeared in recent years are unique and have not previously been built in HM Ships, such as those of the 'Weapon' and 'Daring' class destroyers, the forward funnels of which are more like exhaust pipes of large diameter curved at the top and built inside the lattice mast. The principle of ventilation of the casing remains much the same however.

In all destroyers the ship's galley is just in front of the forward funnel and its chimney is led sometimes into the uptake, and sometimes, as in the 'Tribal' class destroyer shown in (4), round the outside of the casing and up to above the cage. Often more than one chimney is led into the uptake and out above the top as in the funnel of the 'Algerine' class minesweeper shown in (6). Escape pipes from the safety valves of the boilers are nearly always a prominent feature as shown in six of these examples, although in the later cruisers only the tops of them are visible, the pipes being led up inside the after end of the streamlined casing, as in the 'Dido' and 'Southampton' classes. When they are led up outside, the upper ends of the pipes above the clamp that holds them to the funnel casing are unpainted, and the metal, which is invariably copper, is given a high polish for the sake of appearance in peace time. In war all such 'bright work' is painted over. Other external pipes lead steam to the sirens of which there are two. These are of brass and are also highly polished. Access to them is gained from the siren platform which is shown in most of these examples except in the case of the battleship, as, at the period when ships of this class had two funnels, one of which is shown, the sirens were fitted high up on the legs of the tripod foremast. The funnel of the cruiser of the 'Cardiff' class (3) seems to be rather short compared with the others which is partly owing to the fact that it rises from the superstructure, whereas in destroyers it rises from the deck.

Funnels are built of thin plating in two or three sections divided horizontally, the plates overlapping at the seams in some, while in others it is connected by an internal butt strap. They are stiffened vertically by small angle bars, the riveting of which shows on the surface, as indicated in (5), (6) and (7). Where the funnel stays are connected a reinforcing band is riveted on for strength, the stays being sometimes furnished with porcelain insulators as in (5). The funnels of cruisers of the 'Dido' and 'Colony' and 'City'

classes are constructed so as not to require stays. In addition to the stay band, where fitted, is an upper band at the top of the casing to take the eyebolts for the small blocks through which are led the chains for hauling up stages for repainting the funnel, which is required more often than in most other parts of the ship owing to changes of temperature affecting the paint. In the older ships all the chains were rove and secured to cleats above the bottom flange as in (2) and (3), a very characteristic feature in all classes except destroyers from 1895 to 1939. A very beautiful model of a funnel can be made from thin tinplate over a wood former by soldering, the detail being added in thick and thin wire, great exactness and high finish being attainable in this medium.

Cowls and Ventilators

The ventilating arrangements of a warship are a prominent feature, more so than in a merchant ship as the watertight subdivision of the former has to be more extensive and elaborate, for strict rules are laid down that the transverse bulkheads are not to be cut through by ventilation trunks, a precaution that is necessary against damage by gunfire or torpedoes. The consequence of this is that the openings of supply and exhaust ducts are all carried up to the weather decks or superstructure in groups between the main transverse bulkheads. In a merchant ship they would be more widely distributed and there would usually be fewer of them.

In earlier ships of the Royal Navy the engine and boiler rooms and the flats and mess decks were ventilated by large cowls with or without steam driven fans connected to them. They were a very striking feature in the region of the ship near the funnels and, in most cases, they were of immense size. A characteristic example is shown in (1), the dotted lines indicating that the trunk was often angled to place the opening clear of the funnels. The cowl could be rotated by a rod with a long handle which moved a spur gear engaging with a toothed rack surrounding the base of the movable part of the ventilator, or sometimes by an endless rope passing over a pulley which turned the spur wheel. In coal fired ships the bunkers were ventilated by air trunks leading into the superstructure, the gases generated by the stored coal being vented through louvres which could be closed against the weather by sliding shutters as in (3).

In the majority of ships built just before, during and after the 1914–18 war, the cowls were replaced by the now familiar 'WEMTV' or 'water excluding mushroom-top ventilator' which, in one form or another – and in varying sizes – has become the typical ventilator in HM ships, and also by the rectangular ventilating trunk – examples of which are shown in (4) and (5). The tall ones are usually carried up outside the barbettes of 'B' and 'X' turrets in capital ships with the opening facing inwards, the large short ones, as in (6), being fitted in cruisers as intakes for the 30in engine room supply fans. The exhaust fans, which are at the after end of the machinery spaces are larger, 35in, as they have to discharge a greater volume of air owing to its expansion by the heat of the turbines and steam pipes. The tall 'swan neck' vent pipes (7) are usually exhausts from oil fuel compartments, the shorter ones being often placed along the ship's side near the guard rails.

The ventilation of the boiler rooms of modern warships depends on the 'forced draught' system in which the funnels are the only exhaust. Air is drawn down by powerful turbine driven fans, passed over heaters in the boiler casing and into the furnaces whence it passes up the funnels. The air in the boiler rooms is maintained at a higher pressure than the atmosphere so that, if a furnace door is opened, air will rush inwards and prevent a 'blow back' of flame. To maintain the pressure it is necessary that the hatchways leading in should be provided with an air lock so that anyone entering or leaving opens a door into a small compartment which, on being closed, opens another leading below. The intakes for the boiler room fans in capital ships and cruisers are very large, examples of them being shown in (15) and (16), those for a destroyer's forward boiler room being shown in (19). These are in the forward superstructure just under the signal deck. The openings are covered with a square wire mesh and those represented in (15) and (16) are closed when not in use by roller shutters similar to the shutters of a garage.

In cruisers of the 'Caroline' and 'Cardiff' classes and in many others of that period, the fan intakes were mounted on top of the superstructure between the funnels. They were protected by the usual wire mesh and closed by means of hinged flaps worked by levers from a platform in the downtake trunks inside the superstructure, the platform being reached by small doors leading from the weather decks on both sides. Carley rafts were often stowed on top of them. They are shown in plan and elevation in (13) and (14).

In a warship in commission the incessant hum of

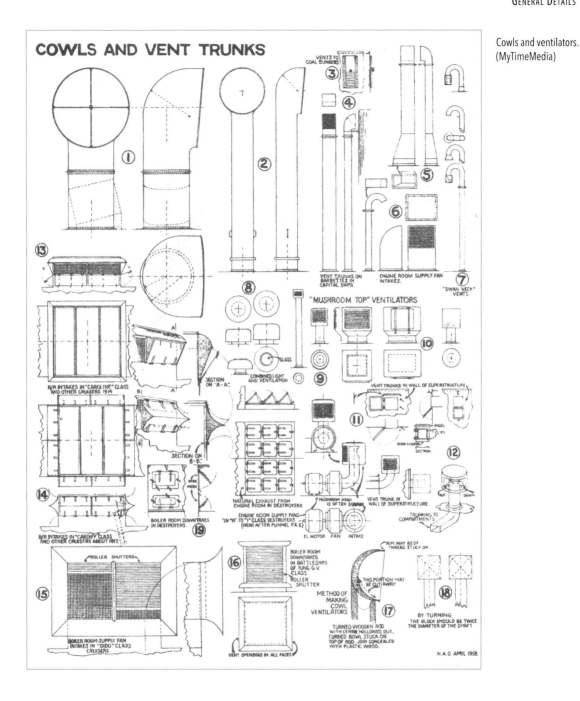

Cowls and ventilators.
(MyTimeMedia)

the fans is a background noise accompanying all life at sea. It is a pleasant, live, busy sound significant of power and activity, and the unnatural quiet in a ship as experienced by visitors to the dockyards on Navy Days is quite unlike her usual condition. As the Navy's ships have to navigate in all the Seven Seas it will be appreciated how large a part the fans play in their habitability in conditions of extreme heat and cold. A man at rest is considered to require from 1,500 to 2,000 cubic feet of air each hour and a capital ship may have a war complement of 1,500 men; in summer in, say, the Mediterranean or the Red Sea, such a vessel will require a lot of air to be sent down below and kept moving especially into the machinery spaces for life to be endurable, and the design of the ventilation system is a heavy responsibility for constructors. This is particularly so in the case of magazines and shell rooms under tropical conditions as cordite becomes chemically unstable when temperature rises above a certain point and special cooling arrangements have to be introduced in the fan trunks leading to these compartments.

Examples of mushroom top ventilators are shown (8), (9) and (10) and the principle by which they take in or discharge air, and exclude water, is sketched in (13). The trunking, which is rectangular in section below the decks, is formed into a circular section to pass through and carried far up inside the mushroom head; it is open at the top and on the side opposite to the opening in the head, which is covered in wire mesh. Air passes through this opening, round to the back and over the top of the trunking and down, or up if it is functioning as an exhaust. Drain holes are cut all round the bottom of the head to allow water from the weather deck or from condensation to flow out. The meshed opening faces away from the region of the ship where the sea is most likely to come inboard. Mushroom vents are made in many sizes and shapes from about five feet in diameter to about one foot or less, and they can be either round or square, short or tall, straight or with bends in the shaft, and the opening can be covered either with wire mesh or by a slatted louvre as is shown in (10) which is an example taken from HMS *Duke of York*. These illustrations are not drawn to a consistent scale as the size of the actual fittings varies so much, but they are of true proportions in themselves.

There are several ways of making a model of a cowl ventilator, two of which are shown in (17) and (18). In the first a bowl is turned from wood on a lathe and stuck on top of a circular rod which has previously been drilled part way down or right through. The connection can be made with 'Durofix', which is waterproof, and when set, the joint can be smoothed over with plastic wood. In the second method the whole thing is turned from a square bar and the cowl is carved from the square part left on the end. It is advisable to do the hollowing out before shaping the outside as this lessens the chance of breaking the thin part of the carving. Another method is to make them of paper. A solid wood model is made first to act as a 'former' and is made slightly greasy with vaseline. Pieces of wet tissue paper are laid on the former and strapped on with 'gumstrip' which is simply brown paper obtainable in rolls at any stationers. The thinnest variety is best for this work. It is sold in 1in

and 1 1/2in widths or larger, and is extremely useful for all kinds of model making. When the whole former is covered with gumstrip a second and third layer may be added, allowed to dry and rubbed smooth with fine sandpaper, thus forming a shell which can be removed by slitting it lengthwise with a razor blade. Once off the former the slit can be repaired with gumstrip. The object of the wet tissue and the grease is to prevent the gummed paper from sticking to the former. When the shell is completed the part covering the opening of the cowl can be trimmed away and the rim added with thread stuck on. The whole should be painted inside and out with model aircraft 'clear dope' which hardens everything and makes it waterproof. The ship's boats can be made in this way and even an efficient working model hull.

Decks and Deck Coverings

Continuing this series of articles on warship detail it is thought that a description of decks should be put in as so much of the character of a model depends on their correct representation, the surfaces being more varied and interesting than is generally supposed, presenting many opportunities for introducing realism into the work. Moreover they are among the first things needing to be completed during the construction of a model.

The decks of ships are always 'strength members' of the hull, as they form the upper and intermediate parts of the built-up girder which it essentially is from an engineering point of view, the outer and inner bottom plating being the lower members. For this reason they are designed to stand great stresses of tension and compression due to the pitching of the ship and of twisting due to rolling, and, in consequence, the strakes of plating of which they are constructed are always worked with the seams in the fore and aft direction as shown in (1) which is a plan of the upper deck and forecastle plating of a destroyer of 1936–45. It is in these vessels that the shipbuilders' art reaches its greatest height. Destroyers are the 'maids of all work' of the fleet. In wartime there are never enough of them; their manifold duties impose conditions of fantastic strain on ship and personnel, and their great power and speed, used in all conditions of weather, require the most accomplished shipbuilding to meet the stresses involved.

The upper deck and forecastle are known as the 'weather decks' and they are invariably 'cambered' to give a rounded surface in the direction at right angles to the centre line. The camber is a segment of a circle of large radius and it usually has a rise of 1/50th of the extreme breadth, so that, in a ship having a beam of 50ft, the centre of the deck would be 1ft higher than the edges. In a working model it is as well to exaggerate this feature slightly by making it 1/25th or 1/30th of the breadth as it assists draining and it gives slightly more emphasis to the form of the hull. In a small model it is difficult for the eye to appreciate so slight a rise as 1/50th. As well as being cambered, the decks of the majority of ships are given a 'sheer', or slowly rising curve from amidships to the stern and a rather steeper curve upwards to the bows. This is a line of the greatest elegance and its gradual upward movement produces, in many cruisers and destroyers, a striking effect of power and speed.

In detail of construction the steel decks show a good deal of variety. In destroyers the wide plate at the deck edges, called the 'stringer' plate, is usually 'flush butted', that is, the ends of each length of plate are brought together and joined underneath by a 'butt strap' or wide strip of steel treble-riveted to each plate end, thus giving a flush surface as shown in (5). The decks are then laid with a centre line strake with three others clinker fashion across to lap on the edges of the stringer plates as shown in section (with the thickness increased for clarity) in (2). This arrangement is not invariably followed, however, as sometimes the strakes are laid in and out like the shell plating of the hull. The ends of the plates are usually 'joggled', that is they are bent up and then down at the after end to form a shallow flange which is then riveted to the next plate and so on as shown in (3). In some of the recent destroyer conversions, where the new structure is built of duralumin, the edges of the plates are joggled along the seam away from the middle line as well. In ships having planked decks the ends and edges of the plates are joggled downwards as in (4) to give a flush surface for laying the wood. In this case, since the projections at the edges lie on the beams the latter have to be joggled to clear them, or alternatively, a 'liner' is fitted to fill up the space between the surface of the beam and the underside of the plate. In all cases the ends of the plates are arranged to come in the spaces between the beams.

Where the weather decks are of bare steel they are covered with footstrips laid in a fore and aft direction along the waist, and in a herring bone pattern or straight across on the forecastle and part of the quarter deck, and they are sometimes placed radially

to the cable holders as in (6). They are short lengths of flat steel about 14in wide and of varying lengths riveted to the deck plating to improve foothold and prevent slipping. They are a very prominent feature and, in a working model, they can be made by hammering softened wire to a flat section and soldering it to the plates.

All round the edges of the decks, usually inside the guard rails in destroyers, is bolted a continuous teak rail about 4in high by 2 1/2in thick, called the 'spurnwater'; its use is to prevent wash deck water from going over the side and streaking the paint, and also to prevent small objects, such as nuts and bolts, from going over as well. It is often of bare wood and scrubbed clean, but is sometimes painted buff colour. When it is inside the guard rails the space outside is usually painted the same colour as the hull.

Large areas of the decks, when they are not planked, are covered in 'Semtex' which is a composition trowelled onto the plates and confined at the edges by small beadings of steel welded on. When dry it presents a matt surface, not very slippery and of almost the same appearance as dry asphalt. It is usually given a coat of paint, either dark green or dark blue, which looks rather handsome, and often, round the base of the whole superstructure where it joins the deck, a wide band is painted about 9in high, of a different colour, dark grey or dark blue, called the 'kicking strip', as shown in (16). If the 'Semtex' is green this is usually blue, if blue it is usually grey. In the *Warspite* in one commission it was dark red which looked very fine in contrast to the planking. It appears that the colour arrangements depend on the decision of the ship's officers. The steel decks are sometimes painted black, or dark grey, and often the forecastle, in front of the breakwater, is treated with red lead paint. In destroyers prior to the 'Tribal' class 'Corticene' was used instead of 'Semtex'. This is a thick plain brown linoleum the same colour as milk chocolate laid down in squares as shown in the half plan of the decks of a destroyer of this period in (6). It was confined at the joins and along the edges by brass strips screwed to the decks as shown in the detail of (6), and it looked very fine when the brass edges were polished. In the most recent destroyers and frigates the footstrips have been replaced by a new non-slip device which consists of rectangular pieces, about 12in x 6in, of material like very coarse emery cloth which is stuck to the deck surfaces, radially all round the gun mountings, and across and in a fore and aft direction in other places as shown in (7).

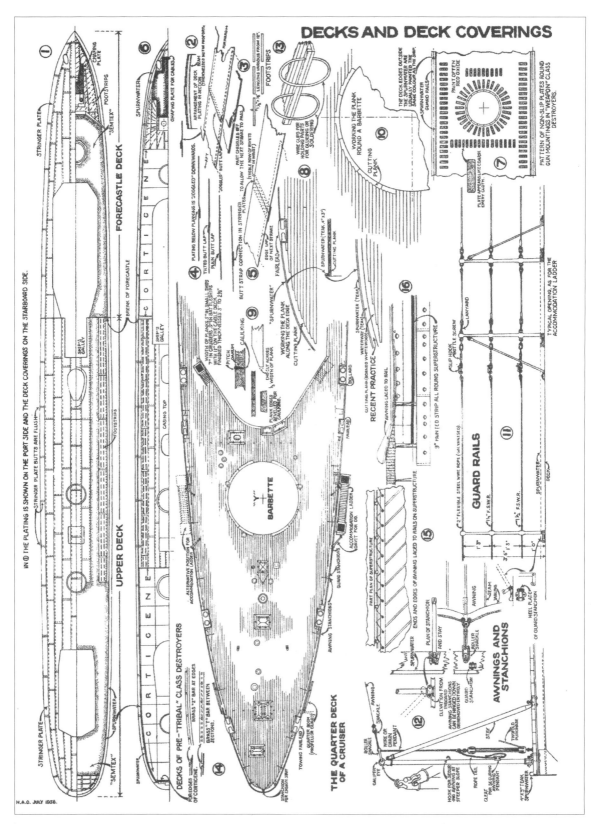

DECKS AND DECK COVERINGS

Decks and deck coverings. (MyTimeMedia)

In representing all this in a model it is important not to make the colours too bright and positive. The effect to be aimed at is a matt surface of subdued dry-looking colour. Where accurate ship model work is concerned the craftsman's worst enemy is shiny paint which spoils definition of form and detail, gives highlights in all the wrong places, and is quite unsuitable where realism is the object. Where it is legitimate is in models of cruising launches and on yacht hulls and deck houses where it occurs in reality, but in one of an ocean-going ship it is out of place.

In large warships, planking is still the universal form of deck covering. It is usually of teak or of Borneo whitewood, the planks being 5in wide in sloops and in the 'Algerine' class minesweepers; 7in in cruisers and 9in in capital ships with the cable deck planks sometimes as wide as 11in. The broader planks have a finished thickness of 3in, and the narrower of 2 1/2in. The edges of the planks are slightly bevelled as shown in (9) to form a V-shaped groove which is filled with oakum, a thick tarred string, three or four lines of which are rammed down to the bottom of the groove with a caulking iron, the seam being finally closed with hot pitch poured along from a ladle, a process called 'paying the seams'. At the ends this is difficult to do neatly, in fact these places are 'the devil to pay', hence the expression which is really a sea term like 'bitter end' which is the end of the cable made fast to the 'bitts', the opposite end to the anchor. The planks are laid fore and aft from the middle line outwards, the butts being 'shifted' so that the ends occur in the same line across only at every fourth plank. Where the ends reach the curve of the side they are notched into the teak 'cutting plank' and not left with sharp ends, as such would be impossible to caulk effectively. By cutting the bevel off at one third the width of the plank a squared end results which is fitted into a corresponding recess in the cutting plank as shown in detail (8) and (9), and in (10) where those fitted round a barbette are sketched. The planks are secured to the steel deck beneath them by deeply countersunk bolts, the holes over the bolt heads being sealed by tapered wooden plugs driven in and cut off flush, so that no metal comes to the surface. In (14) is shown the layout and planking of the quarterdeck of a cruiser. This is the area of the ship that for many centuries has been reserved for the captain and officers and is, by tradition, always aft between the 'quarters' or the two sides of the stern. In ancient ships the navigation was carried on from the high poop, above the tiller or wheel, the centre of control, the officers' cabins and all the small arms (and the wines and spirits) being nearby so as to be under their power in the event of mutiny, the poop being the place of observation of events inboard and outboard in action. In modern warships the stern is lower than the bows and the high poop has long ago vanished, but the quarterdeck is still regarded and still used as the region of authority.

All round the weather decks and the superstructure are the guard rails. Where these are in way of the blast of the heavy guns they are hinged to allow for striking down, as shown in (11) when the ship is cleared for action. They are spaced round the deck edges at intervals of about 8ft and the topmost of the three flexible steel wire rope rails is 3ft 6in above the surface of the plank. The upper rail is of 2in wire (measured, as is all rope, by its circumference), the middle and lower rails being of 1 1/2in wire. The ends are secured by slip hooks to eyebolts in the end guard stanchions and rove through holes in the others. Where the rails pass over large fairleads or bollards they are parted and short lengths put in and fastened by a shackle at one end and a lanyard, or small rope, at the other. At openings a stay is fitted to the stanchions at each side.

Round the deck edge outside the guard rails are the awning stanchions 7ft 6in high and fitted at the top with a 'caliper' eye as shown in (12) to take the roller shackle through which is rove the chain or wire pendant for stretching the awning. The pendant has an eye and a tail rope spliced in the grid, the rope being secured to a cleat on the stanchion or on the deck when the pendant has been hauled taut by the twofold purchase shown in (12). When the pendant is secured the purchase is unhooked and moved to the next stanchion where the operation is repeated. In tropical conditions awnings are spread over the forecastle and along the waist and over the superstructure, so that from overhead the whole ship appears to be covered in canvas. In destroyers an awning is almost invariably spread at the break of the forecastle in the region of the galley to keep rain off those who collect the rations for the various messes. At the ends the canvas is laced to rails on the superstructure as shown in (15).

The fittings of awnings, especially over the quarterdeck, can be an interesting addition to a model. If the scale is 1/8in-1ft and over, they can be made of tracing linen (with the blue starch washed out with soap and hot water), the cloths being represented by pencil lines drawn on. Tracing linen (whether used or new) is of finer mesh than any other fabric readily obtainable; it has the advantage of being 'off-white' when the starch is removed, and it makes a perfect sail-cloth for models. In small scales the tabling of the edges is best done by folding the edge over only once and sticking it down with clear dope, as a twice-folded hem is too clumsy. The bolt rope can then be sewn all round the edge and the pendants represented by fine wire hooked in at the appropriate intervals.

It is not very difficult to represent a planked deck in a working model so that it will not be shiny and yet be quite waterproof. If the deck is made of thin plywood the first step is to rub white paint into the grain to act as a filler, and to give it the scrubbed salty appearance of reality. Model aircraft flat white dope is the best paint for this as it dries quickly. It is put on by the simple expedient of dipping one's finger in the tin and rubbing the paint well into the grain, none being left on the surface of the wood. When dry this surface can be drawn on with Indian ink and a ruling pen to set out the lines and cutting planks, and when dry the whole surface is painted over with clear dope laid on with a camel-hair 1/2in or 3/4in flat or 'one-stroke' brush. The result looks messy for about a minute, after which the dope disappears, at the same time combining with the ink and the filling paint. The result is a matt waterproof surface identical with the real deck scaled down. The method can easily be proved

by an experiment with a waste piece of plywood. The spurnwater can be fixed to the surface of a wood deck by clear dope. To do this successfully requires a large number of clips to be made for holding it in place while the adhesive is setting. These are formed from circular rings as shown in (13) made of fairly strong galvanised wire bent round a rod which acts as a former. When about 20 turns have been put on, the spiral of wire can be sawn into rings by cutting it lengthwise with a hacksaw or file. The ends need to be finished truly square. Their use is shown in (13), but they are also of the greatest value for holding together small parts for sweating or soldering.

Davits

It can be said that the davits, which enable the boats to be hoisted in and out, are universally a feature of warships. They are mainly of two kinds, both of which are shown in the drawing, 'quadrantal' in which the davits are constructed from forged double channel bar, located into a position so that the boat will clear the side, and 'radial' where they are fixed in a vertical position but can be revolved, through a long arc of a circle. The latter are fitted for the sea boats in capital ships and in some destroyers, the quadrantal davits being more commonly found in cruisers for carrying the sea boats and in the majority of other ships. The sea boats are those on each side near the bridge, either before it, as in the 'King George V' class battleships, or abaft it as in the majority of others. Their function is mainly that of rescue and of being available in emergency, and also for taking the picking

Decks on Ough's model of destroyer HMS *Barfleur*. (© National Maritime Museum, Greenwich, London – SLR 1576)

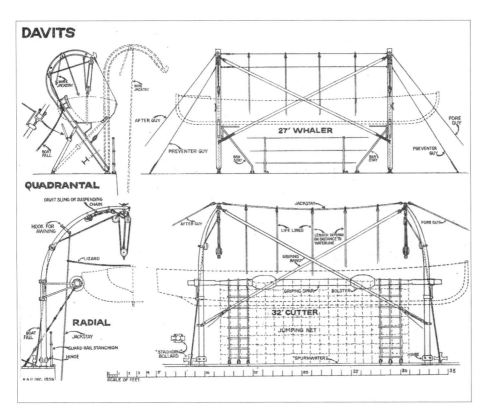

Davits. (MyTimeMedia)

up rope to a buoy when the ship is going to secure to one. In harbour, and most times at sea, they are always swung outboard and, in the former condition, the griping bands that secure them against the rolling of the ship are always cleared away. A long line is passed over the bows of a sea boat and through a fairlead up on the forecastle where it is made fast to a bollard. This is the boat rope and its function is to keep the boat's head pointing forward in the direction the ship is going as she is released from the falls while the ship still has way on her.

The boat most commonly used in the Service today as a sea boat is the 27ft whaler which is shown in outline in the upper part of the drawing and, being fairly light, it is usually slung in quadrantal davits. These are constructed from forged double channel, or 'H' bar, bent at the upper end into part of a circle and hinged at the lower end to plates bolted to the deck. They are stayed with wire rope guys which are led to convenient points on the superstructure, often nearly horizontally, and further stayed by preventer guys leading to eyebolts in the deck and set up taut by 'bottle screws'. Two horizontal jackstays are rigged between the davits with bottle screws at their ends,

one of which carries the life lines, which are ropes used by the crew to steady themselves while the boat is being lowered, and which are made long enough to reach the water when the ship is in the light condition. They have an eyesplice in the upper end which is passed over the jackstay, the standing part being passed through the eye and down into the boat where the slack is coiled down on the bottom boards. A whaler is supported in the davits by her keel which rests in chocks fitted to each end and is held against the griping pads by the bands as shown in the elevation. These are made of 'sword matting' which is very heavy canvas, and they are set up by a lanyard, or by blocks and tackle for heavy boats. The purchase that hoists the boat consists of a double block at the top and a single below, or, in a 32ft cutter, by two double blocks and a single leading block. In a whaler the hoisting ropes, known as the 'falls', are belayed to cleats on the davits; in a cutter they are led through sheaves in the staghorn bollards, and belayed by taking turns round their arms. A wire jackstay is fitted to each davit and led vertically down the side to an eyeplate near the waterline. To this a rope called a 'lizard' is led from the boat to enable the bow and stern to be kept steady as she is lowered. It has a metal thimble spliced in the end to run up and down the jackstay. Chain davit slings are not fitted to whalers as they are supported by the chocks on the davits. In addition to the wire rope guys which steady them in the secure position quadrantal davits are fitted with a bar stay hinged to the deck as shown.

The radial davits shown in the lower part of the drawing are hinged so that they can be laid down on the deck, the boat being often stowed in 'crutches' between them. This is to clear them out of the way of the blast of the heavy guns. Since a cutter, when hoisted in, is supported only by the grass ropes of the falls, a chain sling ending in a sliphook is provided on each davit to take her weight.

Access to the boat is gained by double Jacob's ladders of wire rope with wood rungs, secured by eyesplices to the griping spar and set up in the deck by lanyards. Often a 'jumping net', lashed to the spar, is also fitted as shown. When the boat is to be turned in the spar is unshipped and laid on the thwarts and the davits are swung first further aft. The forward davit is then turned inwards to bring the boat's head over the deck followed by the turning of the after davit to bring her stern in. When they are correctly placed the boat is slung from the chain slings, the weight is eased off the falls, the griping spar and bands are replaced and the guys set up taut. Addition of all these features to a model adds greatly to realism, especially the boat ropes leading to the forecastle, and the life lines with their coils of slack stowed in the bottom of the sea boats. The oars and boat hooks should be placed with

The lower boom.
(MyTimeMedia)

blades forward, and the rudder of a sea boat should always be shipped with its tiller lashed so as to be sure of steering the boat away when she is 'let go'.

The Lower Boom

In any model of a warship lying at anchor, as distinct from a model of one lying alongside a wharf, prominent features that should be shown are the 'lower booms'. These are spread at right angles to the centre line of the ship and are for the purpose of securing boats away from her side to prevent them getting damaged. The reason why the boat booms are a feature of all surface warships at anchor, while they hardly ever appear in merchant ships, is that the former are units of a fleet that has to lie in an open roadstead exposed to the weather while the latter usually make for a berth to discharge passengers and cargo. Warships at anchor need to communicate with the shore for the purpose of getting stores or mail or water on board, to exchange official visits and to give shore leave, so their boats as a consequence are in more frequent use than those of merchant ships. If the boats were secured actually alongside the ship they would soon become battered and strained and worn out in spite of their strong construction, so they are made fast to the boat ropes that run through blocks on the booms and these are adjusted to prevent them touching the ship's side.

The term 'lower boom' is, like so many other nautical phrases, a survival from the days of sail when the fore or main lower studding sail boom, which hinged against the ship's side at deck level, was used

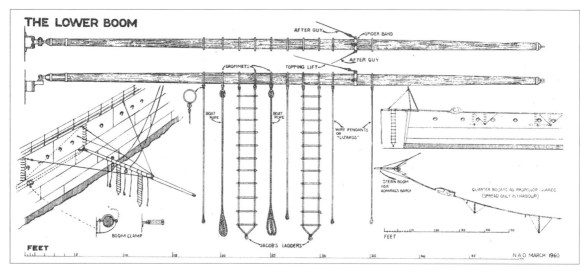

THE LOWER BOOM

N.A.O. MARCH 1960

Ough's model of HMS *Cygnet* depicting the funnels, davits and boom. (© National Maritime Museum, Greenwich, London – SLR 1500)

for this purpose, the boat rope passing through a block on it and leading to a boat which may have brought a guest to the ship, thus being referred to as the 'guest warp', the term 'lower' referring to the fact that it was the boom that spread the foot of the studding sail at deck level, or lower studding sail boom, that was used, the upper boom being attached to the fore or main yardarm. Hence the names 'guest warp boom' or 'lower boom' which are still used.

It will be seen from the drawing, which is of the lower boom of a capital ship, that it was an impressive spar 50ft long with quite an amount of rigging attached. In cruisers it was smaller, about 40ft long, and in destroyers about 20ft long. The greatest diameter of the 50ft boom was 11in and this was at two-thirds of its length from the inboard end, the rigging being of heavy flexible steel wire rope. The perspective sketch shows how it was stowed against the ship's side and clamped in position when not in use. Rings riveted to the plating gave access to the heel of the boom and to the clamp. When swung out the boom was kept level by the topping lift which had a bottle screw at its upper end to adjust to horizontal. It was kept square to the centre line by the fore guy shackled to the spider band and secured to an eyebolt at the deck edge by a sliphook. To prevent movement, the after guy, also shackled to the spider band, was secured to an eyebolt in the deck edge by a slip hook, having been set up taut by a runner and tackle hooked

on to a short tail or loop of wire spliced in the inboard end of the guy. On the topping lift a life line of cordage or wire rope was rigged at waist height and secured to an eyebolt in the side to assist the boat's crew to walk along the boom. The Jacob's ladders which gave access to the boats were shackled at their upper ends to two 'grommets' worked round the boom and a thimble was fitted at their lower ends to take the boat's 'lazy' or short painter. The grommets were rings of wire rope with a thimble eye worked in one place and were parcelled over with canvas and painted white. The boat ropes were of heavy grass line and led through blocks on the boom to bollards or cleats far up on the forecastle. At their lower ends they were divided into two loops for securing to one of the thwarts of the boats. In calm weather the boats were usually made fast to the eye and thimble at the ends of the wire rope 'lizards', but, in a seaway, they were shifted to the boat ropes which, owing to the weight of their long bights, had more give in them and so prevented jerking and straining. The heaviest boat made fast nearest to the spider band to reduce the strain on the boom. Some of the boats of a capital ship were heavy, as they included the two 50ft steam picket boats, the 42ft sailing launch and the 36ft sailing pinnace. When the boat ropes were unoccupied they hung a foot or two above the water and were prevented from running out of the blocks by a wooden toggle worked into the rope.

On arrival in harbour the booms were swung out together, having been completely rigged beforehand with their lizards and ladders, the boat ropes being rove after the booms were set in position. It was usual to swing out the booms at the same time as the anchor was let go, the rigging having been put on just beforehand. It was removed and stowed away again when the ship weighed anchor.

Quarter booms are fitted in some ships to act as propeller guards in harbour. When the ship is under way they are clamped against the side as shown in the sketch. They are not used as boat booms, but only to prevent another vessel berthing alongside at that place and damaging the propeller blades. The small boom at the stern is used for securing the Admiral's barge.

All the booms are of bare Oregon pine but they are sometimes varnished, and all their fittings such as the spider band, the grommets, and the end rings are painted white.

A waterline model of a warship is more impressive if she is represented at anchor with the booms spread, the boats in the water and with perhaps her attendant drifter or MFV [*motor fishing vessel*] alongside. A representation of the ship under way involves the problem of the bow wave and the wash along the sides and at the stem and it takes considerable artistic resources to cope with these successfully.

The Main Derrick

The main derrick was a feature of all warships large enough to carry heavy sailing and steam boats, that is, battleships, battle cruisers and large cruisers, from the early 1880s until the 'King George V' class and *Vanguard* of recent times, which used the cranes normally used for recovering aircraft for working their large boats. It was an immense spar, often over 65ft long, and built of tube with cast steel bead and heel fittings. The rigging consisted of a topping lift for raising the derrick and a purchase for hoisting the boats, a sling to take the weight of the derrick when it was not in use, and two wire guys on each side with tackles hooked to eyebolts in the deck and shackled to each side of the head. These were for swinging the derrick inboard and outboard. The wire rope of the topping lift, purchase and sling was of 4in flexible steel wire rope (4in FSWR) measured by circumference. The drawing shows the main derrick of HMS *Warspite* which was similar to those of all other ships throughout the period. A slight difference was that, in earlier types, as in the 'King Edward VII' class

battleships of 1902–6 for example, the leading blocks on the mast were slung freely from a shackle secured to a vertical steel pin fitted between the upper and lower bracket plates. In the example shown, which is typical for recent times, the wires of the derrick tackles were taken over the sheaves of trunnion blocks on the mast. These consisted of two bracket plates into which were inserted pivots or trunnions projecting from the housing which carried the sheave or sheaves, the bearings of which were so placed that the wire rope coming off the sheave ran exactly down through the hollowed centre of the lower pivot of the housing, thus allowing the derrick to be swung through an arc of 180 degrees or more for lowering or hoisting the boats. An enlarged plan and elevation of the trunnion blocks is shown in (1), detail of the upper trunnion block, which was double, being enlarged to twice the scale again in (2) the derrick itself being drawn to twice the scale of the general arrangement in (6) with detail of the head fittings, joints in the end castings and connections for the guys in (7). The original scale of the general drawing is 1/32in·1ft, the enlargements 1/16in·1ft, and the detail of the upper trunnion block 1/8in·1ft. The wire ropes from the blocks on the mast led down vertically through holes in the deck to the machinery space below.

This drawing also shows some of the detail of the rig of a capital ship. The main mast consisted of the lower mast, a topmast, a topgallant mast and wireless aerial yard, and a flag pole. The lower mast was a built-up steel tube 2ft 6in in diameter which rose to a bracket structure 80ft above the deck. This was known as the 'starfish' and is shown in plan and in enlarged detail in (3) and (4), its function being to spread the rigging of the masts above it. The lower mast was stayed by five 4 1/2in flexible steel wire rope shrouds on each side, the upper ends of which were shackled to the spider band near the masthead as shown in (5), their lower ends being made fast with a slip hook and bottle screw as shown enlarged in (8), the slip hook passing through a shackle secured to the eye of the shroud plate which was riveted to the side of the superstructure. The mast was stayed forward by the mainstay which was made portable to allow for the working of the derrick. It was secured to the deck by a slip hook and bottle screw like those of the shrouds.

The starfish, which is shown in plan (3), consisted of a platform supported by a six-pointed star built of flat triangular bracket plates stiffened along their upper edges by angle bar. The platform and brackets

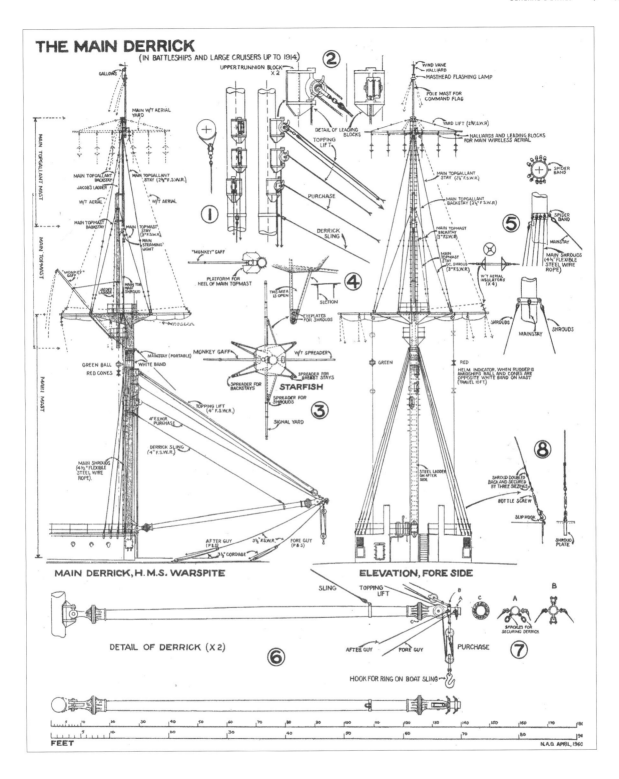

THE MAIN DERRICK
(IN BATTLESHIPS AND LARGE CRUISERS UP TO 1914.)

MAIN DERRICK, H.M.S. WARSPITE

ELEVATION, FORE SIDE

DETAIL OF DERRICK (X 2)

N.A.O. APRIL, 1960

FEET

served also to support outriggers or short spars which extended secondary wireless aerials and carried blocks for a few signal halliards. The six ends of the starfish structure was plated over for a short distance and on these plates were fixed the eyebolts for the ends of the stays, shrouds and backstays of the top and topgallant

The main derrick. (MyTimeMedia)

masts. Below the railed platform of the starfish, on the after side, was a second smaller platform through which passed the heel of the topmast and to which was secured the heel of the 'monkey' gaff which carried the white ensign when the ship was under way at sea. Slung under the two cross outriggers of the starfish were the leading blocks for the wires of the helm indicator which consisted of a green ball on the starboard side and two opposed cones on the port side, painted green and red respectively. When the helm was amidships the ball and cones were horizontal and were opposite to the white band painted on the mast. When the helm was put over to port the cones rose and when over to starboard the ball rose, the cones going down; the travel was 10 feet for full helm from the central position either way. On the after side of the mast was an iron ladder reaching to the platform housing the heel of the topmast with rungs above it leading to the starfish platform or main top. Further rungs let into the sides of the mast near the main derrick leading blocks gave access to them for oiling and maintenance.

Above the maintop and leading through it was the main topmast and to this, in the majority of capital ships in the 1914 war, was slung the main wireless aerial yard, as, with the additional height of the topgallant mast, they would have failed to clear the Forth Bridge in making for or leaving the base at Rosyth. In the drawing the full rig is shown including the topgallant mast and the pole for the command flag. The topmast was stayed forward by steel wire rope stays, laterally by shrouds of the same size (3in FSWR) and by similar backstays aft, all these being divided into three parts lengthwise by inserting porcelain insulators. Their upper ends were eye spliced and shackled to the eyebolts in the spider band, their lower ends being made fast by slip hooks and bottle screws of the same type as those for the main shrouds as shown in (8) but smaller. At the head of the topmast were the fittings for housing the topgallant mast, one at the masthead and one for its heel lower down, both masts having a Jacob's ladder leading up them on the after side, and on the same side of the topgallant mast was slung the wireless aerial yard. At the head of the topgallant mast in similar housings was the pole for the Admiral's Flag at the top of which was the masthead signal lantern and the 'gallows' for the wind vane which carried a single block for hoisting the lantern. On the main topmast was a bracket for the after electric steaming

light with a block underneath it and two guide wires leading down to the main top for hoisting an oil light should the electric light fail.

It will have been noticed how, in the technical terms used in this description, that many survive from the days of sail, such as maintop, shrouds, stays, backstays, gaff, yard, leading blocks, topping lift, and purchase, etc. On board warships, especially on cruisers and destroyers, until quite recently one was surprised at the amount of seamanship gear that was in evidence.

The Forebridge and Spotting Top

In a capital ship the spotting top and the forebridge were her eyes and brain. From here the main and secondary armament and the anti-aircraft guns were controlled and the ship was navigated and manoeuvred. The spotting top was placed as high as possible on the tripod foremast to enable the gunnery officers to get the widest possible view in action for observing the fall of salvoes and broadsides from the big guns, its commanding height enabling them to be well clear of funnel smoke and of cordite smoke from the guns. In probing for the range of the enemy's ships usually a salvo of four guns was fired in which one pair was set to fire a slightly greater distance than the other. If this resulted in 'straddling' the target, with two shells falling beyond it and two on the near side, a close approximation of the range was found. In the next salvo the guns firing 'over' would be slightly depressed and those firing 'short' slightly elevated so that, theoretically, the next would hit the target. A salvo consists of the fire of two or more guns but not of the whole of the main battery. When this was fired, all eight guns, as it was when the range was found, it was called a 'broadside'. The ship's rangefinders could measure the distance with much accuracy but not sufficient to make sure of hits, so the method of trying for a 'straddle' was used for final adjustment. The hundred feet high white columns of water and spray thrown up by the impact of the great shells were, while they lasted, visible marks which showed where one pair of guns was ranging short and the other over and corrections could rapidly be made, the operation being known as 'spotting'. For the main armament the forward central part of the spotting top was used, the two wing projecting compartments being used for spotting for the 6in guns of the secondary battery, communication being by numerous voice pipes which were led down the outside of the mast and the struts of the tripod. On being straddled the gunnery officers of the enemy's ship were, of course, aware of the significance of the manoeuvre and they would alter course in order to avoid the predicted range of the next salvo, but, in so doing, would throw their own rangefinding out of adjustment. Thus victory in a hard battle depended, ultimately, upon the rival captains' skill in anticipating the fall of the enemy broadsides and in avoiding them by alterations of course while keeping their own guns correctly ranged, responsibility that, in the overpowering noise of battle, called for the highest qualities of coolness and cunning to sustain. Where a great sea power was concerned a fleet engagement could have a decisive effect on the course of a war. Once the enemy's battle fleet was crippled or destroyed its power to protect the cruisers engaged in raiding the convoys was removed and, once gone, the power to starve an island nation into submission went with it. So the fate of a nation could depend, and, in the past *did* depend, on the efficiency of the training in co-ordination between the spotting top and the compass platform.

The drawing shows the foretop and bridge arrangement in the ten battleships of the 'Queen Elizabeth' and 'Royal Sovereign' classes, six ships of which fought in the battle of Jutland, four of the former and two of the latter. In HMS *Hood* the spotting top was more streamlined and it was of a different shape in *Repulse* and *Renown* and in *Nelson* and *Rodney* it was embodied in the high bridge structure. In the five 'King George V' class battleships it was not fitted as a visual observation position as their heavy guns were ranged by RADAR. It consisted of a steel house built on the 'starfish' arrangement of supporting brackets secured to the top of the tripod and with glass windows on all sides. It is shown in plan in (1) in elevation in (2) and with a rear elevation in (3), its relation to the tripod and to the whole of the bridge structure being shown in profile in (4) and in front elevation in (5). The roof was open around the pedestal of the anti-aircraft gun director tower and towards the back of the structure. Below the spotting top was the platform for the director tower for the main armament of 15in guns and from this position they could be laid, trained and fired, similar directors for the 6in guns of the secondary battery being placed on either side of the compass platform, these batteries being used for defence against torpedo attack by destroyers. At the forward end of the platform was an enclosed raised wooden platform, vulgarly known as 'Monkey Island' which carried the standard or magnetic compass and the Gyro compass, both of which were placed in a central raised area and surrounded by a wood grating. Voice pipes led down from the compasses to the captain's sea cabin and to the wheelhouse which was situated on the platform below as shown in (7) and on which, outside the canvas covered guard rails, was carried the upper pair of bow lights. Below this was the signal searchlight platform which was fitted with a shelter for the crews of the visual signal and observation instruments placed there. It was surrounded by a guard rail covered with canvas with a steel wall round the projections at the after end. Below this again was the conning tower platform with the signal, or flag, deck at its after end. The armoured conning tower, with its hooded rangefinder on top, the former built of 11in plating and the latter of 4in plating, occupied the forward end of the deck as shown in (8), access to the conning tower being by a heavy armoured door running on a semi-circular track in the deck. Built round the vertical strut of the tripod was an additional chart house and the Admiral's sea cabin with ladderways through the deck on each side leading down to the compartments below, and with two large ventilation trunks near them. This platform also carried two 24in signal searchlights and six flag lockers at the after end, the dotted lines in this area and on the plans of the other platforms showing the run of the beams and brackets supporting them. Below the conning tower platform was the shelter deck, the fore end of which was enclosed by the armoured barbette of 'B' turret as shown in (10). At the two after corners of this deck were fitted the massive stanchions for the 35ft wooden ammunition embarking derricks, and it also carried heel fittings for the sounding booms and the paravane derricks. Other features were the two sounding machines, hawser reels, mushroom top ventilators, two large Carley rafts and the four 3pr saluting guns which could be unshipped and fitted to mountings on the 50ft steam picket boats. The guns are shown enlarged in (12). Projecting from the screen walls that supported the shelter deck were the winch barrels for working the paravane and the 35ft derricks, the electric machinery of these being situated inside. It is probable that, in later commissions, all the platforms were covered in 'Semtex', an anti-slip

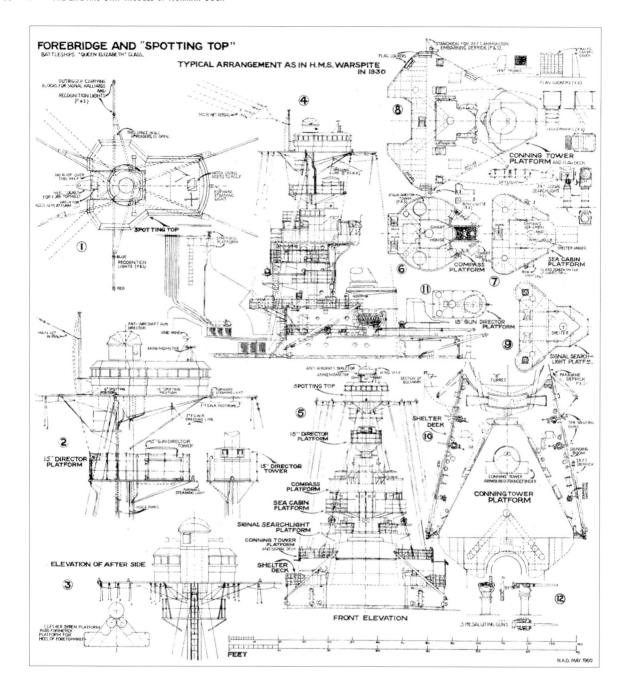

Forebridge and spotting top. (MyTimeMedia)

composition dark grey in colour and of matt surface.

The whole array of the forebridge and shelter deck in these vessels, which were among the last to be built in the old tradition as ships-of-the-line, consisted of nine decks and platforms above the forecastle, and, when seen in perspective with a foreground of the huge guns of 'A' and 'B' turrets, presented a sight to cause awe and wonder in the beholder.

Anchors

The previous article on 'Anchors and Cables' did not really give enough detail of the anchors themselves, and since most of those used in the Royal Navy are also used in the Merchant Service this present article should cover a fairly wide field, although the period described is only from about 1900 onwards. A great deal is known about the anchors of ancient ships, for they date from before the dawn of history, some having been preserved, also drawings and paintings of them, but they are outside the limits of this series.

Anchors are made in great variety and in an astonishing number of sizes, the Byers anchor, for example, being listed in the Admiralty 1912 Manual as being made in 119 different weights and consequently sizes, and the others in almost as many. There are seven main types, Byers', Wasteneys Smith's, Martin's, Hall's, the Admiralty patterns of boat and stream anchors, and those for small craft such as Danforth's and the 'CQR'. Within each type also there are minor modifications of design. To detail them all would fill numerous pages, mostly with columns of figures of dimensions, so these are only given in outline for a few different weights which are always stated in hundredweights, those shown being for the largest, the smallest, and for an intermediate size about half-way between. If the dimension 'A' or 'A-B', as shown on the drawing, is known this can be used to make a scale of inches which is used to find all the other dimensions of the anchor. In most cases, however, this dimension will not be known but an approximation may be reached by noting that the height of the guard rail from the deck is 42in. If dividers are set to this height as it appears in a photograph of a ship and then moved to the crown of the anchor its width may be obtained and a scale of inches made which will give all the other dimensions from these drawings, which are in true proportions.

The parts of an anchor are the 'anchor ring', which is the heavy shackle to which the cable is attached, the 'shank', which is the central arm, the 'crown', which is the enlargement at the end of the shank to which the 'arms' are welded, the 'blades' or 'flukes' which grip the sea bed, and the 'stock', which is an iron bar, or wood in ancient ships, fixed to the shank at right angles to the plane of the arms and blades to ensure that they tilt into the ground. In stockless anchors this function is carried out by the 'tripping palms', which are large projections from the crown, and, in later types, the whole crown, which is essentially a wide thick plate, as shown in the modifications of Hall's anchor in (5) and (6), and performs the same function. There is also the 'gravity band' fixed at the centre of gravity on the shank with shackles above and below for slinging the anchor. The arms of a stockless anchor tilt either way to an angle of between 43 and 45 degrees but not more,

that is, they can swing round the swivel pin to an angle of about 90 degrees.

Before 1914 most of the heavy ships carried Martin's or Inglefield's anchors as shown in (3), (9), (10), (11) and (12). In battleships these were stowed on sloping beds recessed into the forecastle deck and chained in position. They were brought in by the anchor davit which was fitted with leading blocks for a single wire rope which was taken to the middle line capstan. In cruisers this davit was replaced by short catheads which served the same purpose, and their anchors were either stowed vertically as in (9), or horizontally, as in (10). Two of the securing chains led round the anchor to a rod with projecting arms over which the last links of the chains were passed. The rod, being rotated to tension the chains, was held by a third arm which entered a steel cup with part of its side cut away to receive it. When the cup was rotated by the rod leading to a lever on the deck it clamped the securing chains, when rotated the opposite way it released them. Additional chains were also passed round by hand and tensioned by rope lashings, some of them being placed by way of a watertight port for bousing in. It can be imagined how difficult and dangerous this operation must have been in bad weather and how liable the anchors must have been to work adrift in heavy seas coming over the bows.

Since about 1914 the stockless anchor, which could be drawn right up into the hawse pipes, thus abolishing the clumsy earlier methods of securing, has become universal and the drawing shows the main types in use in the Royal Navy and in the Merchant Service since then.

The Byers and Wasteneys Smith anchors were characteristic of capital ships, but they were also carried in cruisers and there seems to have been no general rule, so perhaps availability on fitting out was the deciding cause in allocating them. In the Byers anchor the crown, the arms and the tripping palms are all one large steel casting connected to the shank by the swivel pin, while in the Wasteneys Smith the crown is part of the shank forging, the arms being fixed to the swivel pin by positioning bolts, the pin passing right through them and through the crown. Hall's anchor was more complicated as, although the crown is one casting, the shank and its pin are passed through an oblong hole of appropriate size carrying the pin with it into a deep slot with rounded edges, the pin being held in by massive blocks positioned by securing bolts as shown in part section in (4), or by bolts passing through the

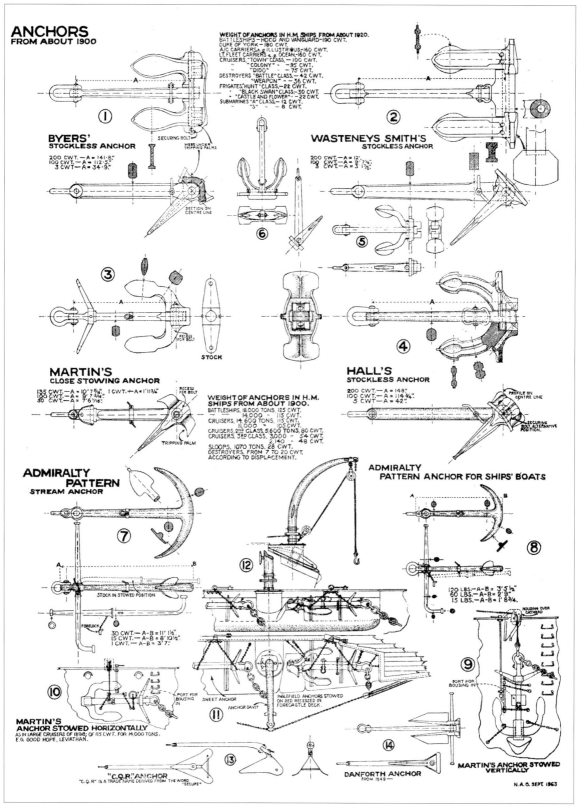

ANCHORS
FROM ABOUT 1900

WEIGHT OF ANCHORS IN H.M. SHIPS FROM ABOUT 1920.
BATTLESHIPS – HOOD AND VANGUARD–190 CWT.
DUKE OF YORK – 180 CWT.
A/C CARRIERS, e.g. ILLUSTRIOUS–160 CWT.
LT. FLEET CARRIERS & g. OCEAN–160 CWT.
CRUISERS, "TOWN" CLASS, – 100 CWT.
        "COLONY"   " – 95 CWT.
        "DIDO"   " – 75 CWT.
DESTROYERS "BATTLE" CLASS, – 42 CWT.
        "WEAPON"   " – 36 CWT.
FRIGATES,"HUNT" CLASS,– 28 CWT.
      "BLACK SWAN" CLASS,–30 CWT.
      "CASTLE AND FLOWER" – 22 CWT.
SUBMARINES "A" CLASS, – 12 CWT.
        "S"   " – 8 CWT.

BYERS'
STOCKLESS ANCHOR

200 CWT. – A = 141·8"
100 CWT. – A = 112·5"
3 CWT. – A = 34·9"

WASTENEYS SMITH'S
STOCKLESS ANCHOR

200 CWT.– A = 12"
100 CWT. – A = 9·7¼"
3 CWT.– A = 3 1⅛"

MARTIN'S
CLOSE STOWING ANCHOR

135 CWT.– A = 10'7¾", 1 CWT. – A = 1'11¾"
100 CWT.– A = 9¾"
50 CWT.– A = 7'6⁹/₁₆"

**WEIGHT OF ANCHORS IN H.M.
SHIPS FROM ABOUT 1900.**
BATTLESHIPS, 18,000 TONS, 125 CWT.
      14,000   " 115 CWT.
CRUISERS, 14,600 TONS, 115 CWT.
      11,000   " 105 CWT.
CRUISERS, 2ND CLASS, 5,600 TONS, 80 CWT.
CRUISERS, 3RD CLASS, 3,000 " 54 CWT.
       2,140   " 48 CWT.
SLOOPS, 1070 TONS, 28 CWT.
DESTROYERS, FROM 7 TO 20 CWT.
ACCORDING TO DISPLACEMENT.

HALL'S
STOCKLESS ANCHOR

200 CWT.– A = 148"
100 CWT.– A = 114·¾"
5 CWT.– A = 42"

**ADMIRALTY
PATTERN**
STREAM ANCHOR

**ADMIRALTY
PATTERN ANCHOR FOR SHIPS' BOATS**

120 LBS.–A–B = 3'5½"
60 LBS.–A–B = 2'9"
15 LBS.–A–B = 1' 8¾.

30 CWT. – A–B = 11' 1½"
15 CWT. – A–B = 8' 10½"
1 CWT. – A–B = 3'7"

**MARTIN'S
ANCHOR STOWED HORIZONTALLY**
AS IN LARGE CRUISERS OF 1898; OF 115 CWT. FOR 14,000 TONS.
E.G. GOOD HOPE, LEVIATHAN.

**MARTIN'S ANCHOR STOWED
VERTICALLY**

"C.Q.R." ANCHOR
"C.Q.R." IS A TRADE NAME DERIVED FROM THE WORD "SECURE"

DANFORTH ANCHOR
FROM 1949 –

N.A.O. SEPT. 1963

Anchors. (MyTimeMedia)

crown as shown in the view with the blade canted. This anchor, or modifications of it, as in (5) and (6), was common in cruisers and aircraft carriers. The type shown in (6) is a modification where the pin is inserted above the crown which has become a large flat plate, shaped as shown, with a heavy rectangular boss underneath it. The type shown in (5) has the same kind of crown but the arms are passed right through it, each having an internal shoulder to receive the block that holds them in place, the arms being also shouldered above the plate. These two kinds were very common in HM ships of less displacement than capital ships in the period between the wars.

The Admiralty Pattern anchors are older than the Admiralty itself and, in some form or other, as in the 'fisherman's hook', they go back to remote antiquity. The Admiralty kind are more massive and they have a close-stowing stock but otherwise they differ little from those of past centuries. The large size are used as stream anchors for keeping a ship in position in a tidal stream and they are usually stowed lashed up to some part of the superstructure. The boat anchors need no description. The Danforth anchor has its stock passed through the crown in which it also serves as a swivel pin. It is thus 'stockless' since it can be hauled into a hawse-pipe yet it has a fixed stock to lay the blades and tripping palms in place for cutting into the ground. It is used in small craft as is the 'CQR' which consists of a shank attached to two ploughshares with a stay between them, the connection with the shank allowing them some sideways movement. For a light anchor it has great holding power. The name CQR is a pun on the word 'secure'.

Watertight Doors and Hatches

The hatches and skylights and watertight doors of warships are a universal feature, common to all classes of ships. They are also characteristic, being unlike those of merchant ships or yachts, and, in a detailed model, even of a very small scale, they need to be shown so that their functions are distinguished. By making clear what these functions are this drawing, which is to scale, should help those who work from photographs to know one from the other. The scale of the original is 1/2in and 1/4in to 1ft.

Warships being usually faster, heavier and lower

in the water than merchant ships and liners, their superstructures receive rough treatment from heavy seas, so the doors, windows and vent openings have to be made watertight by clipping them home against a rubber seating by means of handles that can be rotated from outside or in and which, in the closed position, ride over wedge-shaped pieces of steel on the outside of the door.

The drawing shows in (1) the elevation and section of a watertight door of the type common to all of HM ships from the eighteen nineties down to 1914. The opening in the bulkhead is plated well above the deck surface and it is reinforced all round inside and out by a wide flange of angle bar, the angle projecting outwards and inwards. The outer projection forms the seating against which the rubber strip round the inside of the door is pressed by the clips or handles. The door is shown in section and with enlarged detail of the hinges and clips. When the latter are turned on closing the door the underside of the handle slides along the wedge-shaped pieces of steel, thus pressing the rubber seating hard up against the edge of the angle bar lining. Turning the clips the other way, either from inside or out, and clear of the door, takes off the pressure and allows the door to open. There are 10 clips, evenly spaced all round to ensure equal pressure, and the hinges are made so as to allow enough movement inwards to permit this. The outward surface of the door is 'dished' into a shallow sunken panel and its edges are rounded. It is stiffened inside with two bent-angle bars placed back to back. The rubber strip is held in position by two long strips of galvanised steel held on by screws. This makes a white line all round the inside of the door which is painted ship-grey on both sides. Doors of this type continued to be fitted in HM ships up to the last of the 'County' class cruisers of 1929.

In the 'Leander' class cruisers of after 1929 and in the later 'Southampton' and 'Dido' classes, and in all since, watertight doors of the later type shown in (2) were fitted. The principle of securing by clips and the hinges was the same as in the earlier type, the differences being in the four-fold panelling of the dished recesses and in the larger radius given to the corners. Welding was used in their construction instead of the former riveting when this came in with the 'Leander' class ships. The angle bar stiffeners were replaced inside by a deep flange welded on all round inside the rubber lining and reinforced by wedge-shaped plates as shown in the enlarged section of the hinge. The bending over of the edges of the door is carried beyond a right angle so as to hold the outer edge of the rubber. When closed these doors are a handsome fitting, and they make a striking addition to the appearance of the superstructure. They show up well on an 1/8in scale model.

In a warship there are no large hatches such as those giving access to cargo spaces in merchant ships, the largest of them being the torpedo embarking hatch shown in (10). This is usually only found in those capital ships which had submerged torpedo tubes and they were placed aft of the quarterdeck turret and near the foremost turret. They were longer than the other hatches and they had a massive hinged davit near them and a 'stag-horn' bollard, usually of polished bronze, next to it for belaying the falls of the tackle used in lowering the torpedoes.

The ordinary deck hatches are all much alike and are almost unchanged since towards the end of last [nineteenth] century, except that riveting has been largely replaced by welding. They consist of a coaming about a foot high which is a long strip with rounded corners fitted into the steel deck plating which is connected to it by angle bar. If the deck is planked the latter is hidden as the planking goes over it and tight up against the coaming. The hatch cover, which is hinged to the coaming, consists of a flat steel plate that extends about two inches beyond the coaming all round. It has the same kind of white rubber lining as in the watertight doors and is held on by steel strips thus making a white line going completely round on the inside and in such a position that the centre line of the rubber coincides with the edge of the coaming. The cover is clamped home by screws with 'butterfly' nuts on them which hinge up and down. When vertical the screwed shank tilts into a slot in the projecting lugs on the cover as shown in (3). The cover, when open, is held upright by a stanchion which has a projecting eye on top at one side. This goes into a fitting on the cover having two eyes and a steel peg passed through them locks it in position. The hinges are extended right across the cover to act as stiffeners, one end being formed into the notched lug for the clamping screws, and the other into an eyeplate which forms the centre part of the hinge, the material for them being either angle bar or 'T' bar, as in (8). The vertical part of the angle is cut away to a slope downward towards the lug end to reduce weight. The hatch leading below from the quarterdeck is surrounded by a portable brass handrail and the ladder inside is fitted with a teak handrail supported

at the upper end from inside the coaming by a brass stanchion as shown in (3). Some hatches have sloped tops as shown in (5) and some have a manhole in the cover as in (8), which is secured with clips as in a watertight door. Some of the deck hatches had to be placed near the muzzles of the big guns and the huge pressure wave that passed over the deck when they fired could start the coamings away from their fastenings. For this reason the hatches in that area were fitted with 'blast plates' which were sloping strips of steel going from the deck to part way up the coaming to prevent the shock wave from getting a hold. Inside these were filled with fir or some other timber as shown in (4) and (6). They were fitted not only to the hatches beyond the gun muzzles but to those near the turrets as well, since the blast acted in both directions. In (9) is shown a quarterdeck hatch with the frame for its canopy in place. This was of canvas, painted ship-grey, and it spread across the top, down the sides and back and had a roll-up canvas curtain in front.

Skylights are constructed in the same way as hatches and with the same kind of steel covers and securing screws. They could be either single as in (7), or double as in (6), the former being generally placed against a bulkhead. The glass is usually frosted and framed in teak which rests on angle bars fixed to the coaming and it is opened by lifting rods with holes in them to go over a peg as in many domestic windows. The two halves of a double skylight are separated by a channel bar which takes the castings for the hinges and for the two stanchions for holding the covers open, the channel bar being fitted against the bulkhead, in a single skylight. Both types are shown in section and with an elevation of a double one fitted with a blast plate. There are many skylights on the weather decks and on the superstructure for lighting the wardroom galley and the ship's galley, the bakery and the blacksmith's and coppersmith's shops and also the recreation spaces.

The openings for light in the ship's sides and in the superstructure can be either circular ports or rectangular windows. The round ports are known as sidelights or 'scuttles' and they are closed from inside by steel covers called 'deadlights', the windows, which are 18in x 24in, being covered from outside by steel plates having the same character as small hatch covers with the usual hinges, clamping screws and rubber lining strips. Nearly all have just above them, a curved gutter, called a 'rigol' or 'eyebrow', the former word

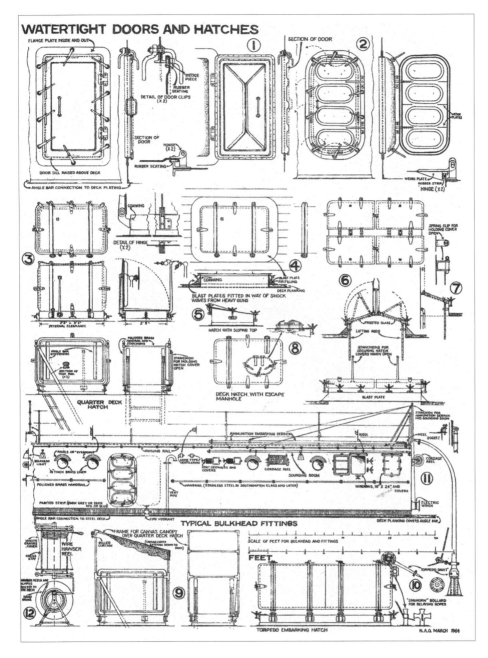

Watertight doors and hatches. (MyTimeMedia)

having descended from the name of the carved ornamental fitting over the ports of the old wooden walls. The openings of the ventilation trunks in the walls of the superstructure are also closed by doors of the same kind but smaller, the openings being covered by steel wire mesh set vertically and horizontally.

In (11) is shown a general view of typical external bulkhead fittings drawn to half the scale of the rest of the sheet. At the right hand is a massive stanchion which carries the topping lifts for the ammunition embarking derrick or the paravane derrick and also for the sounding boom which is just below it. These swing about heel sockets and are supported by chocks when not in use. Along the top of the screen wall is the awning rail which is a steel bar carried at intervals by short stanchions and it is used for lashing the inboard edge of the awning by a spiral serving passing round the bar and in and out through eyelet holes in the

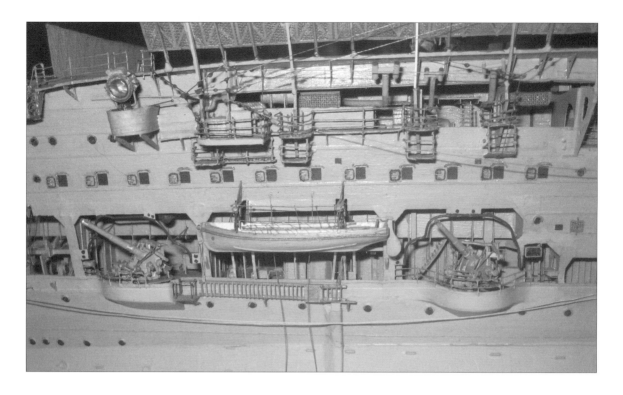

Detailing on the starboard side on Ough's model of HMS *Glorious*. (Author's collection)

doubling of the canvas. Along the bottom of the wall is a painted strip to make good the wear and tear caused by things on the deck knocking against it. It is a prominent feature and it may be either dark grey, dark red or dark blue, the colour seeming to be at the choice of the ship's officers. It makes a clear defining line all round the upperworks and it contrasts elegantly with the deck colour. About half way up is a polished brass or stainless steel handrail for holding on to in heavy weather. In peace-time it is kept bright and it makes a fine accent in a model, but in war time it is painted over with the ship's grey. Another feature of the bulkheads are the 'gooseneck' vent pipes which allow circulation of air in oil fuel compartments, shorter ones than that shown being placed along the ship's side outside the guard rails, the curved part usually being turned to face aft.

The weather decks are illuminated at night by the shaded lights on the bulkheads. These are shown on the drawing and in elevation and plan at the left hand end. Those on the quarterdeck were given shades of polished brass in peace-time. Another feature is the cordage reels. They are for hemp rope and are placed

near the boat davits on the nearest bulkhead, one for each davit where they take up the slack of the boat falls, and they are also placed near booms and derricks, for stowing the cordage belonging to them.

Lastly, and usually placed at the forward end of the superstructure on the forecastle and similarly on the deck down aft, are the hawser reels. They are always placed on deck as they are much heavier than cordage reels and they are used for stowing the ship's galvanised steel berthing wires. Both types are covered with canvas, often painted white, when not in use. The hawser reels are worked like a hand winch by a handle at both sides, one being fitted with a spur wheel which engages with teeth on the inside of a large gear wheel fixed on the end plate concentric to the bearing shaft. A hand brake is fitted for controlling the rate of spin of the drum veering wire.

All these details are part of the essential character of HM ships of the past 80 years as all the large external surfaces are broken up by them; omitted from a model it becomes more like a diagram. A knowledge of what they are enables the modelmaker to recognise them even from poor photographs.

7
❖ CRUISERS ❖

I t appears that there are five model cruisers made by Ough still in existence and four of these are held in the Imperial War Museum (IWM) collection. There is also correspondence held by the IWM regarding an order for a model of HMS *Hawkins* but it is unknown whether this was in fact built as there is no further record of her. Another two, both of the 'Cardiff' class cruiser HMS *Curacoa*, cannot be traced at the time of writing.

Some of Ough's articles on cruisers are included later in this chapter, as are those for other ship types in their own respective chapters, but it will be noted that these vary in content. The two articles on HMS *Dorsetshire*, depicted in No. 14 Dry Dock, are full of information, while the one on HMS *Dido* reveals little about the ship itself but concentrates very much on how Ough gleans information for his drawings and plans. Some of his work occasionally becomes repetitive,

often using original material taken from one article for use again in another article, or in a different publication. With this in mind it was decided not to reproduce his articles on 'Cardiff' and 'Southampton' class cruisers as, other than the actual plans of the ships, very little is different from articles already reproduced. Full details of all his articles referred to, whether reproduced or not, are listed in the Bibliography so they can all be traced for further use.

Ough working on a waterline model cruiser – believed to be HMS *Curacoa*. (Courtesy the Ough family)

Ough's working model of HMS *Curacoa* (1/96 scale). The semi-flash boiler, turbines and the actuator for radio control are shown in the foreground. (MyTimeMedia)

Ough with his working model of HMS *Curacoa*. (MyTimeMedia)

HMS *Curacoa* (1917)

It is known that Ough made at least two models of this 'C' or 'Cardiff' class cruiser. One of his photographs, showing his part-completed model of the aircraft carrier HMS *Glorious*, also depicts an unfinished waterline 1in-16ft model of *Curacoa*. We know that his model of *Glorious* was made during 1931–2, therefore the *Curacoa* must have been made, or at least started, during the same years. Another photograph also depicts Ough working on the same vessel but there are no pictures or records of the finished model. It is unknown if, or whether, she was commissioned by a private buyer or an institution: no trace has been found of this particular model in any of the major museums.

The second *Curacoa* model that is known to have been made by Ough is completely different apart from the fact that its life, or eventual fate, is also unknown. Constructed in 1951 as a fully working steam-powered model with semi-flash boiler, two turbines and radio control she was to a scale of 1/8in-1ft, giving her an overall length of just over 56 inches. According to an article about Ough and the model in the February 1956 edition of *Model Engineer* magazine: '... the remote control will enable him to carry out thirty different actions with the model from distances up to a quarter of a mile. The guns of the model can be fired by remote control and will shoot for a distance of 100yds with sufficient force to pierce 3/16in plywood.' I would love to think that this *Curacoa* is waiting to be discovered in some loft or barn somewhere!

Obviously a superb piece of engineering with working guns, steam turbines, and so on, there is a piece of film, dating from 1955 and approximately two minutes long, showing Ough working on the model. This can be viewed on the British Pathé News archive (www.britishpathe.com/video/model-ship-curacoa).

HMS *Penelope* (1936)

This waterline model to 1in–16ft scale of an 'Arethusa' class cruiser is believed to have been made by Ough in 1947 for the IWM, where she still remains (Catalogue No. MOD 153).

HMS *London* (1927)

Commissioned by the Royal United Service Museum (RUSM) as part of the series of waterline models depicting the principal types of ships in the Navy of the day, this 'County' class cruiser was built to a scale of 1in–16ft. When the RUSM was disbanded in the 1960s the model was acquired by the IWM which now holds her in their collections (Catalogue No. MOD 563).

HMS *Vindictive* (1897)

Historically this model, commissioned by the IWM, is in some ways one of Ough's more important works. A waterline model of the 'Arrogant' class protected cruiser *Vindictive*, built during 1927–8 to a scale of 1in–16ft, she is depicted as she appeared on

Turbines (port and starboard) for the model of HMS *Curacoa*. The ahead and astern motors are on the same shaft of each engine - the larger end of the casing containing the ahead motion. (MyTimeMedia)

Inside Ough's working model of HMS *Curacoa*. (British Pathé)

Part-completed model of HMS *Vindictive* in Ough's workshop. (Courtesy the Ough Family)

23 April 1918 when used in the Zeebrugge raid. Although the operation was only a partial success, such was the fighting that eleven Victoria Crosses were awarded plus a further fifty DSOs and DSCs. The model is very much an example where first-hand knowledge, and therefore probable historical correctness, makes it an important record. Various notes have been made by Ough on the reverse of his own photographs depicting the *Vindictive* and they confirm some of the research he undertook to maintain his usual meticulous detail. He makes a point of mentioning that the model was made from a 'photostat' of Admiralty 'as fitted' drawings and also from information obtained from a constructor and one of the shipwrights at Chatham Dockyard who had been involved in the ship's alterations. These included showing the bower anchors slung to make space for Carley rafts in the anchor beds, the gangways for lowering on to the Zeebrugge mole, the mole anchors, flame thrower hut, 11in howitzer, foretop covered with splinter mats, arrangement of the gangway deck and ramps leading to it plus the storming ladders. It appears that such care had been taken to keep the ship's preparation from the enemy that the shipwrights were kept in ignorance and the drawings destroyed as soon as the work was completed. Because of this it is believed that this model may be the only accurate record

of the ship as she went into action on that April day in 1918. The model is still held by the IWM in their collection (Catalogue No. MOD 352).

HMS *Hawkins* (1917)

Although mention has been made of a model of *Hawkins* possibly being commissioned from Ough by the IWM only one has come to light during research, and this was held in private ownership. On 10 May 2016 it was put up for auction by Charles Miller Ltd of London.

This *Hawkins* waterline model was believed to have been built by Ough in 1926 to a scale of 1in-32ft and the presumption is that it was made as a private commission. Mounted on a raised cloth-covered plinth and shown in a glass case it displays a maker's plate plus name and scale plates. To the top left hand corner of the glass case is affixed an exhibition label which reads 'H.M.S. HAWKINS. 9,800 tons, Modelled by Norman Ough, Esq. Formerly Chief Modeller at the National Maritime Museum'. It would appear that this label was added afterwards by a third person as Ough usually referred to himself as Norman A. Ough. The title 'Chief Modeller at the National Maritime Museum' is also unlikely to have been used by him as the majority of his models now held by the National Maritime Museum (NMM) were originally built for the Royal United Service Museum and acquired by the NMM at a later date. It should also be noted that the NMM was not founded until 1937, more than ten years after the model was allegedly built.

HMS *Dorsetshire* (1929) and Dry Dock Model

This is probably Ough's *magnum opus* as it appears he derived a great amount of joy in constructing not only *Dorsetshire* herself but also the model of No. 14 Dry Dock, Portsmouth, in which the ship sits. It took Ough about eighteen months of full-time work to complete, beginning in September 1947 and finishing in March 1949 when she was handed over to the IWM who had commissioned her. Built to a scale of 1in-16ft, the complete model is over four feet long. It was originally displayed under the clock in the cross gallery of the museum; unfortunately it is now kept in storage (Catalogue No. MOD 269).

The two articles that Ough wrote for *Model Maker* magazine in 1963, describing the construction of both the model of the ship and the dry dock, are reproduced below. One rather amusing anecdote was told to me by Richard Eddy, who, as a young Sub Lieutenant in the Royal Navy, had visited Ough in his workshop in Charing Cross Road in 1960. Ough told him that on completing the model he had been visited 'by some people from a security department' who wanted to know how he had received clearance to visit the ship during her refit. Apparently he took particular delight in telling them that if they checked dockyard records they would find that *Dorsetshire* had never been refitted in that particular dry dock!

A few of the articles on cruisers written by Ough for *Model Maker* magazine, and mentioned earlier in the chapter, are reproduced below.

HMS *Dido* (1939)

One of the reasons why comparatively few models of ships of the Royal Navy are attempted by

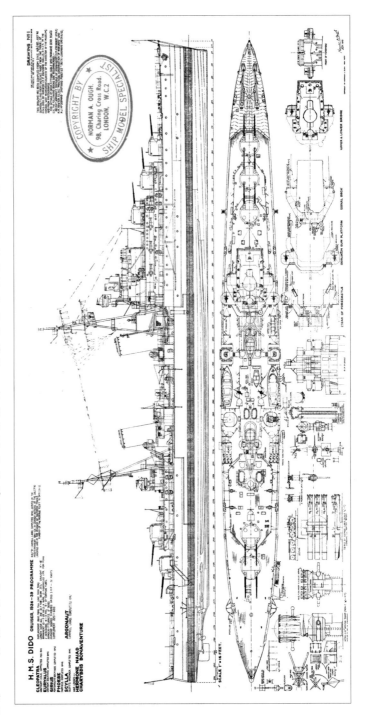

modelmakers is the fact that there are no detailed drawings of them.

To my knowledge the plan reproduced here is the only one in existence of a modern cruiser available to the public. I say 'to my knowledge', because for the

Ough's plans for HMS *Dido*. (ss Great Britain Trust)

past thirty years I have had letters from modelmakers all over the world asking for plans showing detail, and, had any been discoverable, I should probably have found them in that long time. In the course of my work for the Royal United Service Museum and the Imperial War Museum I have had access to the official drawings, but my tracings from these have all been returned to the Admiralty after each model has been finished and, in replying to letters, I have only used information that is available to anyone who has the time (and the money) to search for it – a tedious and costly business.

Nevertheless, a drawing like this of HMS *Dido* (which covers a class of ten ships – cruisers which broke the power of the Axis in the Mediterranean) can be put together with considerable accuracy without reference to official information. The sources are text books and photographs and such small plans as are sold to the public by the Admiralty and the Institution of Naval Architects. A study of builders' models is useful as well, provided that one does not take them too seriously, and many popular accounts have been written describing the principles of torpedoes and naval gunnery. Also there are illustrated memoirs by naval officers and many novels and stories about the modern navy, including such classics as *The Cruel Sea* by Monsarrat and *The Ship* by Forester. This latter is probably the finest description yet written about the organisation of a cruiser and its application to battle conditions, the ship in question being HMS *Penelope* and the flagship HMS *Cleopatra*, a sister ship to the *Dido*.

The text books give descriptions of how a warship is built and a great deal of detail about plating, ventilation, deck coverings, drawings of typical sections and many illustrations of fittings. Up to 1917 the best-known work on the subject is N. J. McDermaid's *Shipyard Practice as Applied to Warship Construction*, and for the present day, R. N. Newton's *Practical Construction of Warships* (both Longmans, Green & Co.). The current Admiralty *Manual of Seamanship* (two volumes, HMSO, 1952) gives some fine drawings of boats and davits, full descriptions and plans of cable holders and the layout of the forecastle, descriptions of paravanes and their gear, rigging of masts and derricks, towing arrangements and so on. The second volume is a book of great general interest as well, as it has chapters on astronomy, the weather, on tides and charts, map projection and a host of other subjects.

In modelmaking photographs are essential, and in the thirty years in which I have been making models

I have collected thousands of them from the agencies in Fleet Street, from the dockyard ports, from the Naval Photograph Club, and from newspapers, books and periodicals. The collection is a by product of commissions for models; as each one has been finished the pile has grown.

Since I have had a good deal of training in art (which, curiously enough, is important in this connection) and some in engineering and ship draughtsmanship, it seems logical to turn it all to account and make a series of plans for modelmakers. I know they are wanted; apart from other evidence, the number of enquiries I got at *The Model Engineer* Exhibition last autumn conclusively proves it.

I can only make drawings of those ships I knew well and of which I have a lot of information, so that most of them will be before 1940. This is in order to cut guesswork down to the absolute minimum. Each drawing will include a 'lines' plan and a scheme of plating which must necessarily be guessed, but, since the text books and the *Manuals of Seamanship* give typical sections, they will probably not be far wrong. Production will be rather slow, as, although there is nothing in the mere drawing, the piecing together of hundreds of scraps of information into a unified whole is a lengthy process. It takes about ten weeks of full time to make a set of plans of a cruiser that is of any use to modelmakers – about a month for a destroyer.

A model made from a drawing that is as nearly as possible accurate can have historic value in the future. For the *Revenge* has gone now, and Lord Beatty's flagship the *Queen Elizabeth*, and the *Renown* and hosts of others that were the very stuff of our recent naval history. Because of them we are free today from slavery. The contemporary world is generally blind. Nobody thought of making a set of sketches of the *Victory* or the *Temeraire* after they paid off from the Trafalgar campaign, and there were scores of artists who could have done so. Nowadays we have cameras that can take hundreds of pictures at the cost of a pound or two, but nobody had the vision to record the *Nelson* and the *Rodney* in this way at the end of their last commission. It is too late now.

HMS *Dorsetshire* (1929) and Dry Dock Model – Pt 1

The model illustrated here was one of the writer's dreams that came true – a happy outcome for all worthwhile dreams. Ever since, as a small boy, more than fifty years ago, hanging about near No. 1 Dock at

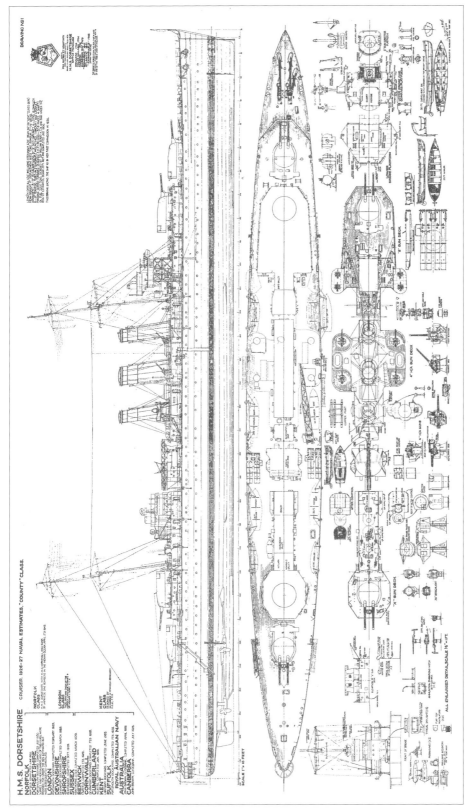

Ough's plans for HMS
Dorsetshire.
(MyTimeMedia)

Kowloon in China, a dock large enough to take the Royal Navy's capital ships in those days, and later, on many visits to Portsmouth Yard, it had always seemed to him that a warship in dry dock is one of the most impressive sights in the world, and with his acquiring some skill in model-making, it seemed an ideal subject, dreamed about and thought about for half a century. Perhaps such thoughts attract the means for realising them for there came a day in 1947 when the Imperial War Museum commissioned him to build just such a model, in full detail, as a historical record of both ship and dock.

The one chosen, No. 14, leading out of No. 3 Basin, is one of the busiest in Portsmouth Yard and also, for a dock able to take large cruisers, one of the widest, thus allowing the magnificent lines of the ship, the 10,000 ton cruiser HMS *Dorsetshire*, to show to great advantage. A dry dock is nearly all straight line geometry and this makes a fine contrast to the long elegant slow-moving curves of a large fast cruiser, for it is this contrast that shows off the form of the ship in high relief.

HMS *Dorsetshire* and her sister ship HMS *Norfolk*, the last of the thirteen 10,000 ton cruisers, was designed by Sir William Berry, KCB, who was responsible also for the four preceding ships, *London*, *Devonshire*, *Shropshire* and *Sussex*, and she belonged to the best period, from the point of view of appearance, of British warship design, being completed in 1930, and perhaps there has never been a time in our naval history, as successive Fleet Reviews between the wars showed, when so much splendour has been seen at sea. A journalist, describing a Review, wrote that never in his life till then had he realised the pictorial beauty of the Fleet, and indeed few who were present on those occasions failed to be awed by the majesty and latent power of these ships. The fate of nations depended on them as the next few years were to show.

The 10,000 ton cruisers were built under the limitations imposed by the Washington Treaty on gun calibre and displacement. Their high freeboard allowed for spacious 8ft high decks and unrivalled accommodation. In profile they were all nearly alike except for the position and shape of the bridge, the 'Kent' class having 21ft more beam and slightly inclined sides with a short armour belt which distinguished them from the later 'London' and 'Norfolk' classes. They were big ships, longer but of less displacement than the heavy cruisers of the period 1900 to 1914. Including the sternwalk their

length overall was 635ft with a beam of 66ft and a mean draught of 17ft. They carried eight 8in guns, two quadruple 21in torpedo tubes and a fairly strong anti-aircraft armament which was later greatly increased. The drawing shows HMS *Dorsetshire* as in her first commission but the model shows the modifications added during her 1937 rearmament, during which the single 4in H/A guns were replaced by twin mountings and the battery was more widely spaced. These ships attained high speeds on their trials - 32.25 knots - and some of them exceeded this in service. HMS *Dorsetshire* was built at Portsmouth Dockyard and completed in July, 1930. She served in the Atlantic and Home Fleets from 1930 to 1933, on the Africa Station from 1933 to 1935 and on the China Station to 1939. She was not destined to have a very long life for, after twelve years of commissions, she was sunk by Japanese dive bombers in the Indian Ocean on April 5th, 1942, whilst in company with HMS *Cornwall*, another 'County' class, which was also sunk in the same action.

The dry docking of a ship is a process requiring a number of precautions apart from the problem of manoeuvring her through the dock gates. When the dock leads from a basin as does No.14 at Portsmouth the placing of the ship in the entrance is comparatively easy, for there is no tidal stream in the basin to interfere, though high winds may. There are usually three tugs in attendance on a large ship, and these are kept secured until her bows are well into the dock and have been taken over by the fore guys which work her along the dock by means of a succession of capstans or mechanical bollards.

Dry docks are provided with large numbers of keel blocks in three long rows and spaced about two feet apart. They consist of five large baulks of timber, stacked one above the other, and chained to the bottom of the dock and to each other, the lowermost of the five and the one above it being shod with steel plates, the latter having a bevel at each end to admit large iron wedges to be driven in so as to force the upper blocks hard up against the keel. The bottom of the dock is slightly inclined downwards towards the entrance for draining so the ship must have enough water over the sill of the dock to enable her to clear the blocks at the forward end. When destroyers are docked some of the blocks at the after end of the side rows are removed to clear the propeller blades as these project below the keel in such vessels, and one or two are removed from the middle line to allow for

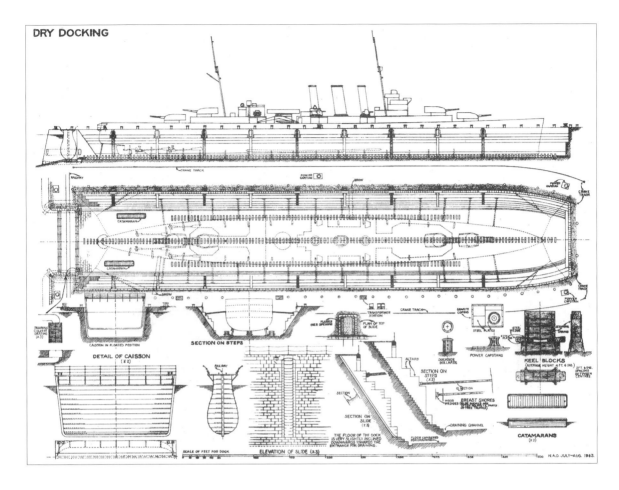

DRY DOCKING

the placing of the 'cut up' shore which supports the overhang of the stern. When the ship has been brought to the correct position in the dock, and this is shown by a painted white mark on the stonework at each side, she is centred over the middle line of keel blocks by the bow and stern lines, final adjustment being made against a wire with a plumb line hanging

from its exact centre and run across the dock at stem and stern. To make the positioning of the ship certain a tackle called a 'handy billy' is fastened to each bow and stern line and hauled taut till stem and stern coincide exactly with the plumblines.

When the ship is truly centred the 'catamarans', which are long wooden pontoons surrounded by a

Ough's plans for Dry Dock model to incorporate HMS *Dorsetshire*. (MyTimeMedia)

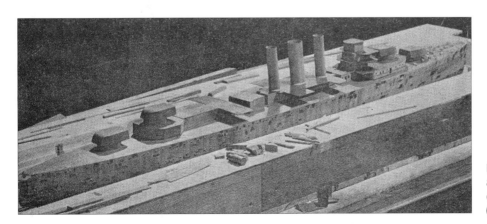

Model HMS *Dorsetshire* and Dry Dock under construction. (MyTimeMedia)

❖

HMS *Dorsetshire* under construction in Ough's workshop. (Courtesy the Ough family)

heavy rope fender, and which are kept in the dock, are brought alongside and from them men paint white marks on the hull exactly on the waterline at stem and stern with others six inches above them. These are called 'suing' marks and their purpose is to show if the ship 'sues' on a level keel fore and aft as she settles down on the blocks when pumping begins. As the water falls ratings from the ship with long-handled scrubbing brushes clean the hull, great care being taken to keep the heavy catamarans clear of the propellers as they work round the stern. At the same time the breast shores, which are long timbers laid from the 'altars' of the dock to the hull, are lowered

into the water by the travelling crane on the dockside. Each shore has a line attached at each end, one line going to the ship and the other to the dock for moving them into a position normal to the curves of the hull. The shores are always set against a deck edge or against a transverse bulkhead so as not to exert a thrust against unsupported shell plating. When they are in position heavy wedges are driven between the heels of the shores and the masonry of the dock to support the ship when she no longer has buoyancy and until the bilge shores are placed. They are all numbered with white painted figures and an abbreviation of the ship's name, their length being

determined approximately before docking from drawings of the ship and the dock.

As the water is pumped from the dock the seacocks for flooding compartments such as magazines and the spirit room are uncovered and these have their gratings removed by the engine room staff and they are connected to the shore hydrants, till finally all the water is cleared and the dockyard 'mateys' cut up and erect any bilge shores that are required for parts of the hull unsupported by the outer rows of keel blocks, the ship's company meanwhile sweeping the dock bottom and altars clear of mud and rubbish.

Finally the 'brows' or gangways are placed in

position and hoses and cables are connected between ship and dock to provide fresh and salt water, electricity and telephonic communication and earthing arrangements. These last are necessary as the ship is insulated by the wooden keel blocks when they dry, and an earth wire is needed in case of lightning striking. All this accounts for the maze of wires, cables and hoses connecting ship and shore. Some of these cables come from the small sheds along the dockside, which are the transformer stations supplying current for the electric welding gear. A number of slopes called 'slides', cut vertically through the masonry of the dock, are for lowering the shores and the planks

Ough working on the *Dorsetshire* / Dry Dock model. (Courtesy the Ough family)

for the painting stages to convenient positions. The ship's cables are cleared entirely from the cable lockers and ranged along the bottom of the dock for examination. Canvas covers are lashed over the funnel tops to keep rain out of the furnaces. After a few days of refitting the ship looks rather forlorn and neglected but, nevertheless, the scene is very colourful – a fine subject for a marine artist. Contrasting with the pale blue-grey of the ship's sides, the broad black stripe at the waterline and the dark red below are the vivid patches of orange-red oxide on scraped metalwork,

the white streaks left by the welders and the occasional hint of bright green weed on the hull set in a ground of brown-grey granite and the mud colour of keel blocks and shores and timbers. But all this seems to vanish overnight when the refit is over and the ship is commissioned again.

There is a lot of work involved in the construction of a model like this requiring hundreds of hours, about 18 months of full time, it having been begun in September, 1947, and completed in March, 1949, when it was handed over to the Imperial War

HMS *Dorsetshire* model in Ough's workshop. (Courtesy the Ough family)

Museum. A description of the methods used and drawings of the dock need to be the subject of another article. The whole work is just over four feet long and the scale is 1in-16ft.

HMS *Dorsetshire* (1929) and Dry Dock Model – Pt 2

The drawing gives a fairly detailed view of the ship after she has been docked down, and of the characteristic features of a dry dock such as No. 14 at Portsmouth Yard, although it is not quite identical. The scale of the original is 1in-50ft so it will be seen that the dock is an immense civil engineering work 700 feet long, measured from inside the caisson, 130 feet wide at the top and 40 feet deep. It is a noble work of architecture as well, being lined throughout with large granite blocks which are finely proportioned in the construction about the nine sloping grooves, five of steps and four of 'slides' for the timber used for cradling the ship, that descend through the steps or 'altars' of the dock down to the granite pavement of the bottom. Such a dock was large enough to take the capital ships of the Navy up to 1914, but since then their greater length, and also that of the battle-cruisers, has required them to be accommodated in 'C' Lock which leads from the harbour into No. 3 Basin. Capital ships being much heavier than cruisers are designed with as large an area of the bottom plating as possible to be built flat so that they can be supported by three rows of keel blocks. For cruisers, which have a noticeable 'rise of floor', the outer rows are not required and they are supported by the bilge shores thrust up against the bilge keels as shown in the sectional drawing which also shows the breast shores supporting the ship laterally. These run from one of the 'altars' of the dock, as the great ledges in its sides are called, to the ship's side, always being placed against a deck edge (shown dotted) and they are driven tight home by wooden wedges placed between the heels of the shores and the masonry.

It will be seen from the plan view that the steps and slides leave great rectangular holes in the dockside so these are planked over with heavy timbers when not in use. A guard rail of stanchions and chains goes all round the edge of the dock and the outer track for the crane runs just inside these, the inner track being thirty feet away beyond the bollards, the crane thus bestriding most of the fittings on the ground. The three small sheds on the starboard side are the transformer stations for the electric welding gear and

these are also well inside the crane tracks. The object on the port side beyond the ship's mainmast in the general view is the 'plate-rack'. It is a structure of channel girders used to hold the spare plates required for a ship undergoing major repairs. On each side of the dock entrance and also half way along and at the fore end are the power capstans which are used for warping the ship along the dock and keeping her over the centre line. They are surrounded by steel plates giving access to the machinery, the plates being surrounded by a granite coping. All along both sides are quantities of wire and grass rope coils, manifold fittings taken off ships, old masts and spars, great drums of electric cable, oil and paint drums, piles of coal and stacks of timber for shores and stages and painting and graving platforms – an orderly disorder of interesting 'junk' which, incidentally, is an old naval term for condemned rope. This was sold at the dockyard gates to ship chandlers who sold it again, with miscellaneous marine oddments, bits of brass, gunmetal, etc., from small shops in the town – whence the term 'junk shops'. Another feature is the long rectangular tool chests, painted dark grey and lettered in white with their owners' names, lying about on deck and around the dock. These are the shipwrights' tool chests, and, among them, here and there, are large interesting-looking packing cases marked 'S.N.S.O. H.M. DOCKYARD, PORTSMOUTH', but what they contain is only *somebody's* business. 'SNSO' means 'Superintending Naval Stores Officer'.

Finally there are the two 'brows' or gangways from ship to shore, one to the quarter deck for the officers and the other, on the port side amidships, for the ship's company and the dockyard workers. These have handrails each side and wheels in the middle for moving them along.

There is a little artistic licence in this model for the boats are always removed from a ship before docking and taken to the boat basin where they can be hauled up on a slip and run into sheds for repairs, but for the sake of completeness of the model of the ship as such they are shown on board. Slung along the ship's side are the paint stages, and the platforms for reaching the propellers for cleaning and burnishing can be seen under the starboard quarter in the close-up view of the stern. The two 'catamarans' belonging to the dock are shown on the plan view near the stern. They are of heavy unpainted timber and are surrounded by a double length of very thick grass rope to act as a fender.

These and all the other appurtenances of a dry

dock are mellowed by decades of grime which, in some lights, gives a splendid colour harmony, a joy to the eye of an artist.

The most important single item in the dock is the caisson or entrance gate. These are of several kinds and in old time docks the opening was closed by two huge wooden doors which met at the centre in an obtuse angle so that the pressure of water outside would force them together and ensure a water-tight seal. Nowadays the most usual type is the one shown on the drawing, the floating caisson, which is in fact a small ship able to be towed into the entrance and sunk into a groove in the masonry. For making the seal it has a massive flange which fits easily into the groove, the water pressure forcing the flange against the inner face of the groove when the dock is being pumped out. A diver is sent down before the caisson is worked into position to make sure there is no rubbish fallen into the groove to prevent it sinking properly as its deck needs to be flush with the ground since a railway runs over it to and from other parts of the yard. Just inside the dock near the caisson is a tunnel in the masonry large enough to allow a man to walk through. This is the flooding culvert which admits water from the basin outside when the ship is to be floated out, and it is a fine sight to see the water rush through at full bore into the dock, clearing from its path the accumulated rubbish left by the refitting of the ship. At the bottom of the dock, in the extreme corner below the flooding culvert, is the draining culvert, a rectangular cavity covered by an iron grating, leading to a tunnel to the basin by way of the pumping machinery. The drawing shows the ship as she would be after pumping has finished, with the bilge and breast shores and the 'cut-up' shore supporting the stern in place, and the bow and stern lines, used for centring her over the blocks, in position with the 'docking tackles' for final adjustment on them. There are 148 keel blocks along the middle line and 90 in each of the two side rows, 328 altogether.

In building this model the writer began with the hull of the ship, which was made of American whitewood to give a good deck colour on its upper surface, and this was given a coat of priming all over, except the deck, and then 'plated' with strips of typewriter paper to represent the strakes, the paper having first been painted to waterproof it against the dilute Seccotine used for holding it to the hull. The ports were cut in by punching indents in the paper and inserting discs of thin perspex cut with the same punch, the material having first been painted black on one side. This method gives a perfect representation of a scuttle, the 'rigols' above them being formed of bent wire stuck on. The planking of the deck was then lined off with a hard pencil and the surface was painted with model aircraft clear dope which fixed the lines and darkened them without making them over emphatic.

The hull being completed, the keel blocks were next made and laid out on a heavy sheet of plywood which had previously been marked with a scriber to represent the masonry of the dock floor, the whole being eventually lowered into the completed model of the dock with the model invisibly screwed on to it and with the bilge shores and the 'cut-up' shore in place. The keel blocks themselves were all made of separate timbers machined out on a power saw and cut up into the right lengths, that is 1,640 separate pieces and 656 smaller ones to represent the steel wedges. The chains had to be shown by fine cotton, the blocks being gummed together. The masts and spars of the ship model were all made from brass or steel wire ground to the appropriate taper and assembled by fine soldering. The 8in guns were turned from duralumin.

The dock was coated with white priming paint preparatory to adding the broken colour for the masonry, the lines defining which were scratched through this colour with a scriber so revealing the white. The whole was then streaked down with a very thin oil mixture of burnt umber and black by a process known to artists as 'dragging' and which is done with a nearly dry brush. It was here that the writer's training as a figure and landscape artist helped, for in a work of this kind, which is in the context of art as well as craft, the control of tone in the colour is critical, any very positive colour being 'off key'. However, the exposure of the model to the atmosphere of the workshop during the months leading to completion helped the unity of tone.

There is not much to add about the construction of the dock as it was straightforward carpentry, but the multitude of steps were made by cutting lengths of them with a home-made miniature 'spindle' and cross cutting them to fit.

8
❖ DESTROYERS ❖

It would appear that there are at least six model destroyers made by Ough that are held in various museums but others, like many of his models, seem to have disappeared without trace since the 1960s.

HMS *Daring* (1932)

The first model of *Daring* that we know of was commissioned by Lord Mountbatten, its being his first command. A waterline model was built by Ough to a scale of 1in-12ft, which is larger than his usual 1in-16ft work, and was made during August 1934 to February 1935 from Admiralty 'as fitted' drawings and from sketches made on board.

Mountbatten mentions in a letter he wrote in July 1979 that Ough

lived on board *Daring* for a number of days getting the specialised particulars of the ship for although he had all the Admiralty drawings of the class obviously the *Daring* herself was different and he even made a model of the little Vosper jolley [*sic*] boat I used to use for water

ski-ing which was onboard. I was told by the maker of the model of HMS *Hampshire*, also on display, that other model makers considered Norman Ough, the greatest master of the craft of this century.

This particular model of *Daring* was exhibited at the 1951 Model Engineer Exhibition in London. It was then loaned to the museum at the Royal Naval College Dartmouth for a while before being returned to the Mountbatten home at Broadlands, in Hampshire, where it is still cared for.

The other *Daring* model known to be in existence is also a waterline version but made to the smaller scale of 1in-16ft. A plaque on the display base states it is a model

Ough working on model of HMS *Daring* for Mountbatten. (Courtesy the Ough family)

HMS *Daring* under construction in Ough's workshop. (Courtesy the Ough family)

Below: Part-finished HMS *Daring* in Ough's workshop. (Courtesy the Ough family)

Bottom: Completed model of HMS *Daring* for Mountbatten in Ough's workshop. (Courtesy the Ough family)

of 'HMS *Daring* – First Destroyer Mediterranean Fleet, April–December 1934'. It now forms part of the National Maritime Museum (NMM, Collection No. SLR 1504).

HMS *Cygnet* (1932)

This waterline model of a 'C' class destroyer is built to a scale of 1in–16ft and shown in a diorama, on a shared scenic base, with HMS *Queen Elizabeth* (NMM Collection No. SLR 1414) and an Admiralty steam drifter HMS *Crescent Moon* (as described in the chapter on 'Capital Ships'). *Cygnet* was built from Admiralty 'as fitted' drawings in April 1933 for the Royal United Service Museum (RUSM) and remained there until the museum closed in the 1960s. It may well have been at this time that the model was incorporated into the diorama by Ough and

Model of H. M. S. Daring,
1st Destroyer Flotilla,
Mediterranean Fleet,
Scale 1" = 12'.

Made for
Commander Lord Louis Mountbatten K. C. V. O., R. N.,
Captain.

View of starboard
quarter.

Norman A. Ough.
Late. 1934-35.

Made from Admiralty "as fitted" drawings, and
from sketches made on board.
August 1934. — Feb. 1935.

Wallace Heaton Ltd
30 Conduit Row 86.
New W. photo

Ough's writing on the back of his picture of Mountbatten's HMS *Daring* model. Note the early NAO logo stamp. (Courtesy the Ough family)

Letter from Mountbatten to Ough's cousin about the model of HMS *Daring* (Mountbatten was assassinated a month later). (Courtesy the Ough family)

when he also updated the model of *Queen Elizabeth. Cygnet* has an individual collection number (SLR 1500).

HMS *Barfleur* (1943)

The 'Battle' class destroyer *Barfleur* was originally built by Ough for the RUSM as a waterline model to the scale of 1in-16ft. She was later displayed in a scenic base with the model of HMS *Illustrious* (NMM Collection No. SLR 1544), mentioned in the chapter on 'Aircraft Carriers', and was eventually acquired by the NMM (Collection No. SLR 1576).

HMS *Warwick* (1918)

This model is another one that has been 'adapted' from one configuration to another during its lifetime. Originally *Warwick* was built by Ough as a waterline model to a scale of 1in-16ft for the RUSM. She was depicted in her original configuration as a minelayer, bearing pennant number D25, but was later altered by him to her appearance as in the Zeebrugge raid in 1918, showing the flag of Vice Admiral Sir Roger Keyes, and her pennant number changed to H43. The model is now in the possession of the NMM (Collection No. SLR 1446).

BROADLANDS,
ROMSEY,
HAMPSHIRE.
SO5 9ZD.

TELEPHONE
ROMSEY (0794) 513333

20th July, 1979

Dear Mrs Taylor,

Thank you for your letter of the 12th July. I am so glad you enjoyed your visit to Broadlands.

How interesting that the great model maker, Norman Ough, was a cousin of yours. He actually lived onboard the DARING for a number of days getting the specialised particulars of the ship for although he had all the Admiralty drawings of the class obviously the DARING herself was different and he even made a model of the little Vosper jolley boat I used to use for water ski-ing which was onboard.

I was told by the maker of the model of HMS HAMPSHIRE, also on display, that other model makers considered Norman Ough, the greatest master of the craft of this century.

Yours sincerely

Mountbatten of Burma

Model of HMS *Cygnet*
under construction in
Ough's workshop.
(Courtesy the Ough family)

HMS *Nestor* (1915)

This model is also discussed in the chapter 'Capital Ships' under HMS *Repulse* (1916). Both these models were auctioned by Christie's at their South Kensington Maritime Auction in May 2006 and, unfortunately, it has not been possible to ascertain who bought the models or where they are now. *Nestor* was an 'M' class destroyer that was sunk on 31 May 1916 at the battle of Jutland. Ough's waterline model of her was built to a scale of 1in–32ft, displayed on a plinth and sealed within a glazed wooden display case. The base of the plinth had been signed by Ough although no date of build appears to have been given.

Ough published various articles on destroyers, two of which are reproduced below. As mentioned in the chapter on 'Cruisers', it has been decided that not all need to be included as they often repeat what he had written in other articles. These 'omitted' articles are listed in the Bibliography for those who wish to refer to them at a later date.

Ough's photograph after his alteration of the HMS *Warwick* model. (Courtesy the Ough family)

Model of HMS *Warwick* as originally built by Ough. (Courtesy the Ough family)

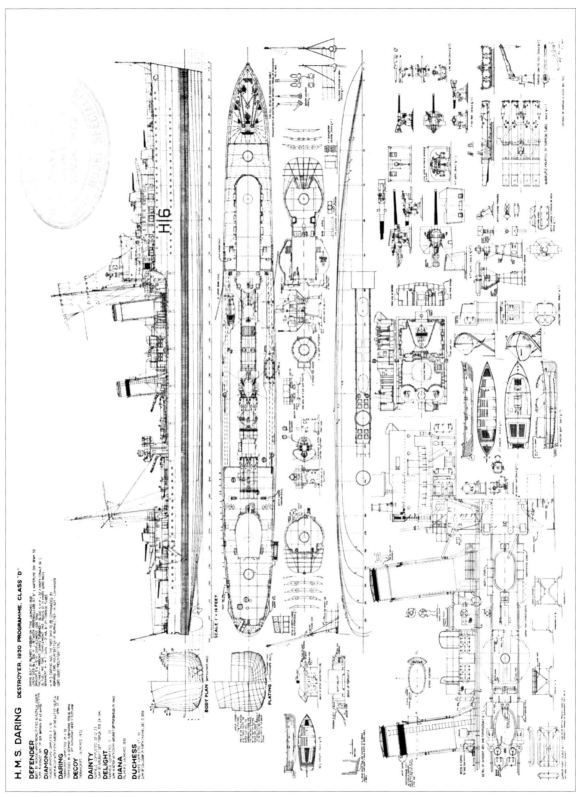

Ough's plans for HMS *Daring*. (ss Great Britain Trust)

Ough's 1in-32ft scale model of HMS *Nestor*. (Bridgeman Images – CH2644968)

Drawings of Warships - HMS *Daring* (1932)

Since my drawings of warships have been published, I have had letters from all over the world requesting prints from the originals. This is most gratifying, as the drawings are intended to be a small service to the hundreds of people who are interested in the ships of the Royal Navy *of our own time*, and who can never get detailed (and reasonably probable) plans of them. Once again, without recourse to official information, here are the essential facts, for modelmakers, of a typical destroyer of the immediate pre-war period – ships that did tremendous service in the years 1939–1945.

With only slight differences, which can be seen in photographs, this drawing covers the 'A', 'B', 'C', 'D', 'E', 'F', 'G' and 'H' classes of destroyers, about sixty ships, since each class built consisted of about eight, except the 'C' class (*Crusader*, *Crescent*, *Comet* and *Cygnet*) of four, and which had slightly different bridgework.

The information for making this drawing came largely from photographs of a model of *Daring* I made in 1934 for Commander Lord Louis Mountbatten (now Admiral Earl Mountbatten of Burma) as the ship was his first command. The model, which was exhibited in the *Model Engineer* Exhibition in 1951, is now at the Royal Naval College at Dartmouth.

Perhaps no destroyers in the Navy have ever so combined the appearance of power and efficiency with such elegance and beauty of proportion.

A model built from the original of this drawing, to a scale of 1/8in-1ft, would be 3ft 5 1/8in long overall, and have a beam of 4 1/8in and a draught of 1 1/4in; the calculated displacement (without distortion of the hull lines) being between 4 1/2 and 5lb. With all-steel construction and with jelly-acid accumulators, it could be powered to run four or five miles, and the steering could be radio-controlled.

Adding full detail to a working model is perfectly feasible and is very much justified by results. It all shows at distances up to 100ft (about 2 scale miles) and 'at sea' the model is almost indistinguishable from reality.

But to show detail it is necessary to get the information for it, and it is for this reason that I am making my drawings to consist of an upper half showing the general arrangement suitable for a model of scale of 1/16in-1ft or smaller, and a lower half showing enlarged detail of the fittings to a scale of 1/8in-1ft for working models. Modern warships are very long – even a small destroyer is longer than the *Victory* – so the latter scale probably represents the upper limit for most modelmakers.

To make a model that has 'character' it is necessary to show as much as possible of the detail of guns and torpedo tubes, range-finders and bridge fittings and so on, almost endlessly! My collection of photographs covers most of these requirements, which, when embodied in drawings, can have historical value, and the models made from them can also have this value for later generations. The 'old sailor's models' were always of contemporary ships – hence their importance – the ships they modelled were the equivalents of the *Queen Mary* or the *Vanguard* of today.

[*A drawing of HMS* Matabele *of the 'Tribal' class is published elsewhere, in the chapter 'All Steel Construction', thus covering the development of destroyer design from 1916 to just before the war.*]

A True to Scale Working Model of HMS *Vega* (1917)

If there are still some who think that it is necessary to enlarge the shape of a working model in order to give it sufficient displacement and stability, this surely is the final answer to them.

The model shown in the drawing is to scale in all respects (8 feet to the inch) and has rather more detail than a number of builders' models, especially in the armament. She is, moreover, built entirely of steel with the same number of strakes and the same method of plating as the real ship. A destroyer of this class has sixteen strakes a side (excluding the outer keelplate), with two more to make up the height of the forecastle. These are all shown on the model, the 'out' strakes being of 0.006in tinplate (which is sheet steel tinned both sides) and the 'in' strakes 0.012in to give longitudinal strength. It is not possible to use sheet brass as it does not give enough strength for weight. About a dozen flat frames were worked in after the model was taken off the former and four transverse watertight bulkheads added for safety in operation. These are pierced near the top with a round hole glazed with perspex to allow the light in the engine room to shine aft and illuminate the ports of the wardroom and after cabins, and also those in the superstructure through a hole in the deck below 'X' gun. In the same way a light in the forecastle shines upwards into the wheelhouse, sea cabin and W/T office, and lights the shelter deck ports. You can imagine that it is a pretty sight to see the gleam from the portholes reflected in the waves alongside when the model is running at dusk. A fairly strong light is needed to show well when the model is a couple of scale miles away, which is about 100 feet.

In building an accurate working model of a destroyer or cruiser, three primary conditions must be satisfied, and everything else subordinated to them. They are: (1) power, (2) stability, and (3) seaworthiness. It is the second of these, stability, that is most often neglected.

A model of a destroyer requires power, and lots of it, and also a large radius of action. After some searching for an efficient motor, and after experiments with different kinds, I found that the best is the 'Permag' marine motor, sold by Messrs. Bassett-Lowke. It has a heavy permanent magnet made of a special alloy and gives an astonishing performance at low voltages. It will run on two volts, at four gives a very strong torque, while at six, with reduction gearing, it is likely to damage the propellers if they strike anything. At eight volts the torque is excessive for anything less than a five foot model. I am told that this is about its limit of efficiency, not much increase of power being gained by supplying a higher voltage. In this model, with reduction gearing of two to one, and driving twin screws, it consumes current at one ampere; on heavy load (not reached in the model with scale propellers) it takes up to 5.75 amperes. Only one of these motors is

required to drive a model of a large cruiser. In a twin screw model the propellers must turn opposite ways (clockwise for the starboard screw looking forward) so that four gear wheels are needed to connect them to the motor, one on the end of each shaft, one on the motor, and an idle wheel to cause one of the shafts to turn the opposite way. Since, in motor ships, the shafts do not come inboard parallel it is better to make a box for the gears and drive them by a disc on the gear spindle with two holes in it engaging two pegs on the shaft, thus overcoming the difficulty of driving nonparallel shafts by parallel gear spindles.

Having made the gearbox it occurred to me that two sets of gears could be fitted to the spindles, one set being a reduction gear of two to one, and the other driving direct, so obtaining two speeds. By having three changes of voltage supplied to the motor a range of six speeds was the very satisfying result. In the first gearbox I made the gears of brass, but these would not stand the stresses imposed by the 'Permag', so in the second version I made them of mild-steel. For the direct drive the gears have 64 teeth, in the reduction gear 42 and 81. I have done the whole thing again with an improved method of changing so that it can be worked by radio.

The second consideration, stability, may be bracketed with the third, seaworthiness, for the two are inseparable. The decks in radio controlled models have to be removable over large areas, and if the model heels over like a yacht when she gets a wind on her beam she is liable to founder. To get stability it is necessary to keep all heavy weights such as motors, gearbox and accumulators, and any radio equipment, as low in the hull as possible, and to make all the superstructure of very thin steel. No metal thicker than 0.006in is used above the forecastle and upper deck. The resulting model is so light that when held in the hand she feels as if she were made of paper, but when all the weights are on board it seems impossible that she should float. Nevertheless she does, showing the right amount of black line above water. Her full load draught is 1 3/4in. It should be 1 1/2in but the incorrect extra 1/4in was accepted in order to carry the third battery for high speed. The portable part of the deck, which is most of the model, formerly was made to rest on a flange 1/16in below the edge of the topstrake of the upper deck, but after a near disaster during trials this was altered so that the deck now goes on to the model like a lid fitting into a rebate so that the connection is nearly invisible. The model is perfectly stable. The forecastle deck still goes on to the internal angle, but she takes very little water

Ough's plans
for HMS *Vega*.
(ss Great
Britain Trust)

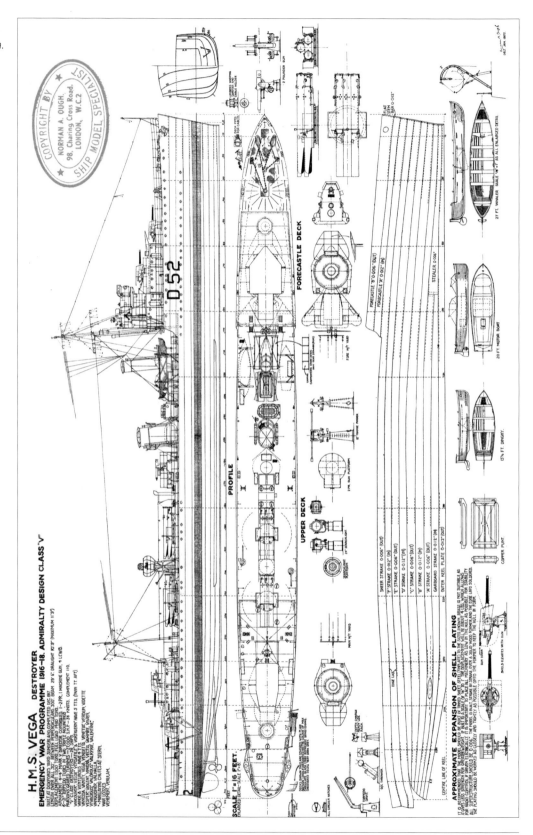

over the bows even in a heavy sea on account of the pronounced 'flare' that all destroyers have, and which can be seen in section No. 30 on the drawing.

In the Exide 'PRA3S' 2 volt jelly-acid accumulators lies the solution of the stability problem. Three of these in series give the 6 volts for full power and if the motor is taking 1 ampere they will drive it for 3 hours. They weigh 11ozs so the three are only just over 2lb and, with the motor and gearbox, they give a concentrated weight well below waterline. The present retail price of the 2 volt cells probably compares favourably with the cost of other small unspillable accumulators, and they have a steady discharge rate for a long period, the falling off occurring right at the end of a run. On a bench test of the destroyer the revolutions were nearly constant till the end of the third hour, falling off occurring after that, the motor stopping after 3 1/4 hours. A wet acid accumulator which has to stand upright is quite useless for driving a true to scale model of any destroyer (even the 'Tribals') of this scale. At full power the three cells will drive the model 400 scale miles – about as far from Lambeth Bridge to the Tower.

The picture was taken by *The Model Engineer* photographer under difficult conditions. Owing to the wind on the Round Pond it was unsafe to let the model go free, so she had to be bridled with an ignominious piece of line through the bow fairlead. The wind was strong, rising to squalls, and I had to keep pulling at the line to keep her in range of the camera, at the same time trying to avoid dogs, swans, small boys and chairs with people in them, on the edge of the water, so we could not get a completely full speed picture. And the model is under way with the anchor fly flying at the bows, a bad mistake! The 'A' flag at the yardarm means that she is still running trials. All the same, the photograph of her at nearly full speed is very fine, as it was taken in a few seconds of calm, and it shows the grace and elegance of a destroyer and the beautiful form of the bow wave as it curves along the pale blue-grey side. The two black bands on the after funnel denote that she belongs to the 2nd Flotilla of the Mediterranean Fleet.

Destroyers are the 'maids of all work' of the Fleet, but in peace time they are always immaculate, and no other warships give so strong an impression of vicious power and speed. As C. S. Forester has said of light cruisers, 'they are eggshells packed with sledgehammers'. Only the most perfect shipbuilding enables them to stand the strains of their never-ending duties in time of war. The famous 'V' and 'W' classes were in their day, in the early twenties, the most powerful destroyers afloat, and many of them served in the two great wars, and all over the world in the years between.

Working model of HMS *Vega* under way at the Round Pond, Kensington in London. (MyTimeMedia)

9
❖ OTHER COLLECTIONS AND ❖
MISCELLANEOUS MODELS

Although individual models have been mentioned in previous chapters, the following sections relate to 'multi-model' collections of Ough's work, which are known either to have been in existence in the past or can still be found at various locations, also other models that have a connection with Ough but that have not been included elsewhere.

Mountbatten Collection

Although Ough was commissioned by Lord Louis Mountbatten to build a model of HMS *Daring* in 1935, as mentioned in the chapter on 'Destroyers', he was also asked to build smaller models of all the ships that Mountbatten had served in. These twenty 1in–50ft scale models are now displayed in the 'Ships' Passage' at Broadlands, the Mountbatten family home in Romsey, Hampshire. This unique miniature 'fleet' includes the first ship he joined, Admiral Sir

1. HMS *Lion* (with missing centre turret). Served as Midshipman. Midshipman of the Fore-Top Division. 1916.

2. HMS *Queen Elizabeth*. Served as Midshipman 1917–18. Returned to this ship as a Lieutenant and also Lieutenant Commander serving as Assistant Fleet Wireless Officer. 1928.

3. HM Submarine *K.6*. Served as a Midshipman for training (lent from HMS *Queen Elizabeth*). 1918.

4. HMS *P.31*. Sub Lieutenant (acting as First Lieutenant). 1918.

5. HMS *Renown*. Sub Lieutenant and Lieutenant. Aide-de-Camp to Prince of Wales for his tour to Australia and New Zealand in 1920 and to the Far East in 1921–2.

6. HMS *Repulse*. Lieutenant. Served as Assistant Torpedo Lieutenant. 1921.

7. HMS *Weymouth*. Lieutenant. Served as Flag Lieutenant and Fleet Wireless & Signals Officer. 1926.

8. HMS *Warspite*. Lieutenant. Served as Assistant Fleet Wireless Officer. 1927.

9. HMS *Resolution*. Lieutenant Commander. Served as Fleet Wireless Officer. 1928.

10. HMS *Stuart*. Lieutenant Commander. Served as Fleet Wireless Officer. 1932.

11. HMS *Daring*. Commander. Commanding Officer. 1934.

12. HMS *Wishart*. Commander. Commanding Officer. 1935.

13. HMS *Kelly*. Captain. Commanding Officer. Captain (D) 5th Destroyer Flotilla. 1941.

14. HMS *Illustrious*. Captain. Commanding Officer. 1941.

David Beatty's flagship HMS *Lion*, depicted as she was after the battle of Jutland with her centre gun turret missing. It also comprises HMS *Renown* in which Mountbatten, first as a Sub Lieutenant and then Lieutenant, accompanied his cousin the Prince of Wales as an *aide-de-camp* on his tours of Australasia in 1920 and the Far East in 1921–2. The models are displayed in a series of floodlit dioramas with painted backdrops of the Grand Harbour Malta, the Firth of Forth, Spithead and Portsmouth. Earl Mountbatten started his naval career as a 16-year-old midshipman and rose to become an Admiral of the Fleet, eventually becoming First Lord of the Admiralty like his father before him.

The pictures show the ships displayed and also the rank Mountbatten was when he served in them.

The Jutland Fleet – Imperial War Museum

While at Exeter Art School Ough began a model of the Grand Fleet, on a scale of 1in-100ft, and applied to the chief of the Naval Section of the British Government Pavilion

17. HMS *Surprise* (Commander in Chief's Dispatch Vessel). Admiral Commander in Chief Allied Forces Mediterranean. 1954.

18. HMS *Glasgow*. Admiral. Commander in Chief Mediterranean Fleet. 1954.

15. HMS *Sister Anne* (Headquarters Ship). Acting Vice Admiral - Chief of Combined Operations. 1943.

19. HMS *President*. (Borne on Ship's Books at various times.)

16. HMS *Liverpool*. Rear Admiral and Vice Admiral. Flag Officer 1st Cruiser Squadron. 1949.

at the 1925 Wembley Exhibition. As an example of his work he showed a small-scale model of HMS *Hood* to the adjudicator (a 1in-100ft model described in the chapter on 'Capital Ships') and was told that if he finished his model of the fleet in time he could show it at the Exhibition. Although this was a remarkable undertaking, Ough did in fact finish the model on time and it was shown at the Wembley Exhibition, after which he sold it to the Royal United Service Institution.

The Grand Fleet model was intended to show the composition of the fleet at the battle of Jutland and depicted the 151 British ships that took part in the engagement. When the Royal United Service Institution museum closed in 1962 the model was acquired by the Imperial War Museum where it is now held in storage. It appears that some of the individual ship models have become detached from the baseboards and the whole diorama now requires a major restoration to achieve its former state. The

ships were set on four panels each measuring 80in by 13in and, at the time of the Wembley Exhibition in 1925, it was displayed in a glass case. It would have been a fitting tribute to Ough if this model could have been restored for the centenary of the battle of Jutland in 2016.

The ships depicted in the diorama are:

Battle fleet

2nd battle squadron

1st division: *King George V, Ajax, Centurion, Erin.*

2nd division: *Orion, Monarch, Conqueror, Thunderer.*

4th battle squadron

3rd division: *Iron Duke* (Fleet Flagship), *Royal Oak, Superb, Canada.*

4th division: *Benbow, Bellerophon, Temeraire, Vanguard.*

1st battle squadron

5th division: *Colossus, Collingwood, Neptune, St. Vincent.*

6th division: *Marlborough, Revenge, Hercules, Agincourt.*

Cabinet at the RUSM displaying Ough's 151 ships of the Grand Fleet at Jutland. (Courtesy the Ough family)

Attached battle cruisers

3rd battle cruiser squadron: *Invincible, Inflexible, Indomitable.*

Cruisers

1st cruiser squadron: *Defence, Warrior, Duke of Edinburgh, Black Prince.*

2nd cruiser squadron: *Monitor, Hampshire, Cochrane, Shannon.*

Light cruisers

4th light cruiser squadron: *Calliope, Constance, Caroline, Royalist, Comus, Boadicea, Blanche, Bellona, Active, Canterbury, Chester.*

Destroyers

12th flotilla: *Faulknor, Marksman, Obedient, Maenad, Opal, Mary Rose, Marvel, Menace, Nessus, Narwhal, Mindful, Onslaught, Munster, Nonsuch, Noble, Mischief.*

11th flotilla: *Castor, Kempenfelt, Ossory, Mystic, Moon, Morning Star, Magic, Mounsey, Mandate, Marne, Manners, Michael, Martial, Milbrook.*

4th flotilla: *Tipperary, Broke, Sparrowhawk, Achates, Contest, Porpoise, Shark, Spitfire, Acasta, Unity, Ophelia, Garland, Christopher, Ambuscade, Owl, Ardent, Hardy, Fortune, Midge.*

Attached to battle fleet: *Oak, Abdiel.*

Battle cruiser fleet

Fleet flagship: *Lion.*

1st battle cruiser squadron: *Princess Royal, Queen Mary, Tiger.*

2nd battle cruiser squadron: *New Zealand, Indefatigable.*

5th battle squadron: *Barham, Valiant, Warspite, Malaya.*

Light cruisers

1st light cruiser squadron: *Galatea, Phaeton, Inconstant, Cordelia.*

2nd light cruiser squadron: *Southampton, Nottingham, Dublin, Birmingham.*

Destroyers

1st flotilla: *Fearless* (light cruiser), *Acheron, Ariel, Attack, Hydra, Badger, Goshawk, Defender, Lizard, Lapwing.*

13th flotilla: *Champion* (light cruiser), *Nestor, Nomad, Narborough, Obdurate, Petard, Pelican, Nerissa, Onslow, Moresby, Nicator.*

9th and 10th flotillas: *Lydiard, Liberty, Laurel, Landrail, Moorsom, Morris, Turbulent, Termagent.*

Seaplane carrier: *Engadine.*

Royal Albert Memorial Museum

Ough's modelling career really started at the Royal Albert Memorial Museum (RAMM) in Exeter. When he was at Exeter Art

College he built a working model of a sailing ship that he used to sail in Dawlish Bay, Devon when he was a boy. The model was shown at the Exeter Museum and as a result the then curator commissioned Ough, in the mid-1920s, to build a series of models showing the development of ships through the ages. He built fourteen models; in fact one of them, an Elizabethan galleon, had not yet been finished when he was interviewed for *Ships and Ship Models* magazine in 1932. The present curators at Exeter Museum were most helpful when approached with a request for help in tracking down these models but it appears they could give only a possible identification to five models that may have been donated to the museum. These were:

Roman Merchant Ship (accession no. 11/1924)
Norman Ship Model (accession no. 18/1924)
Kings Great Ship Model (accession no. 70/1924)
Viking Ship Model (accession no. 80/1924)
Caravel Ship Model (accession no. 1/1925)

This suggests that only the above were donated but, unfortunately, their location is now unknown as they were not identified during the collections inventory held in 2005. They may have been loaned or transferred elsewhere, but records are incomplete. It appears that the museum does have a number of ship models in storage which have lost their associated accession numbers and it may be possible that one or more of them could be an Ough model. The museum holds in their archives:

Old display label for the Roman Merchant Ship giving some detail.
Old display label for 'Rigged Model of an English Hoy 1700–1730' loaned by Ough.
Old display label for two ships donated by others but 'restored by Ough'.
Small number of letters between Ough and Rowley (Curator).

Exhibition Catalogue (1931) of model ships – all loaned items but limited detail given.

The museum staff are very much aware that their ship model collection requires further research to positively identify their models and to investigate the provenance and significance of each one of them. Loan collections are by their very nature difficult to keep track of. As an example, it is known from family papers that in 1927 Ough supplied the Exeter Museum Loan Collection with a 1in-32ft model of HMS *Revenge*. This model appears to be the one now held by the Imperial War Museum (Catalogue No. MOD143).

Another model that appears to have had connections with the RAMM, but has now been identified as being held by Plymouth City Museum, is that of a full hull model of HMS *Hood* built to a scale of 1in-32ft. One of Ough's photographs depicts this model; written on the back is 'Dr Worthington Collection. Exon. 1927'. Robert Alfred Worthington FRCS (1878–1945) was the son of Arthur Worthington FRS, professor of physics successively at HM Dockyard School, Portsmouth, the Royal Naval Engineering College, Devonport and the Royal Naval College, Greenwich. This appears to be where the naval connection lies even though Robert himself was a surgeon and, in his spare time, an accomplished artist. He was appointed a governor of the Exeter Museum and loaned a number of pictures and other items to them. The model of HMS *Hood*, which appears to have been his, is now part of the Harmsworth Collection at Plymouth City Museum. Ough's name and address feature on the base of the mount and the dates of when it was made is given as July to October 1927.

The Royal United Service Museum
The Royal United Service Museum (RUSM) has been mentioned in other chapters with regard to Ough's individual models, and the diorama model depicting

Top: Ough's model of HMS *Revenge* in his workshop. (Courtesy the Ough family)

Left: HMS *Hood* in Ough's workshop (model now held at Plymouth City Museum). (Courtesy the Ough family)

the 151 ships of the Jutland Fleet, which was sold to the museum after its display at the 1925 Wembley Exhibition, was described above.

The museum used to be located in the Banqueting Hall of the old Whitehall Palace, London. In the crypt a series of models was displayed depicting the introduction of steam into the Navy, as well as more modern versions. Ough built a series of waterline models of the principal types of ships in the Navy of the day, that is, the 1920s–30s, specifically for the Museum. Captain Altham RN, the then curator, said in an interview for *Ships and Ship Models* magazine in April 1932:

they are probably the most accurate and detailed ship models in existence. They are 1/16ins scale, and have been reproduced, by courtesy of the Admiralty, from the original ship's drawings. So exact are they in every particular, including the colouring and metal work, that a photograph of one of these models against a suitable background is indistinguishable from the ship herself.

The series of ships displayed included the battleship *Queen Elizabeth*, the cruiser *London*, the destroyer *Warwick*, the submarine *Osiris* and a sloop minesweeper plus the aircraft carrier *Glorious*.

In 1962 the government of the day reclaimed the Banqueting Hall for their own use and all the exhibits, including the ship models, were dispersed or sold off. *Queen Elizabeth* and *Warwick* were acquired

❖

Top: Model 'Admiral's Barge' believed to have been restored by Ough. (Courtesy the Ough family)

Left: Model 32ft naval cutter believed to have been restored by Ough. (Courtesy the Ough family)

by the National Maritime Museum (NMM), *Osiris* went to the Imperial War Museum (IWM) and *Glorious* is now held by the Fleet Air Arm Museum at Yeovilton. The 'sloop minesweeper' could well be HMS *Dartmoor* (1917) modelled by Ough and now held by the IWM (Catalogue No. MOD840). In addition it is believed that the model of the destroyer HMS *Barfleur*, now held at the NMM, was originally built for the RUSM.

Ough also restored models for the RUSM and among his photographs are two depicting models of an Admiral's barge and a 32ft naval cutter, both to the scale of 1in-4ft (1/48). His notes state that they were restored by him in 1933 and that they were 'Admiralty models of boats belonging to a model of HM Frigate *Medway* (1730)'. This frigate appears to be the *Medway* actually built in 1693. She was a 60-gun Fourth-Rate ship of the line, rebuilt in 1718 and hulked in 1740, and was used by Vice Admiral Sir Stafford Fairborne while he commanded twelve ships in the North Atlantic during the Spanish War of Succession in June 1704.

Admiralty Drifters and HMS *Crescent Moon* (1918)

When displaying his waterline models on scenic bases Ough often incorporated different types of smaller vessels within the diorama. These were often ship's boats or picket boats, but he also often included models of Admiralty steam drifters. Examples of these can be seen alongside the models of HMS *Glorious* (see chapter on 'Aircraft Carriers') and the battleship HMS *Queen Elizabeth*. This latter one was actually named by Ough as HMS *Crescent Moon* and it depicts a 93ft Admiralty steam drifter that was completed in 1918 and used for minesweeping duties during the Second World War (Pennant No. FY5 – later Z28). She is a waterline model built to the same 1in-16ft scale as *Queen Elizabeth*.

Miscellaneous Models

Another model, which appears to have been restored by Ough but there is no proof, is that of a three-decker ship of the line made on the typical French Prisoner of War style. Painted in 'Nelson checker' suggests a date after 1803 but unfortunately the figurehead is very indistinct in the photographs, making it difficult to positively identify which ship she depicts. It is also unknown where this model now is or whether it is in fact still in existence.

There are two other models of ship's boats that we do know were made by Ough: a 16ft naval dinghy, to a scale of 1in-8ft (1/96) and built from 'visiting card paper', and a 32ft naval cutter to the same scale and believed to be built from card and notepaper. The fate of the dinghy is unknown but the cutter is now held by the National Maritime Museum (NMM) (Object ID – SLR1819). For this latter model there is an accompanying plaque stating that it was 'Made from an Admiralty drawing and from the sketch of sails and rigging in the 1932 Manual of Seamanship'. It is known to have been constructed in 1933 by laying 'planks' over wooden moulds; when the hull was completed the mould was withdrawn and ribs were then put in. The sails were made of tissue paper.

Unidentified 'three-decker ship of the line' believed to have been either built or restored by Ough. (Courtesy the Ough family)

Steam drifter HMS *Crescent Moon* incorporated within the diorama of HMS *Queen Elizabeth* and HMS *Cygnet*. (© National Maritime Museum, Greenwich, London – SLR 1414)

Ough's model 16ft naval dinghy (1/96 scale) built from card. (Courtesy the Ough family)

The completed model is mounted in one of Ough's handmade glass display cases, but unfortunately one panel of glass in the case has been broken at some stage.

It is at the close of this chapter that the search for other models constructed by Ough must end, or at least be held in abeyance, for the time being. There are certainly more of his models to be 'rediscovered' at some stage in the future, whether they be in private houses or perhaps lying, unrecognised for what they are, in some archive vault of a museum. Hopefully, this book may stimulate others to re-examine models, whether previously catalogued or unidentified, with a view to identifying their true provenance and, perhaps, discover models that have originated from Ough's workshop.

10
❖ SUBMARINES, FRIGATES ❖ AND MINESWEEPERS

A gain, as in groups of ships mentioned in other chapters, very few models of this type by Ough appear to have survived, or if they have, their whereabouts are unknown. At present, only three models that fall within this grouping can actually be illustrated, and of those three only two can be identified as still being in existence.

HMS *Dartmoor* (1917)
This model of an early 'Hunt' class minesweeper, of 'Ailsa' design, was believed to have been built by Ough in 1930. Constructed to a scale of 1in–16ft and depicted as a waterline model, she is at present held by the Imperial War Museum (IWM, Catalogue No. MOD 840). Unfortunately, she appears to be in a sorry state of repair at present with broken rigging and a missing funnel.

HM Submarine *Osiris* (1928)
Commissioned by the Royal United Service Museum (RUSM), this model was built by Ough in 1929 using Admiralty 'as fitted' drawings. Shown as a waterline model to a scale of 1in–16ft, she was acquired by the IWM after the RUSM closed in the 1960s (Catalogue No. MOD 833).

HM Submarine *E.29* (1915)
This was another model commissioned by

the RUSM and built to their 'standard' scale of 1in–16ft. Ough made her from plans published by the Institute of Naval Architects and she is depicted in full hull configuration. The date of construction and the fate of the model are both unknown.

The following articles, written by Ough, were published by *Ships and Ship Models* magazine. Although the technical aspects of building working model submarines probably appear somewhat naive to us in the twenty-first century, in his day Ough was certainly at the forefront of model making technology and appears to have readily adopted the innovations of the day.

'O' Class Submarines (1926-1928)
The 'O' class ships are handsome vessels with a good deal of external detail to interest the miniaturist, while their great length and magnificent lines make them an admirable subject for a dry dock model.

The scale of the original drawing is 1/8in-1ft and if a working model of this size is made it will have a length

Ough's model of HM Submarine *Osiris*. (Imperial War Museum – MOD 833)

Ough's cased full hull model of HM Submarine *E.29*. (Courtesy the Ough family)

of 35 3/8in and a surface displacement of 3.89lb, the scale speed being 1.75 knots to represent 17.5 knots of the real ship on the surface.

If the scale is increased to 1/4in-1ft the displacement will be about 30lb and the scale speed 2.5 knots. This does not seem very large for a model nearly six feet long, but the block coefficient of a submarine, arrived at by calculating from the published figures in *Jane's Fighting Ships* is quite low, 0.498, which is less than that of a destroyer.

The block coefficient, sometimes called the 'coefficient of fineness', is a ratio which can be expressed as a decimal. It is the difference in volume between the amount of water displaced by the immersed part of the hull of a ship and the volume of an oblong block or rectangular prism of the same dimensions the length of the latter being usually that of the length between perpendiculars, the breadth the extreme beam of the ship and the depth that of the draught at the load under consideration. It is often possible to find its approximate value from the figures published in *Jane's Fighting Ships*. Once the value of the ratio is found it is quite easy to estimate the weight of a scale model. The calculation, from the published figures, for HMS *Olympus* is as follows:

Length 283 minus 9ft (as 9ft of the ship before the foremost bulkhead is open to the sea). Beam 28ft and draught 13ft 6in. So that the volume of the block is 274 x 28 x 13.5cu ft = 103,572cu ft. This can be reduced to tons by dividing by 35, since one ton of salt water equals 35cu ft, so the figure corresponds to 2,959 tons. The published displacement of the ship at a draught of 13ft 6in is 1,475 tons so the ratio is 1,475/2,959 which reduces to 0.498.

The block coefficient of an 'O' Class submarine is 0.498 or just under one half. Thus obtained it can be

applied to the calculation of the weight at surface trim of a model of any scale. At the same scale as the original drawing 1/8in-1ft, the figures are as follows: length 34 1/4in x beam 3 1/2in x draught 1 3/4in = 210cu in. So that the volume of displacement is approximately 210/2 = 105cu in. This can be converted to lb weight as 1lb of fresh water is 27cu in, in volume 105/27 = 3.89lb, which is too small for a working model.

Increasing the scale to 3/16in-1ft the figures become: 51in x 5.25in x 2.3in which give a displacement of approximately 11.9lb, a value which allows scope for fitting radio control and a fairly large radius of action. Also the model being over 4ft long, it would look better on the water.

Increasing the scale once more to a 1/4in-1ft the figures are: 68in x 7in x 3 1/2in which correspond to a displacement of 30.1lb nearly.

It will be seen from all this how useful the idea of the block coefficient is in making approximate calculation to decide the scale of a working model, and the use of it has shown that building to the scale of the drawing is really not feasible except as a feat of virtuosity.

To make the templates for a 1/4in scale model from this drawing a convenient method is to take a photograph of the body plan and enlarge it to twice the linear dimensions. By tracing from the photograph and sticking the tracings on to 1mm plywood a set of templates can be made, all the other measurements being taken from the plan and profile by dividers which are turned over once to double the distances.

If riding at the exact trim, shown by the surface water line on the drawing, the row of holes just visible in the free-flooding part of the bow plating coincides exactly with the drawn line on the profile. The displacement of 8lb is for this water line at 1/8in scale.

Ough's plans of HM Submarine *Olympus*. (ss Great
Britain Trust)

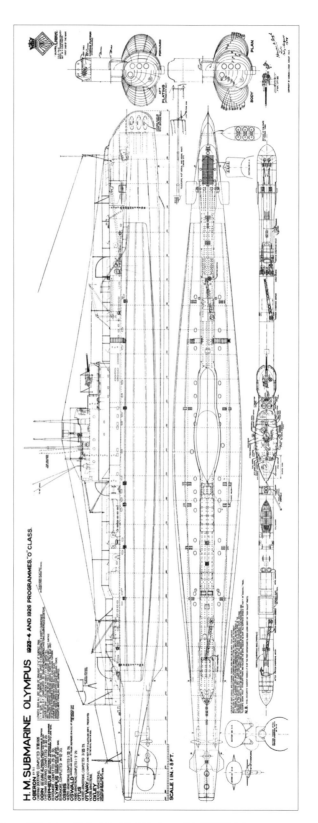

One of the numerous consequences that have
resulted from the publication of this series of plans is
that many craftsmen who have never before made a
ship-model have begun with models built of tinplate
and plated like the real ship from these drawings, and
quite a few have begun with that more difficult and
exacting of all working ship models, a submarine.

Corrections to the above in a subsequent article by Norman Ough

'Would you be so kind as to publish the following
corrections to the figures of the displacement of the 'O'
class submarines given in my article. Those quoted were
from *Jane's Fighting Ships*, but information has just
come to hand that shows that the surface displacement
of the 'O' class was 1,782 tons and not 1,475 tons as
published. Applying this to the calculation shown in my
article the 'block coefficient' becomes 0.61, which is
much bigger than 0.498 derived from the figures given
in *Jane's*. This makes the surface displacement of an
1/8in scale model about 4.6lb and one 3/16in scale
about 13.8lb while that of the 1/4in scale model
becomes about 41.8lb. The figures are, of course, only
approximate, but, even so, they are very useful in
enabling the model maker to estimate the buoyancy
available at a given scale. A further correction: the
volume of 1lb of fresh water should have been given as
27.7cu in and not 27.' – Norman A. Ough.

HMS *Marvel* – 'Algerine' Class Minesweeper (1944) – Pt 1

Continuing my series of detailed plans of HM ships of
the present day, this of an ocean minesweeper is
representative of a very large number of vessels of the
same type. Of the 'Algerine' class there are 85 ships in
commission or in the Reserve Fleet, in the Royal
Canadian and Royal Ceylon Navies and in the South
African Naval Force. All are alike in design except for
minor differences which can be seen in photographs,
as, for example, some have Oerlikon guns instead of
the 40mm Bofors, and a good many have a range-finder
on a small tower platform amidships.

This drawing appears bolder and easier to read than
the others that have been published. The reason is that
as HMS *Marvel* is a small ship, the original could be

made entirely to the scale of 1/8in-1ft and the necessary reduction to fit the two pages needed to be to only about 2 1/4 of its length. It would be quite easy to make a model to any scale from it by reading from the scale of feet on the reproduction to any convenient scale of feet on a ruler or strip of paper suitably divided. A general arrangement drawing such as this, however, does not contain enough information for a detailed model, so a second sheet showing the lines and a scheme of plating, and detail of the boats, armament and elevations of the back and front of the bridge will be published in the second part. In *Model Ships and Power Boats*, an important description of a model of an 'Algerine' class minesweeper, including the calculations for displacement and stability, details of the method of construction of the hull in metal, and of the machinery for electric drive for the twin screws and radio control, was published in April, May, June, and July, 1952. The articles were by Lieut. G. C. Chapman, RN, who served in one of these ships for two years, and who built the radio equipment and parts of the model which was shown working at the *Model Engineer* Exhibition in 1950, and on the stand at the *Daily Express* National Boat Show in January. My drawing has been based on his, the detail being added from photographs that I took on board HMS *Marvel* at Portsmouth in July, 1954. The lines and profile of my drawing are slightly different from those of Lieut. Chapman's, as these were based on the assumption that the length over all of the ship was 225 feet. In the published figures, this is the length between perpendiculars, the length over all being 235 feet. The addition of the missing ten feet has resulted in 'easier' lines and a slight increase of displacement.

Although it is over 400 years since the invention of the submarine mine, happily the evil genius of humanity failed to make it a fully effective weapon until 1904, when it caused devastation in the Russo-Japanese War. The inevitable counter-measure, the minesweeper, was introduced into the Royal Navy in the form of steam trawlers, adapted for the work in 1907. In 1914, it was the fishing fleet that first swept the German mines from the East coast, the heavy casualties among them amounting to the loss of a ship every week. In 1915, the first regular war-built sweepers, the 'Flower' class, appeared, and by the end of the war, the minesweeping flotillas had been expanded to over 1,000 ships, based on 51 ports throughout the world.

The war years 1939–45 produced new types of mines, including the magnetic and acoustic, and sweeping was made more difficult by having to deal with combinations of these as well as the moored mine. The task of clearing them was divided among ships of three classes; small ships for harbours and entrances, slightly larger ones for the shallow coastal areas, the deeper water being assigned to the ocean minesweepers – the 'Algerines'. With the end of the war, our forces diminished, but in 1951, when the Cold War intensified, great attention began to be given to our defences, and the first priority was minesweeping, the mine being at that time regarded as the greatest single threat to the safety of the nation. The Inshore Flotilla of minesweepers based on Harwich is a most active part of Britain's contribution to the naval forces of NATO.

In appearance, the 'Algerines' are, compared with the ugly 'Loch' and 'Castle' class frigates, quite elegant small warships. They would have looked really fine if the transom had been rounded and given a rake aft, and if a fashion plate had been fitted to cover the sudden drop from the end of the forecastle to the upper deck. A slightly larger and taller mainmast raked parallel with the tripod would have completed what has the makings of a fine profile, but in spite of this, as seems appropriate for ships that have to carry out the awful dangerous drudgery of minesweeping, their appearance has the great characteristic of staunchness.

HMS *Marvel* – 'Algerine' Class Minesweeper (1944) – Pt 2

This second drawing of HMS *Marvel* is characteristic of all the others where the lines and detail have to be extended to another sheet. Combined with the photographs and the general arrangement drawing it should give fairly complete information for building a detailed model.

It may have been noticed that, in all these plans the 'boot topping' or the dark band along the water line is shown. The effect of this is to pull the drawing together and make it into a portrait of the ship. For a model, however treated, should be a true portrait, and, depending on the artistic sensibility of the craftsman, and the right selection and emphasis of detail, often is, and always may be, a considerable work of art. What the model will look like can to some extent be seen from the profile on the drawing, and for this reason the explanatory lettering is kept away from it, and confined to the detail.

Perhaps the ideal of ship modelmaking, the logically complete result of it all, is the fully detailed

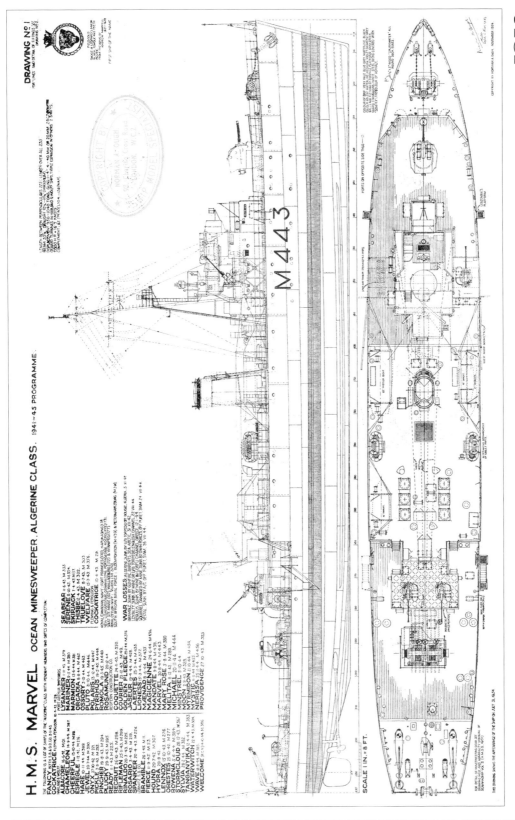

Ough's plans of
HMS *Marvel*.
(ss Great
Britain Trust)

❖

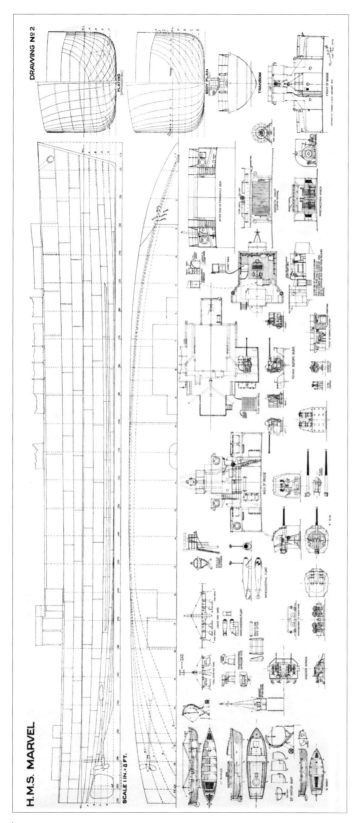

Plating and details plans for HMS *Marvel* drawn by Ough. (ss Great Britain Trust)

working model, either power-driven or sailing, with radio-control. Such a model would combine all the qualities, and include all branches of the art, even to the glass case in which it would be kept. These plans are meant to be inclusive of this ideal, and, since the greater includes the less, they should, in theory, cover all the other requirements. These are equally important, and, as historical records, more important, as they include miniatures, scenic and dry-dock and waterline models of many scales.

These plans are all of contemporary warships, and it must seem that, since they are published fairly often compared with those of other ships, the draughtsman has a 'one-track' mind, without sympathy with other interests. This is far from being the case, since I began with square-rigged models and steam merchant ships more than thirty years ago, and have always tried to guard against 'one-track' tendencies by keeping up an interest in the arts and sciences and especially in philosophy which latter is the surest of antidotes, since it tries to include the whole of 'reality' in a logical system.

The paradox of research in connection with ships of the Royal Navy of today is that one is always looking for information in several places when it already exists in full elsewhere, but in that place is inaccessible. Since most of the information is in London and is in the form of photographs scattered among the Press agencies in Fleet Street, at the Central Office of Information and at the Imperial War Museum, or in the form of builders' and other authorised models, the provincial craftsman does not have much chance to do his own research unless he comes up to London and stays for a week or more – an expensive undertaking. Moreover, it takes a good deal of experience, both of modelmaking and of real warships to piece all this together, combine it with an Admiralty plan from 'P' Branch and reduce it to an intelligible detailed drawing. Even supposing the unhappy modelmaker is also a draughtsman, it would take many months of his spare time before he could begin the model. And spare time is precious. Most craftsmen want to make models in their leisure hours rather than turn into a kind of detective!

These plans are, in their limited way, meant to overcome some of these difficulties. A little research is needed, as photographs always help in putting character into the work, and the purchase of Admiralty Manuals of Seamanship, especially the recent ones, will prove very illuminating in regard to the boat gear, paravanes, derricks and cable arrangements, and many other things besides.

An example of how useful both a photograph and a textbook are is the picture of the minesweeping floats and kite-otters on the stem of HMS *Marvel*. These are shown detailed on the drawing here, but on pp. 441–453 of Vol. II of the *Admiralty Manual of Seamanship* (1951) is a description of the working of the gear, and drawings of the multiplane kite and the marker buoys. The same volume contains information on the working of the bridge fittings (with sketches) and another chapter gives a great amount of detail concerning the boats with their hoisting and stowing arrangements. The perspective drawings of a cutter and a whaler hoisted in the davits which illustrate this section are very fine indeed. Vol. I costs 8s. 6d. and Vol. II £1 0s. 0d., but anyone who buys these books will be well rewarded as, apart from indispensable information for modelmakers, they contain a vast amount of interesting reading of a general nautical character.

Returning to the 'ideal' model before mentioned, which should be fully detailed, power driven, radio controlled, and built true-to-scale from steel (tinplate) with the same strakes and plating as the real ship, thus having all the qualities, this of HMS *Marvel* would be an excellent example. Moreover, apart from the full detail it has already been made and described by Lieut. G. C. Chapman, RN, in the articles referred to previously. The extra weight involved in bringing the fittings to exhibition standard would be negligible, only an ounce or two, assuming the scale to be 1/8in-1ft, slightly larger than Lieut. Chapman's model which was one-hundredth of the linear dimension.

It will be seen in the drawing that the plating is in short lengths as is often the case with small ships. These could be cut from tinplate of 0.006in thickness, giving a very light hull, easy to build over a wood former on which the strakes had been set out from the plating diagram. The frequent 'end laps' or 'butt laps' of the short lengths of plating would tend to give the hull vertical strength. It would require a good many flat transverse frames apart from the bulkheads, as experience has shown that a model hull made from this very thin tinplate requires reinforcement vertically, but these are easily made from flat strips of heavier tinplate (about 0.012in) about 1/8in wide closely soldered inside the shell plating. The curves of the plates can be formed exactly by laying them on a cloth pad on the bench and pushing the wooden handle of a screwdriver to and fro along them. In a few seconds the plate will be given the required curvature.

On this scale (1/8in-1ft) the real ship will be, volume for volume, 884,736 times larger than the model!

11
❖ 'ALL STEEL CONSTRUCTION' ❖

These seven articles, written by Ough in the late 1950s, deal with making working models using tinplate construction and focus on the destroyer HMS *Matabele* as an example. They highlight his metalworking skills as well as his lateral and mathematical thinking when scaling up working drawings.

Some of the plans that illustrate this chapter have had to be copied from the original *Model Maker* magazine as the originals are not available. Although not of the same quality as those in the 'Warship Detail' series, which have been taken from Ough's original work and are now held at the Brunel Institute (ss Great Britain Trust), they are, hopefully, clear enough to illustrate what Ough is writing about.

Various metal working techniques drawn by Ough. (MyTimeMedia)

Part One – Hull Construction

Some readers may be interested in trying a few experiments in one of the most exciting aspects of model engineering, for in these articles a method will be outlined whereby working models of ships may be built from the same material as the real vessels, that is, from sheet steel in the form of tinplate. Those who have tried this method of 'ship building in miniature' are unanimous in saying that they would not again go back to more conventional methods. For it is very much more interesting than carving a model from a block of wood, or building it 'bread and butter' fashion, moreover the finished hull is a shell no thicker than a visiting card, so that there is no loss of internal space, and also, when ports are drilled through the thin strakes and glazed with perspex, the most wonderful effects result from internal lighting, and the completed hull, when the watertight bulkheads are fitted, is exceedingly strong and light, a requirement of the first importance where accurate working models are concerned.

The raw material for the building of working ship models is available everywhere at no cost at all, since it comes from one of those unconsidered marvels of the modem world – the humble but ubiquitous tin can! Soup tins, jam tins, cake tins, biscuit tins, cocoa tins, paint tins and tobacco tins can all be used, the smaller ones for the light plating and those of heavier metal, such as contain the produce of Messrs. Huntley and Palmer, for the shell plating of major ships of war and large liners.

Tinplate is the most fascinating material to play with, since as it costs nothing, it is of no consequence if experiments fail, and to work with it requires no additions to the average household tool outfit in order to discover something of what it can be made to do. The light metal may be cut with old scissors (although these are not suitable for dissecting a petrol can!) and it may be 'dished' or worked into hollow shapes to a surprising extent by laying a piece on a block of wood and striking it with a large nail with its end rounded and driven by a hammer – a process known as 'cold' forging – as shown in (13). If it is required to form a ship's plate having a hollow curve, all that is needed is to cut a strip of tinplate of the right shape, lay it on a table with a thick pad of folded cloth under it, and push the handle of a file or screwdriver along it lengthways. By applying some pressure the plate will soon take a lateral and longitudinal curvature, steeper curves being attained by using smaller wooden tool handles. The face of an old flat iron is suitable for an anvil, giving a fairly level surface.

As soon as a few pieces have been cut from a tin can – squares, triangles, rectangles, or discs and ovals, and their edges have been trued with a file, the mere 'feel' of them will suggest to the experimenter the immense potential that he has in hand, for here is a material having almost limitless possibilities of accuracy in the working, and which can be persuaded into almost any structural form. And an hour's trial will convince him of its greatest quality, for steel is almost a synonym for strength.

The material from which a modern ship is built consists of rolled steel plates of thicknesses governed by her size, that is from 1/8in to over an inch, from three to five feet wide and twenty or more feet long. These, in model work, are represented by plates cut from tins. The framing of the hull and the structure supporting the decks consists of rolled steel angle and channel and 'Z' bar of various kinds, and an additional tool to form these is needed to enable long strips of tinplate to be bent accurately. This tool is the 'scorer' and it is shown in operation in (1). It can be made by grinding it from a length of hacksaw blade by means of an emery wheel. In grinding the recess that leads to the cutting point, it is important to keep the blade cold by frequent dipping in water or the fine point will lose temper and be spoilt. In order to bend tinplate accurately along a line, it is necessary to cut away some of the metal of one surface in a 'V' shaped groove, having a section of 90 degrees as shown in (2), thus enabling it to be bent up at right angles to form angle bar. The use of this tool opens up a great new field of model engineering. For example, by scoring the edge of the plate twice as in

(3), and making the second groove deeper, the strip can be bent backwards along the second line and broken off, thus saving shearing which bends the strip. It is then put in a vice and tapped over at right angles along the remaining groove with a hammer, into a length of angle bar. Solder can then be run along the throat of the angle as shown in (4). The result is a scale model of the commonest unit used in shipbuilding. In (3) and (5) are shown developments of this simple process that lead to the fabrication of other members of the structural steel work of ships, single and double channel bars and 'T' and 'Z' bars. These are built up from angle or single channel soldered back to back as shown in the section in (4). The connecting members, known as 'gusset' plates, are cut from the flat metal as shown in (6). By combining these few elements the most intricate steel structures may be built, such as the framing under the long 'catwalk' of an oil tanker, or the lattice masts of destroyers and frigates.

The separate items of structure and the plates of the hull are connected together by 'tinmans' or plumbers' solder, the cored solder used by electricians being unsuitable because it is too soft, and, in the author's opinion, the best flux to use is Baker's soldering fluid. This is acid and corrosive so the work should be rinsed in water when assembled, and it is advisable to wash the soldering iron after use as well as the acid attacks it. In spite of this, however, it is far more efficient than the greasy fluxes.

The hull plating of the model (in ship building it is called the 'shell' plating) is worked over a wood 'former' which needs to be an accurate wooden model of the hull, and it can be used several times once made. Wood of poor quality can be used for it so long as it is good enough to shape and most of its length may be just a hollow box with thick sides, top and bottom, as shown in section in (9), the ends being carved from joined slabs of wood connected to it. The shell plating of most ships is laid in long strips called 'strakes', half being on the former and the other half being lapped over their edges as shown in section in (10), (11) and (12), the diagram also showing the methods of connecting decks when they are required to be removable. When the shell is completed it is taken off the former.

Part Two – Hull Construction (cont.)
'I'd a foolishness in my head that ships could be builded out of iron: Yes – iron ships! I'd made me a

liddle toy one of iron plates beat out thin – and she floated a wonder!'

RUDYARD KIPLING
– From 'Rewards and Fairies'.

This was said a few years before the Armada in 1588. But Simon Cheyneys, to whom this strange notion came, a shipwright and a burgess of Rye in Sussex, had an aunt, the widow Whitgift, who possessed the second sight, and she dissuaded him from further experiments, saying that England needed wooden ships just then. But she and his friend Francis Drake (it was before he had a 'handle' to his name) took the notion with entire seriousness, both being possessed of vision.

Well, the Hour struck more than a century ago and today the ships of the world are built in accord with Simon's dream in the time of the first Elizabeth. One can imagine something of the intense thrill that he must have felt in trying the model in the nearest brook or in Rye Harbour - undaunted by the laughter of his fellow shipwrights. How he must have brooded over this vast possibility!

But there is no need to imagine – one can do it oneself. As was said in the previous article, the raw material, 'iron plates beat out thin', are to hand in abundance, requiring only to be worked into the form of a model. But a form implies a 'former', made usually of wood from packing cases, and, for most modern ships of any size, it can be a box with thick sides, top, and bottom through most of its length, the top plank running the whole length, the bottom being slightly shorter to allow for the rake back of the stem. These give support to the short lengths put in between them for carving the bows and stern, as shown in (1). Before joining the planks with screws or glue or nails it is usual to paint the joining surfaces liberally with red ink so that it soaks in to the grain. The planks having been sawn out to the appropriate curvature they are assembled red ink face to red ink face. The former will now have a series of steps all round it in places. These are carved and planed away, but the joins will show as red lines all round the hull, which are of great use in getting it symmetrical. When the carving is finished and the 'fashion' plates at the break of the forecastle have been cut from plywood and set in as shown in (1) the 'station' lines shown in the body plan and profile in (3) and in perspective in (8) can be drawn on, and they may be made indelible by cutting them into the wood with

the point of a knife. When these are set out the lines representing the seams of the plating can be drawn on by transferring the measurements on to the station lines with dividers from the body plan section lines. It is then only necessary to draw in the 'out' strakes, or those projecting, as the 'in' strakes are contained within these bounding lines. When, however, the plates for the 'in' strakes are cut they must be made 1/2in wider to allow 1/16in to slide under the 'out' strake on either side. When all the lines are set out the positions of the 'butts' of the plating can be set out along each strake as shown in (3) the plan part of which shows the deck plating. These marks determine the lengths of the separate plates. Where the superstructure joins the decks all the plating inside the area may be omitted, the walls of deck houses, etc., being cut deep enough to pass through and 1/8in below the decks, thus forming a coaming for strength. This saves weight and allows lighting from below to shine into the superstructure.

The model described in these articles is of a destroyer of the 'Tribal' class HMS *Matabele*, built to the standard scale most convenient for working models of ships in the destroyer category – 1/8in-1ft – and having a full load displacement of 5.5lb. For adequate strength the tinplate required for the hull should be 0.008in thick. It would be advantageous to use thinner metal but this is very difficult to work without buckling arising and it requires stiffening with large numbers of flat frames which partly cancel the saving in weight. Material of suitable thickness may be obtained from condensed milk or soup tins, but it is a great convenience to be able to cut it from tinplate sheet which is sold in pieces of 28 1/2in x 20in of varying gauges from 0.004in upwards to quite heavy plate by Wilbraham and Smith Limited, 260 Gray's Inn Road, London, W.C.1, price about 2s. a sheet. This is the only place known to the author where it can be obtained for certain, although some local ironmongers or tool shops stock it but usually not the useful thin metal. Since most of the structure of an l/8in scale model of a destroyer can be built from less than one sheet of 0.008in plate and a fraction of one of 0.005in, it is clear that 'tin can engineering', as it has been called, is not an expensive hobby.

In the 'Tribal' class, and in all destroyers built since, the shell plating has 'end' laps as shown in (4). This means that the end of each plate is made to lap over the forward end of the next plate aft, the

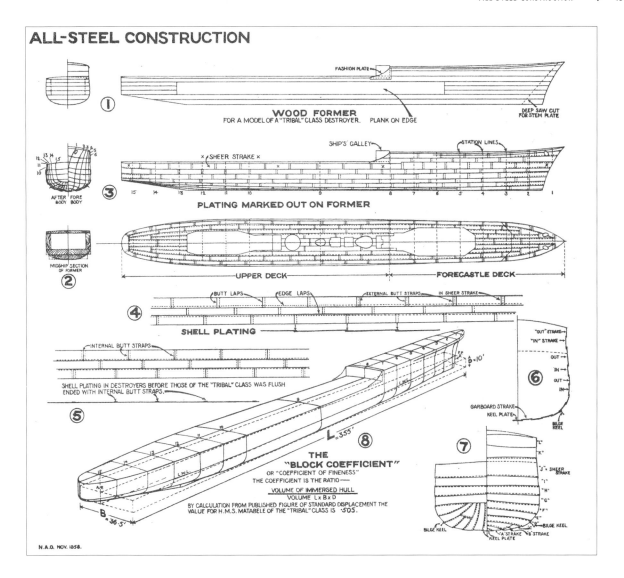

ALL-STEEL CONSTRUCTION

① FASHION PLATE — DEEP SAW CUT FOR STEM PLATE

WOOD FORMER
FOR A MODEL OF A "TRIBAL" CLASS DESTROYER. PLANK ON EDGE

③ AFTER FORE BODY BODY — SHEER STRAKE — SHIP'S GALLEY — STATION LINES

PLATING MARKED OUT ON FORMER

② MIDSHIP SECTION OF FORMER — UPPER DECK — FORECASTLE DECK

④ BUTT LAPS — EDGE LAPS — EXTERNAL BUTT STRAPS — IN SHEER STRAKE

SHELL PLATING

⑤ INTERNAL BUTT STRAPS
SHELL PLATING IN DESTROYERS BEFORE THOSE OF THE "TRIBAL" CLASS WAS FLUSH ENDED WITH INTERNAL BUTT STRAPS.

⑥ "OUT" STRAKE "IN" STRAKE OUT IN OUT IN — GARBOARD STRAKE — KEEL PLATE — BILGE KEEL

⑧ **THE "BLOCK COEFFICIENT"**
OR "COEFFICIENT OF FINENESS"
THE COEFFICIENT IS THE RATIO —
$$\frac{\text{VOLUME OF IMMERSED HULL}}{\text{VOLUME } L \times B \times D}$$
BY CALCULATION FROM PUBLISHED FIGURE OF STANDARD DISPLACEMENT THE VALUE FOR H.M.S. MATABELE OF THE "TRIBAL" CLASS IS ·505.
L = 355' B = 36·5'

⑦ "J" SHEER STRAKE, "L","K","I","H","G","F" — BILGE KEEL — "A" STRAKE "B" STRAKE KEEL PLATE

N.A.O. NOV. 1958.

connection being made by two, three or four rows of rivets or by solder in a model. Prior to the 'Tribal' class the plating was worked flush at the ends, being connected on the inside by a 'butt strap' as shown in (5), the lap over of the horizontal edges of the plates – the 'seams'– being the same in both. As will be seen in (6) which is a section near the after end of the forecastle, the plating is arranged alternately in 'in' and 'out' strakes, the 'in' strakes lying directly on the surface of the former during building. There are no rules as to where to begin the plating; some prefer to start with the keel plate, as in a real ship, and to work away from it on both sides, others lay on the sheer strake, which in a real ship is heavier as it is a main strength member, and to work upwards and downwards from it. As the plating progresses it can be held tight on to the former by binding around with string or with drawing pins. If the strakes show a tendency to lift off the former there is tension somewhere and a few plates should be unsoldered and put back again to remove it or distortion may develop. In all, to complete the hull (without decks), about 380 plates are required. In naval practice the strakes are lettered 'A', 'B', 'C', etc., outwards from the keel plate as shown in (7) the sheer strake being 'J'. This, the keel plate, the garboard strakes, and one along the bilge are of heavier metal than the rest and part of the sheer strake is 'flush butted' with external straps as may be seen in the profile in (3) – a characteristic feature of destroyer hulls, which have

Diagram showing model plating techniques. (MyTimeMedia)

altered very little in form in the past 70 years. Each plate requires to have an exact duplicate made of opposite curvature for the other side, but although there are so many, the majority are rectangles or only slightly tapered and with little curvature. Working them in the short lengths required is a great convenience as it lessens the distortion to which long plates are liable. The plates and seams are connected by 'tinman's' solder (which is the strongest available) run along the edges and ends, both joining surfaces of which need to be 'tinned'. The soldering iron is moved along the seam and followed by a piece of wood held in the free hand to keep the faces together until, in seconds, the metal sets. As some heat goes through plates it is important *not to paint the formers* as the paint will melt and later set and cause the shell to stick to it. If this happens there is real trouble as, even if the shell can be released it may cause damage to remove. The stem plate in the bows is a flat sheet of heavy metal slid into the deep saw cut shown in (1) and cut to the profile of the bow. It is made deep and long where it meets the keel, since it has to receive the shock of collision or of running aground on a hard shore. The plating is lightly soldered to it at first but when the shell is taken off the former more solder is added inside to strengthen the construction. In (2) is a section of the former amidships showing the box arrangement, and the projecting edges of the two planks of the bottom before they are carved away. In (8) is a perspective sketch showing the 'station' lines, the dotted lines being an outline of an imaginary rectangular block of length equal to the length of the model between perpendiculars, depth equal to her draught at full load, and breadth equal to her extreme breadth outside the plating. This is used in calculations for 'displacement' or the amount of water 'displaced' or pushed aside by a body immersed in it, and which is known to be exactly equal to the weight of the body (if it floats) so, if the volume of water displaced by a ship can be calculated the resulting weight expressed in tons, or, in a model, in pounds is the same as the weight of the ship or model. If the weight is increased the model will float deeper thus increasing the 'volume of displacement' which is consequently a function of her draught. In naval architecture the estimation of volume is done by Simpson's Rule which is an application of calculus, but the use of the 'block coefficient' or 'coefficient of fineness' reduces the laborious task to comparative simplicity for fair approximations. The coefficient is

the ratio of the volume of the immersed hull compared to the volume of the imaginary solid L x B x D as shown in (8) and, in the case of destroyers, is almost exactly as 5 is to 10, or 1/2 is to 1, the calculated figure for this model being .505. So the displacement in cubic inches is 1/2 (L x B x D) cu ins and this figure divided by 27 (as 27 cu ins = 1lb of water) gives the weight in pounds, that is 5 1/2lb. If the scale were increased by 50 per cent to 3/16in-1ft the resulting displacement or weight would be about 18lb. These facts are of very great importance as they give the total permissible weight of the models at scale full load, so that if either weighs more she will float too deep. The 1/8in scale model would be just on 4ft long and the larger just on 6ft long. So the builder now knows before committing himself to making a former or to any other work or expense, just how much weight of power plant he may expect to carry in a given true scale hull, the prospect for the 4ft one not being very encouraging. However, if he can transport a 6ft model, the results on the water are far more interesting and impressive, and the larger displacement would give more scope for radio control and, if desired, steam machinery. With Venner accumulators such a model could be driven at full power electrically for 50 miles with one charging. As this might cost 1d. if done at home a voyage of such a distance for this amount is cheap transport!

If the model were kept on course by radio, and allowing for tides, she could cross from Dover to France and back.

Part Three – Scale Distortion, Speed, Colour & Detail

In order that those who would like to build a fully detailed working model of the destroyer under discussion may know what is involved, the drawing here shows the complete profile and plan of the forecastle and upper decks, the bridge, 'B' and 'X' gun decks, the 0.5in machine gun platform, the 'lines' plan and two body plans, one of which shows the run of the plating in relation to the station lines. The ship's badge and motto are also shown, the latter being a phrase, *Hamba Gable*, in the language of the Matabele tribe from which the ship is named. It is a greeting signifying 'go in peace'.

Ough's plan of HMS *Matabele*. (MyTimeMedia)

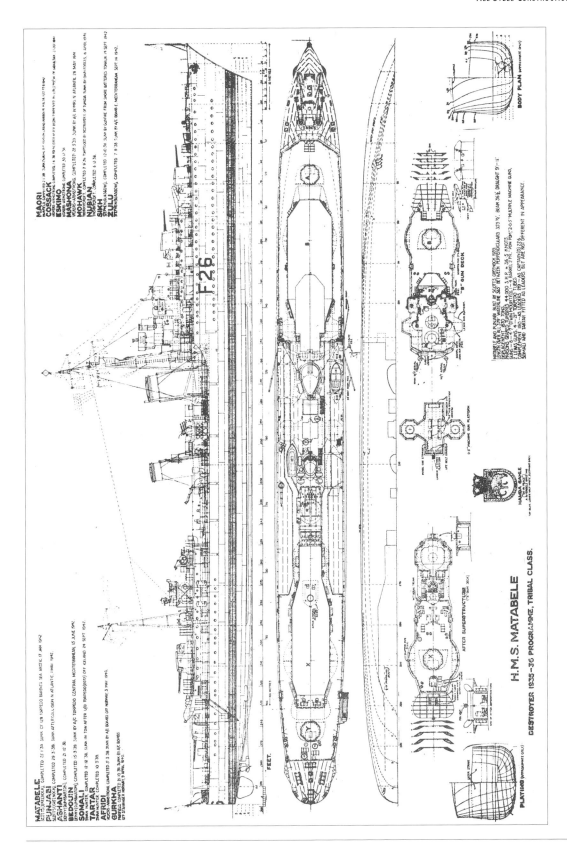

H.M.S. MATABELE, TRIBAL CLASS.

DESTROYER 1935-36 PROGRAMME, TRIBAL CLASS.

The famous 'Tribal' class destroyers were, in their day, the largest ships built in this category for the Royal Navy, and many think them the finest design of all performing the manifold duties of such ships. Their appearance can hardly be overpraised as they were the embodiment of power and majesty and beauty. All saw heavy war service from 1939 to 1945 and, of the sixteen ships, only four, *Eskimo*, *Nubian*, *Ashanti*, and *Tartar* survived, HMS *Matabele* (completed in January, 1939) being sunk by a German submarine in Barents Sea in the Arctic on the 17th January, 1942. Seven ships of a modified 'Tribal' class design are still serving in the Royal Canadian Navy and three more in the Royal Australian Navy.

An idea of the form of the hull of a 'Tribal' class destroyer can be gained from the drawing as it shows the 'lines' plan so often mentioned. This is a view of the hull seen from above with the outlines (dotted) of five horizontal planes spaced at equal distances apart and including the waterline plane. For a model the distances apart of the planes can be the thickness of the planks from which the 'former' is built from the waterline downwards, the dotted lines representing the sawn edges of the planks. The lines plan is also called the 'half-breadth' plan, as since the other side of the ship is the same there is no need to show both sides. These five planes define the shape of the hull below water with considerable accuracy, and a near enough approximation for carving the former into shape could be obtained with only three.

The author has often been asked to draw a set of lines for a hull of much larger carrying capacity but still of a destroyer form. Within narrow limits it is possible to do this without spoiling the model by obvious distortion. For example it might be possible to add 1/2in to the breadth of a 1/8in scale version of this ship, that is 1/4in to each side, and perhaps 1/2in to the draught without this being visible except by measurement. The resulting increase of displacement would be surprising although the model would no longer be a true scale version of the real ship.

The displacement at 1/8in scale with the draught at 1 1/2in (representing 12ft, a very deep load), would be 5.5lbs approximately. With the additional breadth and depth it would be 8lbs approximately, a gain of 2.5lbs with only this slight increase in size. But by increasing the *scale* from 1/8in to 5/32in to the foot and leaving the hull unspoilt the resulting displacement would be 10.7lbs – a really worthwhile gain. The 1/8in scale model would be just under 4ft long, which is rather small for rough weather, but the 5/32in scale model would be 4ft 9in long which is still a convenient size and which would look better on the water, as experience shows that the larger a model is the better she looks 'at sea'. So it is really a matter of opinion or of temperament whether the builder should decide to distort the hull or to increase the scale. The author would say that it is better to increase the scale for this reason: a detailed model of a ship often is, and always may be, a considerable work of art, but it is more than this as it is also an historical record if built true to scale from reliable information.

Much of our knowledge of ships of the past depends on the survival of accurate models such as those that are now the glory of the Science Museum and the National Maritime Museum and other places, and model ships of the present day will have a like value in the future, including working models if they show detail and are not distorted in their proportions. In the Imperial War Museum there are two fully detailed working models of early destroyers, far more elaborate than those of the builders. They were constructed many years before the war by the late Mr. Hugh Oldham, one of the chief engineers of the Rolls Royce Company. As records they are of more value than contemporary builders' models, as the detail came from observation of the ships themselves and not only from design drawings.

Having decided on a scale which will give a model the displacement required for carrying the intended power plant the question arises as to how much power, or rather at what speed must the model of a given scale be driven to represent the maximum speed of the real ship. This can be decided by finding the 'corresponding speed' of a given scale.

It is found by the formula L that is, the speed 's' of the model will be the speed of the real ship 'S' divided by the square root of the ratio of the length 'L' of the real ship and the length '1' of the model:

$$s = \frac{S}{\sqrt{L/1}}$$

For example, if a model is 1/100th of the length of the ship (nearly 1/8in scale), then the ratio

$$\frac{L}{1}$$

will be

$$\frac{100}{1}$$

The square root of 100 is 10 which, divided into the maximum speed of the real ship, that is into 34 knots, gives 3.4 knots. Driven at this speed the model should produce the appropriate wave formation. It is a moderate walking pace which, in the water, looks very fast with a small model. If the scale were 1/4in-1ft the ratio L to 1 would be 48 to 1. The square root of 48 is 7 nearly, which divided into 34 knots gives 4.8 knots nearly. The figures are approximate as it is not very likely that most readers would want to carry out exact scientific experiments.

In the drawing the plan of the superstructure is vertically below the plan of the upper deck and forecastle. The raised deck forward that carries the second gun mounting, 'B' gun deck, or the shelter deck, has the flag deck and wireless office at its after end and above it is the director control platform and the compass platform. The after superstructure carries the mounting for the 4-barrel pom-pom gun, the after control and searchlight platform (from which the ship can be steered if the bridge is wrecked) and 'X' gun mounting. These guns belong to the main armament of four twin mountings named 'A', 'B', 'X' and 'Y' [*which were described in the chapter on 'Ordnance'*]. Amidships between the funnels is the platform for the short range anti-aircraft armament consisting of two 4-barrel 0.5in machine guns, and, abaft the second funnel, is the mounting for the four 21in torpedo tubes. Larger drawings of the upper works will be reproduced and described later as, in this illustration, which is reduced from the original plan at 1/16in-1ft to one-ninth of its area, they are too small to be seen clearly. The large plain areas shown on the upper deck and on most of the forecastle and over the superstructure are covered with 'Semtex' which is a non-slip material trowelled on to the deck and looking rather like dry asphalt. It hides the edge and end laps of the deck plating. It has a matt surface and is usually painted dark green or blue, but this colour should not be very positive in a model but should be given a dull salty look. The cable deck in front of the breakwater is sometimes painted black and sometimes with red oxide, but it spoils the look of a model if this paint is shiny or intense in colour. One way of getting rid of shine is to rub it over with a damp rag and some pumice powder when the paint is thoroughly dry.

Part Four – Detail Problems

It is a much debated question among builders of working models as to whether or not to add detail. But since the addition of it has little effect on performance, and only some on convenience of handling, does not the question become the same as that referred to in the previous article concerning alteration of hull form, resolving itself into a matter of taste or of temperament? What is not doubtful, however, is that more impressive effects are got from a detailed model at moderate distances than from a simplified version, but it is again a matter of taste whether a builder is going to do the extra work in order to achieve the enhanced effect. For these articles the drawings are made with a view to showing as much detail as possible for 1/8in scale, it being assumed that those who do not want it can leave it out. Whatever view is taken, however, it is generally advisable to build a model without adding the detail until her trials are satisfactorily run.

In working models the question of access to the machinery and radio gear is critical. In those of cruisers where the superstructure is fairly large parts of it may be made to lift out, access being gained through the resulting spaces in a permanently fixed deck. In models of destroyers, however, assuming 1/8in scale, it is usually necessary to be able to lift away all the upper deck and most of the forecastle as the superstructure is too small to give enough room to reach in. The two lengths of deck may be bracketed together at the break of the forecastle, the ship's galley acting as a strengthening piece as shown in (3), a method which has the advantage of leaving the masts and funnels, which have many rigging connections to the deck, standing complete with the wireless aerials undisturbed. The section (4) shows how the upper deck is connected to the hull and (2) how the forecastle deck aft of the breakwater is connected. Stiffeners of deep angle bar are soldered fore and aft along under the decks for longitudinal strength. Where these pass over the tops of the transverse bulkheads slots are cut to admit them. The bulkheads should be watertight and there should be a good many of them, and the slots only compromise this function high up at the top. They are helpful in the case of partial flooding due to collision, but they will not keep a model with a portable deck afloat against prolonged attack by seas that flood right over her. Once flooded, an all-metal model has no buoyancy at all, and, in the destroyer here being discussed, there is not enough internal space available clear of the machinery for introducing rubber balloons or corks to keep her afloat. In a model of a cruiser of the same scale this might just be possible.

The flange along the edge of the upper deck, as shown in (4), is lodged in a rebate formed from deep angle bar soldered all round the inside of the hull with its flange on top, the narrow edge plate going on to the rebate as a lid fits on a tin. The upper surface of the flange may be coated with Vaseline before the deck is secured with a few small cheese headed screws (say 8 BA) going into holes drilled and tapped

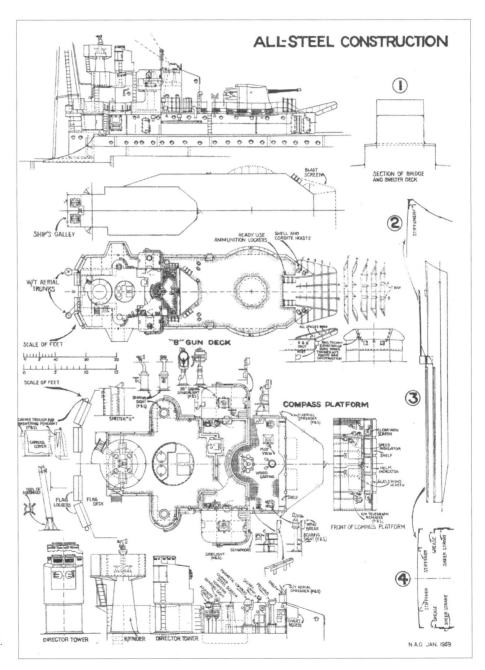

Ough's detailing plans relating to HMS *Matabele*. (MyTimeMedia)

into it, the places where the screws go being thickened by small pieces of brass soldered on underneath to allow more threads to be cut. The resulting greased connection is not fully watertight but it will stand the wash of seas going right over it occasionally. The joint higher up on the forecastle shown in (2) is still less so, but the sheer and flare of the bows will throw away most head seas, only splashes getting on board unless the weather is very severe. When the decks are on secondary access openings may be arranged in the superstructure, as part of 'X' gun deck may be made portable over a fairly large area by lifting it out by the gun mounting, so giving access to part of the engine room. The block forward that contains the wireless office, wheelhouse, chartroom and captain's sea cabin with the compass platform and director control tower on top may be made to lift out bodily, as shown in section in (1), as there are no rigging connections apart from two minor wireless aerials. The resulting aperture allows access to the radio receiver for switching on HT and LT currents and for attaching a milli-ammeter for testing.

For those who like detail, the drawing shows a profile and plan of the forward superstructure or 'shelter deck', the forebridge, director control tower and rangefinder and the compass platform, while below is an enlargement of these latter to double the scale. When the guns of 'B' mounting on the shelter deck are fired on a forward bearing the blast is severe at low angles of elevation and for this reason a projecting screen, stiffened by bracket plates and angle bar frames, is fitted at the end of the deck to cover the area below occupied by the crew of 'A' guns on the forecastle. The drawing shows this in plan and profile and in end elevation with detail of the bracketing. It is known as a 'blast screen'. Where it joins the deck are four small oval hatches. These are the shell and cordite hoists for 'B' guns, used when the ammunition stored in the six lockers shown has been consumed in action.

The forebridge, drawn to enlarged scale, is the position of control both of the ship with her 44,000 horse power and of her gun and torpedo armament. Its eye is the lookout man in the 'crow's nest' high up the mast with whom it is in communication by voice pipe. The compass platform is divided from the rest of the area by a partition the same height as the walls with a communicating door. Most of it is covered by a raised wood grating surrounding the gyro compass

or 'pelorus' and the 'standard' or magnetic compass, both of which have voice pipes leading to the wheelhouse. On the left of the gyro is the 'plot view', a wood structure fitted on top with binoculars for viewing the charts in the room below. Additional charts are kept in recesses in the front of the bridge, the wall and sides of which are topped by a glass windscreen. Just below the compasses is the wheelhouse from which the ship is steered, the helm angles and courses being passed down to the helmsman by voice pipe, so a warship is 'conned' from the bridge and steered from the wheelhouse, where the helmsman is under protection from splinters. At the front of the bridge are the engine room 'tell-tales' giving the number of revolutions of the propellers, the engine room telegraph, the rudder indicator and the repeaters indicating the revolutions of the port and starboard engines, and voice pipes leading to the engine room. Usually near the gyro compass is a tall chair for the captain.

At the after end of the compass platform, on both sides, are the instruments for training the torpedo tubes and for firing the torpedoes, and below, on wing platforms, are the 20in signalling searchlights. The rest of the platform is occupied by the Director Control Tower and its large rangefinder on a conical tower behind it. The flag deck, or signal deck, is below as shown. This has four flag lockers at its after end, to two of which are fixed the canvas troughs for the answering pendants, which are kept on the halliards. The latter run through single blocks on the upper and lower yards and are made fast to cleats at the sides of the flag lockers and on the uppermost guard rails. The deck surfaces on the forebridge and flag deck are covered with Semtex, the wood gratings being left bare and unvarnished. The two chart recesses have canvas covers which are shown rolled up and stowed above them in the drawing, and the flag lockers have similar covers which roll up and are secured on top as shown on the sketch on the left of the plan of this deck. Those who like the complexities of a 'full dress' model will find most of what they will require for the 4.7in. guns of the main armament [*in the chapter on 'Ordnance'*].

Part Five – Mast, Funnels, etc.
Although the author has had the privilege of writing this series of articles, and in that time quite a lot of ground has been covered, it only amounts to about one-fifth of what would be required to treat this vast

Details of masts and funnels for HMS *Matabele*. (MyTimeMedia)

theme adequately from 1895 to date. It is the first time for nearly two centuries that such a work has been attempted, the previous book on the subject, Chapman's *Architectura Navalis Mercatoria*, which includes warships, having been published in 1768, and it is still commanding a world sale. But it seems very doubtful if the present work will be brought to a conclusion, as, although the author has been informed that research for it has been 'approved' by the Board of Admiralty, so far in the past year, only

one item of information has been made available, and this only in part. Some of the material was discovered by the author, purely by chance, in the Library at the Admiralty, and this has been used for the five drawings of gun detail as it is accessible to any student, but the amount there is very meagre so that numerous requests have had to be put in for the missing gunnery and torpedo manuals, and for the specification books of the boats – all to no purpose. It may be months or years before the information is made available, so the prospect is not very hopeful, especially as the long delays have helped to drain away the author's capital. Yet, all over the world, there are thousands interested and not only model makers, as this information is the raw material of the naval history of our times.

Continuing this description of the detail of a working model of a 'Tribal' class destroyer, here are the foremast, the funnels and the platform between them which carries the two 0.5in multiple machine guns of the short range anti-aircraft armament, below which is part of the superstructure containing some of the boiler room ventilators. Near the after funnel are shown the large fans that supply air under pressure to the engine room. The two racks near the funnels are used for the stowage of fenders, lengths of grass rope, etc., for the use of the boatswain and for the stowage of planks belonging to the carpenter's ready use store. Two walking ways covered with Semtex are laid along the steel decks fore and aft where there is much traffic. The davits for the whaler and the 25ft motor boats are also shown. The lockers near the forward funnel are for the stowage of lifebelts, the one with the two doors on the port side being for oilskins. An enlargement to twice scale of the gun platform is shown at the foot of the drawing, and enlargements of the two funnels with details of the plating and riveting are at the top right and left.

The foremast in a 1/8in scale model should have the tripod made of thin tube as solid metal would be an unnecessary weight high above the waterline. The tubes can be made quite easily by folding thin tin round a former of heavy wire or a knitting needle, which would have to be withdrawn before the seam was soldered. The topmast and the two yards are best made from steel wire filed to a taper, soldered in position, and in the case of the yards, assisted by a lashing of thin wire. A useful source of brass wire for the detail of models is the picture wire sold at Woolworths, which is laid up of several strands over an iron wire core. Unlaid it is quite ductile and it is made in more than one gauge. It can be hammered flat or drawn down to a slightly smaller diameter by holding one end in a vice and pulling the other end of a yard long piece till it breaks. It is admirable for making small studded cable such as would be required for this model.

The funnels are best made by folding them round wood formers, the same being used for the uptakes to give them shape, the latter being taken off the formers and pressed to a smaller diameter by hand before soldering the seam which, in the funnel casing, would be made to come in the foreside where it would be hidden by the steam pipes. The uptakes may be extended below decks and soldered into a cylindrical tin container as shown by the dotted line. This can be used for a smoke generator, one end being left open for putting in fuel. One way of making smoke is to buy a 6d. carton of saltpetre at a chemists. This can be dissolved in water in proportion of about one part to five of water. Pieces of rag or newspaper are then soaked in the solution for a minute or two and taken out and dried. When dry, parcels of paper or rag rolled up like a cigar may be made and pushed into the container, one end being lighted. The saltpetre causes the paper to smoulder for some time giving off quantities of smoke of about the right colour to represent oil fuel burning imperfectly, and the volume may be increased by putting a small fan with tin vanes soldered to the shaft of an Ever Ready electric motor near the opening of the container. Since the fan can be controlled by radio, the amount of smoke may be varied from the shore. The smouldering paper or rag gives off some heat, so the connection between the uptakes and the container should be riveted here and there and should be an accurate fit, the joint being kept smoke-tight with asbestos string. The container may be made fast to the deck overhead, so that it is accessible when the deck is lifted off, the fan motor remaining in the hull.

The flanges at the top of the uptakes and at the bases of the funnels are difficult to make, but perhaps the easiest way is to cut out a tinplate collar to fit the funnel and to expand the inner edge by hammering, so that it becomes conical. It can then be soldered on and bent further down and the edge trimmed and filed to shape. Trial and error does it, the advantage of tinplate construction once more showing as it is of no consequence if one or two attempts are failures, as they can be taken off and scrapped. The cages on top of the uptakes are made of brass or steel wire soldered together, but hard soldered in the case of a steam model. The siren platform on the after funnel is made by shaping its rim from wire hammered flat, soldering the rungs of the grating to the edge of the rim and trimming off and filing the ends flush. A piece of wet cotton wool laid on the end of each ring will prevent it coming unsoldered when the next rung is being added, the cotton wool, kept wet, being moved from rung to rung as the work progresses, a similar process being used for making ladders. The finished platform looks best if it is fitted with the rim upwards.

The forward funnel has a large pipe coming from the galley stove, passing round it on the starboard side and leading up to above the cage. Since this would be a considerable weight if made from bent tube, the best way to represent it is to make the curved part by carving it from wood with a tin end rebated in flush so as to appear continuous, and soldered into the galley wall, the straight part of the uptake being also made of tin. The eyebolts for the funnel stays are made from brass wire, passed through holes drilled in the funnel, clenched inside and soldered. The steam pipes, of which there are four on the forward funnel and three on the after, are escape pipes from the safety valves of the boilers. In reality they are of massive copper pipe and, in peace time, are brightly polished above the uppermost clamp that secures them. The sirens are also kept polished, the metal being copper, and the lanyards leading from them to the bridge being of small cotton rope. Just aft of the second funnel is a hooded shelter for the crew of the quadruple torpedo tube mounting, and on the port side nearby is the davit for embarking torpedoes, loading the tubes and recovering them after practice runs. It will be seen that the steel 'dodging' of the gun platform has hinges. This is to enable parts to be thrown down to clear the fire of the guns at low angles. The rest of the platform is surrounded by a guardrail which is usually covered with painted canvas. It is supported on the large trunk fitted with hinged steel doors secured by cleats. When open these admit additional air to the boiler rooms. Next to the trunking are circular hatches leading to the air locks below.

Part Six - Masts
Until the coming of RADAR and, with it, the lattice mast construction, the masting and rigging of warships altered very little since the 1890's. Here are the details of the rig of the 'Tribal' class destroyer which is the subject of these notes. Both masts and yards are made of steel, the tripod of the foremast being of tinplate tube as described in the previous article. Where the tripod ends the foretopmast is inserted. This is stayed laterally by the shrouds, forwards by the breast stays which are shackled to eyeplates on the forecastle deck, and backwards by the foretopmast backstays which have similar shackles securing them to the upper deck. The mast

stays consist of 2 1/2in (measured by circumference) flexible steel wire rope. At the lower end of each stay an eyesplice, lined with a thimble, is worked to receive a shackle to which is attached a 'bottle' screw which in turn is shackled to a quick release hook that also passes through a shackle secured to an eyeplate in the deck as shown in the sketch of detail. The upper end of the stay also has an eyesplice through which passes a shackle connecting it to an eye in the 'necklace' or mast band which has an eye for each stay.

The best way to taper the topmast and the yards is to take a piece of brass or steel rod of the right diameter and length and to file tapering flats, reducing it to a square section at the ends, but leaving the centre round, the flat faces having no width at the round part and broadening until they reach the depth of the required taper at the ends. Four more flat faces can then be filed from the edges of the previous flats giving the rod an octagonal section after which a little more filing will remove the eight edges thus produced. In the case of the foreyard the ends need to be shouldered to take the bands for the yard 'lifts' and to leave room for the yard arm lights. The yards are slung on the mast by a shackle passing through an eye bolt in the band at the centre of the yard, the shackle being secured to another eyebolt in a corresponding band on the mast. They are held at right angles to the mast by the lifts, and the foreyard is kept square by the braces as in the old sailing ships. The stays and braces are cut up into three parts of equal length and the sections are spliced round brown porcelain insulators, called 'coconuts' in naval slang, as shown in the sketch. These are to prevent the long wires from interfering with the radio by acting as unwanted aerials. In a real warship, as the standing rigging is of 2 1/2in wire, its breaking strain is about 18 tons, a precaution by way of strength which is necessary owing to the violent motion of destroyers in a high sea. In a model it is advisable to use strong thread for the rigging as, if wire is used, it is very difficult to make it look straight without a lot of tension being applied in setting it up, and even if this is done successfully, it is easily bent.

The foreyard is fitted with six electric lights, those on top at the ends being white lights and those below red and blue. At night combinations of these lights are used as a challenge to other ships which may be encountered, the answering signal being another combination which serves as a 'password'. Unless the code were known an enemy ship could not reply by

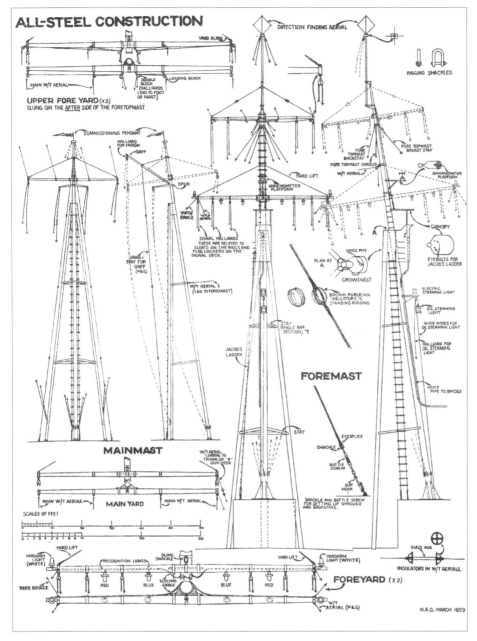

Details of masts drawn by Ough. (MyTimeMedia)

the correct combination so she would be fired on. Hence the name applied to them: 'recognition lights'.

Below the yards are the small single blocks for the flag halliards which are of grass line, best represented by thin cotton, stained rope-colour. There are six of them on the foreyard, four on the upper yard and two on the main yard, and there are also ensign halliards on each side of the 'truck' of the main mast and on each side of the top of the small pole that carries the

directional aerial at the fore. At the main mast head is a small spike which carries the 'commissioning pendant' or 'mast-head pendant', a small tapered white flag with an elongated scarlet cross at the mast end. It is hoisted on the day the ship commissions and it is never struck until the day she is paid off. Few people know it, but the plain white flag, when it is rectangular, bearing the plain scarlet cross, the 'banner of St. George', was, until 1606, the national flag of England and Wales, after which the blue and white diagonal cross of St. Andrew for Scotland was added forming the 'Union Flag', the scarlet diagonal cross of St. Patrick not being incorporated until 1801. The white ensign, which includes all these, with the enlarged cross of St. George – the naval ensign – is flown, when the ship is under way, from the small spar on the mainmast, called the 'monkey gaff', but, in harbour or at anchor, a much larger one is flown from the ensign staff at the stern, the union jack being always hoisted at the bows at the same time, but the latter is always hauled down when the ship gets under way.

The wireless aerials are shackled to the main yard and have a grass rope spliced in the free end which leads through blocks on the upper foreyard, along below to another leading block near the mast and down to cleats on the band at the foot of the tripod, this second block being double (i.e. with two sheaves) to allow the two halliards to pass through it. The minor aerials lead from the ends of the yards to insulating trunks on deck, the main aerial having four leading wires going down to the large trunk under the signal deck as shown in the general arrangement drawing [in Part Three above]. The aerial wires have insulators in them of the type as shown in the sketch at the bottom right of the drawing here. They are easily seen in photographs.

The 'crows-nest' on the foremast is reached from the top of the ship's galley by a 'Jacob's ladder'. This is of steel wire rope with round wood rungs lashed to it. An extension of this ladder goes up the foretopmast starting from the canopy over the crows-nest. Other features of the foremast are the platform for the steaming lights, the anemometer (or wind speed indicator) platform and the small topgallant mast which carries the directional aerial. Electric cables lead up outside the mast to which they are clipped, to these fittings, and also along the backs of the yards to the lights. In the event of a failure of current the steaming light has an oil lantern, which can be hoisted to below the platform along two steel guide wires. 'Tribal' class destroyers did not appear to have a main steaming light which is usually carried in all ships, 15ft above the fore light, if they have two masts of sufficient height to allow this.

Part Seven – Displacement, etc.

A model maker has written to the author about drawings of the ship being described in this series as he proposes to build a working model of her to a scale of 1/2in-1ft, that is, a length of 15ft 9 1/2in. If it is completed in tinplate it will be a good illustration of how effective this method of building is even for a model of large scale. It will be interesting to calculate the displacement of such a model as a way of doing so was mentioned earlier, but not stated adequately. For this serious omission the author apologises and will now hasten to explain the principle.

The 'displacement' of a model, or of a real ship, means its total weight, which must be equal to the weight of the volume of water it displaces while floating. It *must* be, because the only force available to a ship or model for displacing water is gravity or its own weight. If the model is heavy it will make a deep cavity in the water, if lighter the cavity will be shallower. If the water were frozen and the model were lifted out the shape of the cavity left in the ice would be an exact mould of the submerged part of the hull. If an imaginary rectangle were scribed about this cavity, touching it at the sides and ends and along the bottom, it would be simple to calculate the volume of the rectangular prism or block so defined, as this would be its length multiplied by its breadth and again by its depth, or so many cubic inches. The volume of the cavity would be less than this, and if it could be found how *much* less a ratio of volume to volume could be established between them. By a use of one of the rules of calculus this ratio can be found with varying amounts of accuracy, and is known as the 'coefficient of fineness' or as the 'block coefficient'. In the case of destroyers this is almost exactly as 1 is to 2, or 1/2. In cruisers it is rather higher, .55 to 1.00 and, in a modern battleship, .63 to 1.00. Since the volume of the immersed hull is, in this case, now known to be half the volume of the block it will be easy to estimate the displacement of the proposed 1/2in scale model.

The length taken is usually that between perpendiculars, i.e., between vertical lines drawn through the point of intersection of the stem with the water-line, and through the centre of the rudder post.

This, in the real ship, is 366ft, which becomes 183in in the model. The beam (outside plating) is 36 1/2ft, or 18 1/4in in the model, and the full load draught is 12ft or 6in in the model. So the volume of the 'block' is 183 x 18 1/4 x 6 ins = 20,038 cu in. And the volume of the immersed hull is half this, which is 10,019 cu in. This result can be converted to pounds weight by dividing by 27, as 1lb of fresh water is 27 cu in.

$$\frac{10,019}{27}$$

comes to 371. So the total weight of the model at a draught of 6in is 371lb. approximately.

If, in order to gain more speed on a given power, the builder accepts a load draught of 10ft, or 5in, the figures become

$$\frac{183 \times 18\ 1/4 \times 5\ lb}{27}$$

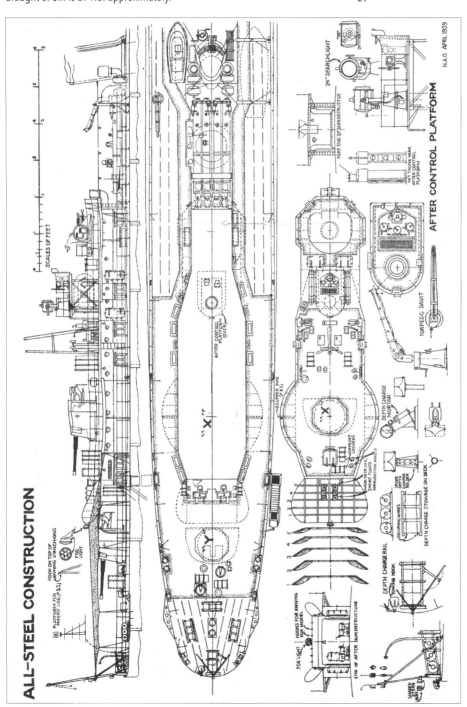

Details of stern and after control platform of HMS *Matabele*. (MyTimeMedia)

which reduces to 309lb nearly; an interesting result, as it shows that he could save 60lb of weight by reducing the draught by one inch. The correspondent mentions that he has machinery in mind for the model, the weight of which is about 150lb, so this calculation, which is, of course, only approximate, shows that she could carry it easily.

It can hardly be over emphasised how important this way of estimating displacement is, as it applies to models of any scale, and it enables the builder who has some particular power unit in mind to know what size true-scale hull will carry it. Stated as a rule of thumb, displacement can be found by multiplying the length BP of the model by her breadth and draught, dividing the result by the 'block coefficient' and again by 27, the result being in pounds weight. The scale full speed for the 1/2in model would be over 7 knots, and it would be 13,724 times smaller than the real ship, a 1/8in scale model being 884,736 times smaller, volume for volume. An approximate estimate of the weight of the complete model as a structure with all fittings, but without machinery, would be 50lb, so that about 300lb of ballast and power plant would have to be added to bring her down to the scale full load waterline. To 'dress up' the large areas of the model with adequate detail would require many sheets of drawings and this seems a convincing answer to those who have advised the author that he puts too much detail into his plans. Quite the contrary, there ought to be twice as much or three times as much, since they are meant for large models as well as small.

* * *

The drawing of detail on these pages completes this survey of the outside of the ship from the construction point of view, as it includes the after superstructure and the quarter deck with their gun mountings and fittings, and the stem, thus covering the whole vessel 'fore and aft', the details of the 2 pdrs and 0.5in machine guns, the torpedo tubes and those of the boats [*shown in the chapters on 'Ordnance' and 'RN Service Boats'*].

It will be seen, in the profile on the drawing, that the superstructure is surrounded by a hand rail, as is that on the forecastle. In peacetime this is of polished brass. Just above it, at the after end, is the ship's name board, usually made of varnished teak, with the name in raised block capitals faced with brass, the

imitation of which is fairly simple. On a 1/8in scale model the letters are 3/32in high. They can be made from brass strip made from a piece of fine brass wire hammered to a flat section, and, if the wire is too hard, it may be softened in a candle flame. This may be cut into the short lengths required with a sharp knife used on a plate of mild steel or tinplate, the bending of the curved parts of the letters being done by using two pairs of tweezers. The most difficult letter to make is a B as this needs two very small curved parts. To make them the simplest way is to bend them from round wire and tap them flat with a hammer. The straight bits forming the diagonal of an N or the V part of an M need have their ends cut at the appropriate angles. A strip of cigarette paper 3/32in wide is cut next and stuck to a board by its ends, leaving most of its length free; it can be kept away from the board by a matchstick. The letters can now be built up on this, one at a time, by flooding a short length of the strip with model aircraft clear dope, dropping the bits of brass in and moving them about with the point of a needle till they make the complete name. In *Matabele* there are only three rather tricky letters, the M, the As, and the B, the rest being straightforward, T for instance, or E. Fine adjustments can be made as the dope sets, the alignment of the letters being ensured by the paper strip which is the same width as their height. When the two names (one port side, one starboard) are complete the strip is cut off the board and stuck with dope to a strip of fairly thick brown paper or card cut slightly wider. This represents the board, and, when painted with dope, it looks like teak, the tissue paper remaining almost invisible. When all is set hard the name boards, with the lettering downwards, are laid on a fine oil stone which should, preferably, be dry. By sliding them backwards and forwards over the stone the faces of the letters are ground smooth and flat, taking a fairly high polish which can be fixed by a thin coating of dope. The two name boards are then cut apart, their corners bevelled and they are ready for sticking on to the paintwork of the superstructure, again with a little clear dope.

It is easier to make the superstructure by bending it about a wood former from a long strip of tinplate rather than trying to build it up piece by piece. If it is made 1/8in deeper than the required height it can be pushed in to an accurately cut opening in the deck and soldered in from below. This leaves the whole of its interior free from obstruction for lighting from the engine room. The camber of the deck may be kept true by two or three angle bar beams soldered across under it, the longitudinal strength being maintained by its soldered connection to the superstructure.

An interesting addition to a model, and one that is hardly ever fitted, is the quarter deck awning. This may be made from old cloth tracings from which the ink and starch have been washed with soap and water. This material is finer in weave than anything else readily obtainable, and, incidentally, is perfect for the sails of ship models. Moreover, it is 'off white', and, when clean, is just the colour of ships' canvas. The awning is fitted along the after edge of the blast screen of 'X' gun mounting and along the sides of this where it joins the plating of the superstructure, and is secured to the tops of the five awning stanchions along the sides of the quarter deck and to the stanchion of the ensign staff at the stern. A wire ridge rope is fitted to the latter and shackled to a point on the blast screen below the foglight. To make it, a template of stiff paper should be cut out and fitted and this is used to scribe a pencil line round on to the material the cutting of which must allow for a 1/8in hem. The latter is made by folding the linen only once and sticking the fold with dope, as a twice-folded sewn hem is too clumsy at 1/8in scale. The 'bolt rope' or edge rope, made of fine rigging cord, is then sewn on all round right on the edge by closely spaced spiral stitching. A series of very small metal hooks are soldered to the superstructure at about 1in intervals and the tops of the awning stanchions are formed with similar hooks pointing outboard. The awning is fitted simply by hooking the bolt rope to these points, and it can be taken off when not wanted. Pencil lines drawn at right angles to the centre line of the awning add the effect of the 'cloths' from which it is made up, these being spaced about 3/8in apart. When the awning is set up the bright-work of the two guns of 'Y' mounting with their prominent breech mechanisms look very impressive in the luminous shade beneath it.

The building of a detailed working model of a recent warship of the Royal Navy in the same material as is used in the real ship and the endowing of it with power and speed and control by radio is a considerable enterprise, and anyone who undertakes such a work will, in the process, learn quite a lot about engineering and ship construction as well as acquiring skill in the working of metals. Surely all these are absolute gains considered as part of life, and, in any case, the acquirement of them must lead to an extension of pleasure and interest and to more knowledge of what goes on in the world generally, and, in particular, something of the naval history of our times. This series has stated the case for 'all-steel construction' only in the barest outline and it could be extended indefinitely, but perhaps enough has been said to establish the principles involved, only one thing more being required to be said in addition, namely, that these same principles apply to the construction of a model of *any* ship built of steel.

12

❖ DRAWINGS AND PLANS ❖

Introduction

Although some people appear to be aware of the length of time a model may take to make, few realise how long it takes to draw up plans of ships and the associated costs. To give an idea of what may be involved, it is interesting to look at Ough's reply to a plea for 'Ironclad' drawings from a reader of *Ships and Ship Models* magazine in March 1954. Ough wrote:

In reply to 'A plea for the Ironclad' by your correspondent Mr R. Fano in the March issue, a letter in which he refers to my drawings of modern warships and expresses the wish that more information about the earlier ships of the Royal Navy should be made available to model makers; I agree entirely, but would be glad if you would allow me space to explain some of the difficulties that arise in producing these drawings.

Incredible as it must seem, this is the first time in the history of England that the work has been attempted at all for the public by a person having enough experience to reach near accuracy.

Since no official information (other than that published) can be used, the research involved becomes the largest item in time and cost, which brings up the question of finance. It is full-time work running to twelve hours a day and six and a half days a week, and excludes the chance of other gainful employment. For the first eighteen months I have financed it out of savings. It takes five or six weeks to draw the details of a modern destroyer properly, eight for a cruiser, ten for a battleship and twelve for an aircraft carrier. So I have to face the fact that if I draw a capital ship it is going to cost me between £50 and £60. The rate of recovery of the outlay is indicated by the fact that, in the first eighteen months, for an expenditure of about £350 I have got back £220. However, some of the worst difficulties of research have been surmounted, but a total of £600 of personal capital will not last very long in a gamble of this kind.

The piles of letters that have come during this time from all over the world show how the public (even allowing for 'security') has been kept starved of this information for generations, and they also show which drawings are most wanted – they are of the very modern ships. If I was free to choose, I would draw the earlier ships by preference as I have information for them. Finally, making these plans is not only a question of

draughtsmanship, but of experience of real ships, and also of the requirements of craftsmen who are interested either in glass case or working models. One has to think of both, in fact of all types of model makers, and also be a model maker oneself.

With regard to the costs Ough was referring to, it may put them into perspective for readers to know that £600 in 1954, when the letter was written, equates to approximately £12,000 in 2015.

Ough's letter was itself replied to in a way which appears to sum up the thoughts of people at the time with regard to his skills. A Mr Laurence Keeble wrote:

Mr Norman Ough reveals the financial hazards involved in the preparation of his magnificent drawings of modern warships. It is disquietening to know that if, and when, their author's private resources come to an end, the work itself must cease.

As a professional designer with experience of model making and research, I do not know of any other drawings which, in their abundance of accurate detail, suggest such clear artistic knowledge. Most engineering drawings are without this quality, and it is Mr Ough's triumph to have given us fact and art in equal measure. There can be no question either of the unique opportunity offered by these drawings to the practical model maker, or by their fascination for historian and connoisseur alike.

The Brunel Institute (ss Great Britain Trust)

Over recent years many maritime historians and model makers have been concerned as to the whereabouts of Ough's plans and

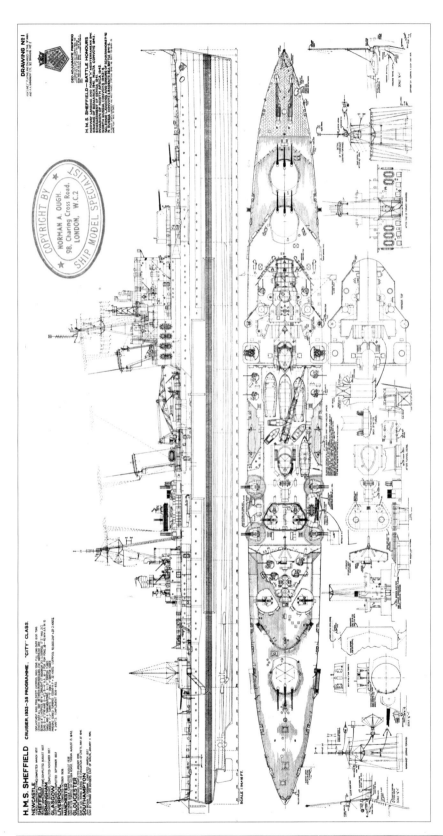

Ough's plan of HMS *Sheffield* now kept at the Brunel Institute. (ss Great Britain Trust)

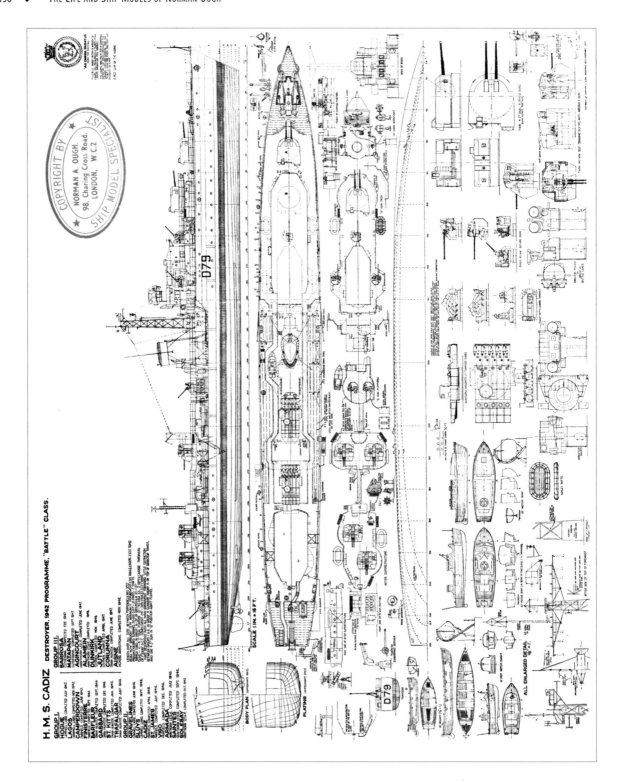

Ough's plan of the destroyer HMS *Cadiz*. (ss Great Britain Trust)

drawings, particularly since David MacGregor's death in 2003. David MacGregor had apparently acquired Ough's plans, with their sole rights, and had been marketing them from the mid-1960s until his own death. Luckily this archive wasn't destroyed as he bequeathed his whole estate, including his plans collection, to the ss Great Britain Trust in Bristol.

When the ships' plans were first acquired by the Trust, as a result of MacGregor's bequest, the full extent of the collection was unknown. It was thought initially that they totalled about 2,500, and the late Michael Stammers, Keeper Emeritus of Merseyside Maritime Museum, assessed the collection to help the Trust gain an insight into how complex it was. There were also tens of thousands of postcards, photographs, films and other items that needed assessment – most of these were MacGregor's own, not Ough's. The plans were drawn or copied on paper, polyester, linen and tracing paper, while the techniques used included photography, diazoprinting, Xeroxing and blueprints. In addition to graphite and coloured pencils, watercolour with pen and ink had also been used by MacGregor and other draughtsmen including Ough. Some of the plans had been stored flat while others had been rolled, sometimes in multiple packs. This diversity meant that great care was required in the way the plans were to be handled, sorted and eventually stored, thus ensuring that the various materials did not interfere with each other and to safeguard the longevity and structural integrity of each individual item.

The plans and other artifacts were stored safely in shipping containers and portable cabins until the Brunel Institute building was completed in 2010. The plans were then brought out of storage, initially listed and briefly identified with the ship's name and what was depicted, and also who had drawn it. They were then sorted to remove damaged or duplicated copies and marked with a unique identity number, known as an accession number. A description of each plan's contents was made (the ship's name, what was depicted in the way of details, scale, lines, measurements, what was represented and who the draughtsman was) and the dimensions measured – some were over two metres in length. The physical composition and condition were also noted for identification, storage and conservation

purposes. A record of all the relevant information for each plan was then entered on to a database. At the end of this stage it was discovered that the Institute had just over 8,000 plans, not 2,500 as first thought; some 300, both original drawings and copies, related to Ough's work.

During the following year the Mobile Scanning Company, a specialist firm, was employed in phased 'blocks' of work to digitally photograph all the plans held. The digitisation process was crucial in providing as much access as possible to the plans, ensuring that those with a special interest, wherever they may be, could use them. The plans are of course also physically accessible to visitors to the Brunel Institute.

The mammoth task of sorting and cataloguing the collection, as well as assessing what further conservation work had to be done, was undertaken by the staff and volunteers at the Institute over a period of three years. At the time of writing a full list of plans held by the Institute, including those by Ough, can be viewed online at the ss Great Britain Trust's website (www.ssgreatbritain.org).

Plans Lists

The plans listed below are those drawn by Ough and now held in the archive of the Brunel Institute (ss Great Britain Trust). 'Hull length' and scale indicate the size of the original drawing, or finished model, and not of the image shown on any digital photographic copies, which would need scaling up to the required size. The coding used by David MacGregor, such as O/S/4A, is shown for historical reference but the Brunel Institute has given its own accession number to each plan photographed; these start with 2012. or 2013., for example 2012.0263, and are listed on the alphabetical named list of plans that was mentioned previously. These accession numbers will need to be quoted if the Institute is contacted regarding specific plans. It should also be noted that the plans held are of variable quality and some may need to be 'enhanced' due to age decolourisation.

Capital Ships

Number	Description	Scale
O/S/1A O/S/1A	**HMS** *Duke of York* Battleship (1941–58) (Hull length 46.5in) Also in this class: *King George V, Prince of Wales, Anson, Howe.* Profile and deck plan Lines, plating and plans of bridge decks	 1/16in–1ft 1/16in–1ft
O/S/2A O/S/2B O/S/2C	**HMS** *Warspite* Battleship (1915–46) as in 1931. (Hull length 40in) Also in this class: *Queen Elizabeth, Barham, Valiant, Malaya.* Profile and deck plan Lines and plating Forebridge and 'Spotting top'	 1/16in–1ft 1/16in–1ft 1/16in–1ft
O/S/3A O/S/3B	**HMS** *Lion* Battle Cruiser (1912–24) as at the Battle of Jutland (Hull length 43.5in) Also in this class: *Princess Royal, Queen Mary.* Profile, deck plan and details Lines, plating and details	 1/16in–1ft 1/16in–1ft
O/S/4A O/S/4B O/S/4C O/S/4D O/S/4E O/S/4F O/S/4G	**HMS** *Hood* Battle Cruiser (1920–41) as in 1933 (Hull length 53.25in) Profile and deck plan Shelter deck and bridge platforms Plan below shelter deck Forecastle deck Lines of forebody Lines of afterbody Quarterdeck	 1/16in–1ft 1/16in–1ft 1/16in–1ft 1/16in–1ft 1/16in–1ft 1/16in–1ft 1/16in–1ft

Cruisers

Number	Description	Scale
O/S/7A O/S/7B	**HMS *Dido*** Cruiser (1939) (Hull length 31.5in) Also in this class: *Cleopatra, Euryalus, Sirius, Phoebe, Scylla, Argonaut, Hermione, Naiad, Charybdis, Bonaventure.* Profile, deck plan and details Lines, plating and further detail	 1/16in-1ft 1/16in-1ft
O/S/8	**HMS *Curacoa*** 'Cardiff' Class Light Cruiser (1916–42) (Hull length 28.5in) Also in this class: *Ceres, Cardiff, Coventry, Curlew, Cairo, Calcutta, Cape Town, Colombo, Carlisle.* Profile, deck plans, lines and details	 1/16in-1ft
O/S/9A O/S/9B O/S/9C	**HMS *Sheffield*** 'City' Class Cruiser (1937) as in 1954 (Hull length 37in) Also in this class: *Newcastle, Birmingham, Glasgow, Liverpool, Manchester, Gloucester, Southampton.* Profile, deck plan and details Lines, plating and details Crane and more boats	 1/16in-1ft 1/16in-1ft 1/16in-1ft
O/S/10A	**HMS *Penelope*** Cruiser (1926–44) (Hull length 31.5in) Also in this class: *Arethusa, Aurora, Galatea.* Profile, deck plan, lines and details	 1/16in-1ft
O/S/11	**HMS *Ajax*** 'Leander' Class Cruiser (1935–49) (Hull length 34.5in) Also in this class: *Achilles, Leander, Orion, Neptune.* Profile, deck plan and details	 1/16in-1ft
O/S/12A O/S/12B	**HMS *Dorsetshire*** 'County' Class Cruiser (1930–42) (Hull length 39.5in) Also in this class: *Norfolk, London, Devonshire, Shropshire, Sussex, Berwick, Cornwall, Cumberland, Kent, Suffolk, Australia, Canberra.* Profile, deck plans and details Lines, plating and further details	 1/16in-1ft 1/16in-1ft

Destroyers

Number	Description	Scale
O/S/13	**HMS** *Vega* 'V' Class Destroyer (1916–45) (Hull length 19.5in) Also in this class: *Vancouver, Velox, Versatile, Vortigern, Vanoc, Venturous, Vanessa, Vanity, Vendetta, Venetia, Verdun, Vidette, Vesper, Violent, Vimiera, Vectis, Vampire, Vivien, Vivacious, Valorous, Valkyrie, Valentine, Vanquisher, Valhalla, Vehement, Verulam.* Profile, deck plan and details	1/16in-1ft
O/S/14	**HMS** *Daring* 'D' Class Destroyer (1932–40) (Hull length 20.25in) Also in this class: *Defender, Diamond, Decoy, Dainty, Delight, Diana, Duchess.* Profile, deck plans, lines and details	1/16in-1ft
O/S/15	**HMS** *Matabele* 'Tribal' Class Destroyer (1939–42) (Hull length 23.5in) Also in this class: *Maori, Cossack, Eskimo, Mashona, Mohawk, Nubian, Sikh, Zulu, Punjabi, Ashanti, Bedouin, Somali, Tartar, Alfridi, Gurkha.* Profile, deck plans, lines and details	1/16in-1ft
O/S/16A	**HMS** *Cadiz* 'Battle' Class Destroyer (1946) (Hull length 23.5in) Also in this class: *Hogue, Lagos, Camperdown, Finisterre, Barfleur, Gabbard, St Kitts, Trafalgar, Gravelines, Sluys, St James, Vigo, Armada, Saintes, Solebay, Barrossa, Matapan, Agincourt, Alamein, Dunkirk, Jutland, Corunna, Aisne.* Profile, deck plans, lines and details	1/16in-1ft
O/S/17B O/S/17A	**HMS** *Kashmir* 'J', 'K' and 'N' Class Destroyer (1939–41) (Hull length 45in) Also in this class: *Jervis, Kelly, Jackall, Javelin, Nerissa, Nizam, Jaguar, Kandahar, Noble, Nonpareil, Napier, Juno, Kelvin, Nestor, Janus, Khartoum, Kimberley, Norman, Nepal, Jersey, Kingston, Jupiter, Kipling.* Profile, deck plans and details Lines plan and plating	1/8in-1ft 1/8in-1ft

Frigates and Minesweepers

Number	Description	Scale

O/S/5A
O/S/5B
	HMS *Amethyst* Modified 'Black Swan' Class Frigate (1943–60)
	   (Hull length 37in)
	Also in this class: *Actaeon, Alacrity, Crane, Cygnet, Hart, Hind, Magpie,
	   Modeste, Nereide, Opossum, Peacock, Pheasant, Snipe, Sparrow.*
	Original 'Black Swan' Class: *Black Swan, Flamingo, Wild Goose, Wren,
	   Woodcock, Mermaid.*
	Profile, deck plan and details
	Lines plan, plating and further details
		1/8in-1ft
		1/8in-1ft

O/S/18A
O/S/18B
	HMS *Marvel* Ocean Minesweeper, 'Algerine' Class (1944)
	   (Hull length 29.5in)
	Also in this class: *Fancy, Cockatrice, Albacore, Chameleon, Cheerful, Espiegle,
	   Hare, Jewel, Onyx, Pickle, Pincher, Plucky, Ready, Recruit, Rifleman,
	   Rinaldo, Rosario, Spanker, Bramble, Fierce, Hound, Hydra, Lennox, Orestes,
	   Rowena, Stormcloud, Sylvia, Tanganyika, Waterwitch, Wave, Welcome,
	   Lysander, Mariner, Marimon, Orcadia, Ossory, Pluto, Polaris, Pyrrhus,
	   Romola, Rosamund, Coquette, Courier, Golden Fleece, Jaseur, Laertes,
	   Lioness, Maenad, Magicienne, Mandate, Mary Rose, Melita, Michael,
	   Minstrel, Moon, Myrmidon, Mystic, Nerissa, Providence, Seabear, Serene,
	   Skipjack, Thisbe, Truelove, Welfare.*
	Profile and deck plans
	Lines, plating and details
		1/8in-1ft
		1/8in-1ft

O/S/6A	**HMS *Hedingham Castle*** 'Castle' Class A/S Frigate (1945)
	   (Hull length 31in)
	Also in this class: *Tintagel Castle, Amberley Castle, Berkeley Castle,
	   Knaresborough Castle, Launceston Castle, Alnwick Castle, Carisbrooke Castle,
	   Farnham Castle, Allington Castle, Lancaster Castle, Oxford Castle,
	   Pevensey Castle, Oakham Castle, Bamborough Castle, Caistor Castle,
	   Leeds Castle, Morpeth Castle, Flint Castle, Hadleigh Castle,
	   Kenilworth Castle, Porchester Castle, Rushden Castle, Dumbarton Castle.*
	Profile, deck plans, lines and details
		1/8in-1ft

Submarines

Number	Description	Scale
O/S/19	**HM Submarine *E.29*** (1915) (Hull length 22in) Also in this class: *E.1–11* and *E.23–55*. Profile, deck plan, lines and details	1/8in-1ft

Number	Description	Scale
O/S/20	**HM Submarine** *L.52* (1919) (Hull length 29.5in) Also in this class: *L.53, L.54, L.56, L.69* and *L.71.* Profile, deck plan, lines and details	1/8in–1ft
O/S/21	**HM Submarine** *Olympus* 'O' class (1930) (Hull length 35.5in) Also in this class: *Oberon, Odin, Orpheus, Osiris, Oswald, Otus,* *Otway, Oxley.* Profile, deck plan, lines and details	1/8in–1ft

Detail Drawings

These drawings were produced by Ough to meet the demands of the really discerning modeller, or the collector interested in ordnance, ship's boats and other details. They show, to a larger scale and in more detail, items on the ship drawings. They are also shown in previous chapters that relate to 'Ordnance', 'RN Service Boats' and 'General Details'.

Ordnance

Type	Drawing No.	Scale
15in Mk 1 & Mk 1 (N) Guns	O/O/1	1/4in to 1/16in–1ft
40mm Twin Bofors Guns	O/O/2	1/2in–1ft
40mm Single Bofors Gun (Mk VII)	O/O/3	1/2in–1ft
20mm Single & Twin Oerlikon Guns	O/O/4	1/2in–1ft
4in Mk XIX Gun	O/O/5	1/4in–1ft
4.7in Twin Quick Firing Guns	O/O/6	1/4in–1ft
4in Twin HA/LA Guns	O/O/7	1/4in–1ft
4in Mk IV Gun	O/O/8	1/4in–1ft
3pdr Mk I Saluting Gun	O/O/9	1in–1ft
21in Quadruple Torpedo Tubes	O/O/10	1/2in–1ft
21in Five Fold Torpedo Tubes	O/O/11	1/2in–1ft

Royal Navy Service Boats

Type	Drawing No.	Scale
50ft Steam Picket Boat	O/B/1	1/4in–1ft
27ft Whaler	O/B/2	1/4in–1ft
25ft Motor Boat	O/B/3	1/2in–1ft
32ft Cutter & Motor Cutter	O/B/4	1/4in–1ft
30ft Gig	O/B/5	1/4in–1ft
42ft Launch & 36ft Pinnace	O/B/6	1/4in–1ft

General Details (scales various)

Type	Drawing No.
Anchors and Cables	O/D/1
Anchors, full detail from 1890	O/D/2
Decks and Deck Coverings	O/D/3
Cowls and Ventilators	O/D/4
Radial and Quadrantial Davits	O/D/5
Main Derrick (Capital Ships)	O/D/
Funnels – General	O/D/7
Funnels – Destroyers and Torpedo Craft	O/D/8
Funnels – Destroyers 1936–60	O/D/9
Boat Booms	O/D/10
Forebridge (*Queen Elizabeth* class)	O/D/11
Dry Dock Details (1in–50ft)	O/D/12
Watertight Doors, Hatches and Skylights	O/D/13
Propeller Design (e.g. HMS *Hood*)	O/D/14

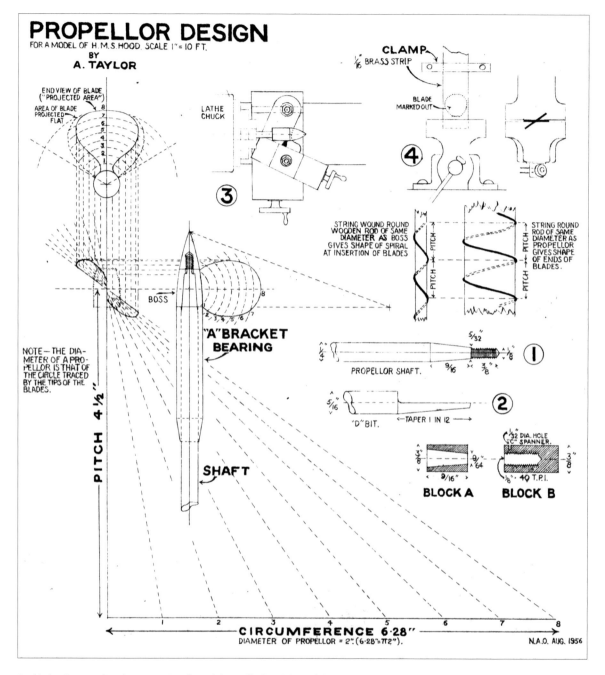

Ough's drawing regarding the construction of a model propeller for HMS *Hood*. (ss Great Britain Trust)

❖ BIBLIOGRAPHY ❖

Arthur-Brand, GW, 'Model Engineers at Work – Norman A. Ough', *The Model Engineer*, Vol. 104, No. 2600, March 1951 (London 1951)

Bennett, Geoffrey, *The Battle of Jutland* (Ware 1999)

Blundell, WDG, *Royal Navy Warships 1939–1945* (London 1971)

Bowen, John (ed), *2012 Shipwright: The International Annual of Maritime History & Ship Modelmaking* (London 2011)

Craine, Lt Commander JH, *Ship Modelling Hints & Tips* (London 1973)

Fox Smith, Cicely, *Ship Models* (new impression, London 1972)

Hobbs, David, *Warships of the Great War Era: A History in Ship Models* (Barnsley 2014)

King, A, Lavery, B, Tanner, M and Young, C (eds), *A Manual of Maritime Curatorship* (Bristol 2002)

Lavery, Brian and Stephens, Simon, *Ship Models: Their Purpose and Development from 1650 to the Present* (London 1995)

Marshall, Percival, *Ships and Ship Models,* Vol. 1. *1931–1932* (Watford 1977)

McNarry, Donald, *Ship Models in Miniature* (Newton Abbot 1975)

Mowll, William, *Thunderer: Building a Model Dreadnought* (Barnsley 2010)

Murphy, Hugh and Oddy, Derek, *The Mirror of the Seas: A Centenary History of the Society for Nautical Research* (London 2010)

Napier Boyd, Norman, *The Model Ship: Her Role in History* (Woodbridge 2000)

Ough, Norman A, see list below

Reed, Philip, *Waterline Warships: An Illustrated Masterclass* (Barnsley 2010)

Roach, Alistair, 'Model Boats in the Context of Maritime History and Archaeology', *The International Journal of Nautical Archaeology*, Vol. 27, No. 2 (2008)

—, 'The Brunel Institute (ss Great Britain Trust): The David MacGregor Ships Plans Collection', *Marine Modelling International*, No. 321 (2013)

—, 'Norman A Ough (1898–1965)', *Model Boats*, Vol. 65, Issue 778 (2015)

Smeed, Vic, *Model Ships* (London 1979)

Wilkinson, PSM, *Royal United Service Museum Guide* (Aldershot 1960)

Ough, Norman A, *Model Maker* (listed below) (Watford – various dates)

'All Steel Construction' Series:

Part One – Hull Construction: December 1958

Part Two – Hull Construction (cont.): January 1959

Part Three – Scale Distortion, Speed, Colour & Detail: February 1959 (HMS *Matabele*)

Part Four – Detail Problems: March 1959 (HMS *Matabele*)

Part Five – Mast, Funnels, etc.: April 1959 (HMS *Matabele*)

Part Six – Masts: May 1959 (HMS *Matabele*)

Part Seven – Displacement, etc.: June 1959 (HMS *Matabele*)

'Warship Detail' Series:

No. 1: March 1958 – Twin 4.7in Naval Guns

No. 2: April 1958 – Anchors and Cables

No. 3: May 1958 – Funnels

No. 4: June 1958 – Cowls and Ventilators

No. 5: July 1958 – 4in Twin HA/LA Guns

No. 6: August 1958 – 4in Mk XIX Guns

No. 7: September 1958 – Decks and Deck Coverings

No. 8: October 1958 – 20mm Oerlikon Guns

No. 9: November 1958 – Twin 40mm Bofors Guns

No. 10: January 1959 – Davits

No. 11; September 1959 – Bofors Mk VII Gun

No. 12: October 1959 – 50ft Steam Picket Boat

No. 13: August 1959 – J, K & N Class Destroyers (note: Series No. correct but not in date).

No. 14: January 1960 – 15in Guns

No. 15: February 1960 – 25ft Motor Boat

No. 16: March 1960 – 32ft Cutter & 32ft Motor Cutter

No. 17: April 1960 – HMS *Duke of York*

No. 18: May 1960 – Lower Boom

No. 19: June 1960 – Main Derrick

No. 20: July 1960 – Forebridge and Spotting Top

No. 21: August 1960 – HMS *Amethyst*

No. 22: September 1960 – HMS *Penelope*

No. 23: November 1963 – Anchors

No. 24: December 1963 – 21in Quadruple Torpedo Tubes

No. 25: January 1964 – Captain's Gig

No. 26: February 1964 – Launches and Pinnaces

No. 27: April 1964 – 21in Five Fold (Pentad) Torpedo Tubes

No. 28: May 1964 – 3 Pdr. Saluting Gun
No. 29: June 1964 – Watertight Doors and Hatches
No. 30: July 1964 – HMS *Hood* – Part 1
No. 31: August 1964 – HMS *Hood* – Part 2
No. 32: September 1964 – HMS *Hood* – Part 3
No. 33: October 1964 – HMS *Hood* – Part 4
No. 34: January 1965 – HMS *Hood* – Part 5

This is the last of Ough's 'Warship Detail' Series. Even though it appears he had planned to continue these articles his health was failing and he was admitted to hospital in February 1965, dying in August of that year.

There were another two 'stand alone' articles written by Ough for *Model Maker* magazine, and these focused on his building of the model of HMS *Dorsetshire* undergoing a refit in No. 14 dry dock, No. 3 Basin Portsmouth Yard. Published in September and October 1963, they are reproduced in the chapter on 'Cruisers' in this book.

Ough wrote occasionally for other magazines, and although not all are listed here those that have been used during the course of research and/or reproduced in this book are shown below.

The Model Engineer (London 1951)
May 1951: HMS *Illustrious* – A New Model for the
    Royal United Service Museum

Model Ships and Power Boats (London 1952/3)
October 1952: A True to Scale Working Model of the
    Destroyer HMS *Vega*
February 1953: Drawings of Warships – HMS *Dido*

Ships and Ship Models (London – various dates)
August 1932: A Model of HM Aircraft Carrier
    Glorious
September 1953: Drawings of Warships – 'D' Class
    Destroyers
March 1954: Drawings of Warships – 'Tribal' Class
    Destroyers
June 1954: The 'Southampton' Class – with notes and
    a drawing of HMS *Sheffield*
September 1954: Drawings of Warships – 'Battle' Class
    Destroyers

December 1954: Drawings of Warships – 'Cardiff'
    Class Cruisers
February 1955: Drawings of Warships – 'Algerine'
    Class Minesweepers Pt. 1
March 1955: Drawings of Warships – 'Algerine' Class
    Minesweepers Pt. 2
June 1955: Drawings of Warships – HM Submarine
    L.52
September 1955: Drawings of Warships – 'E' Class
    Submarines
November 1955: Drawings of Warships – 'O' Class
    Submarines
February 1956: Drawings of Warships – HMS
    Hedingham Castle

Museum Archive Papers

The Hartley Library at the University of Southampton holds correspondence and papers of Earl Mountbatten of Burma as Fourth Sea Lord from 1950 until 1952. One set of papers (MB1/G44) refer to his correspondence with 'Norman A. Ough, model maker, 1951'.

The Imperial War Museum, London holds the following:

Catalogue Number EN1/1/MOD/006 – Correspondence relating to the work of modeller Norman Ough for the Museum. Two subfolders as follows (1) order for model of HMS *Hawkins* and general correspondence re. models of ships required by the Museum (including requests for estimates from Bassett-Lowke) 1925–26. (2) orders for models of HMS *Lion* and *Engadine*, with correspondence about their construction 1926–32. [Author's note: no trace has been found of the models of *Hawkins* or *Engadine*]

Catalogue Number EN2/1/MOD/008 – Sub File 24 – Mr Norman Ough. Correspondence regarding donating and description of models, including No. 14 Dock Portsmouth, arrangements of transfer of Admiralty handbooks to the Museum, supply of drawings for the construction of models, arrangements for the repair of models, commissioning of model of HMS *Dorsetshire*.

❖ INDEX ❖

Note: This index lists RN ship's names only and the relevant pages (page numbers in italic indicate illustrations). In a few cases there is more than one ship of the same name but the index does not differentiate this, e.g. *Nerissa* entry refers to a 1916 'M' class destroyer, a 1939 'N' class destroyer and a 1944 'Algerine' class minesweeper.